KEITH MAGNUSON

THE INSPIRING LIFE AND TIMES OF A BELOVED BLACKHAWK

Doug Feldmann

TRIUMPH BOOKS

Library of Congress Cataloging-in-Publication Data

Feldmann, Doug, 1970-

Keith Magnuson : the inspiring life and times of a beloved Blackhawk / Doug Feldmann.

pages cm

ISBN 978-1-60078-831-4 (hardback)

1. Magnuson, Keith, 1947-2003. 2. Hockey players—United States—Biography. 3. Chicago Blackhawks (Hockey team)—History. I. Title

GV848.5.M33F45 2013

796.962092—dc23

[B]

2013016653

This book is available in quantity at special discounts for your group or organization. For further information, contact:

Triumph Books LLC
814 North Franklin Street
Chicago, Illinois 60610
(312) 337-0747
www.triumphbooks.com

Printed in U.S.A.
ISBN: 978-1-60078-831-4
Design by Amy Carter
Photos courtesy of the Magnuson family unless otherwise indicated

To the Magnuson family

"It is not the critic who counts: not the man who points out how the strong man stumbles or where the doer of deeds could have done better.

"The credit belongs to the man who is actually in the arena, whose face is marred by dust and sweat and blood, who strives valiantly, who errs and comes up short again and again, because there is no effort without error or shortcoming, but who knows the great enthusiasms, the great devotions, who spends himself in a worthy cause; who, at the best, knows, in the end, the triumph of high achievement, and who, at the worst, if he fails, at least fails while daring greatly, so that his place shall never be with those cold and timid souls who neither know victory nor defeat."

—THEODORE ROOSEVELT
"CITIZENSHIP IN A REPUBLIC" SPEECH,
PARIS, FRANCE, APRIL 23, 1910

Contents

Foreword

There isn't a day that goes by when I don't think of Keith Magnuson, but it might surprise you to know that my memories often don't involve hockey.

Keith was my best friend. I met him when I was 10 years old, and we grew up together in Saskatoon, Saskatchewan. We went to the University of Denver together, played college hockey together, played our whole pro career together, and then he became head coach while I was an assistant. When we started our Blackhawk Alumni Association, he was the president and I was the vice president. So we worked together, in one form or another, for 46 years.

Even as a kid, Keith was tenacious. We played on different teams—hockey, baseball, football, you name it—and competed against each other all through high school. He was like a fly—you'd swat him away, but he'd come right back at you. He was probably one of the most determined athletes I ever played with. Keith didn't have all the ability in the world, but he sure made up for it with hard work and desire. He played tough and stood up for his teammates, and that's why he became a fan favorite and one of the best-loved players in the dressing room.

We came out of college at a time when not many NHL players came from the collegiate ranks, so we were looked at a little differently. Keith proved himself by being a genuine person and a hard-working player. I think once he stood up for his teammates a few times, he gained the respect of the locker room and fit in really well.

Keith always had a bit of a mean streak. He didn't fight much when we were kids or in college, because we weren't allowed to. But when he got to the Hawks, he felt he was not going to make it on skill alone. He was a good defensive defenseman, but he didn't contribute much offensively. He figured that he needed to find another way to make his mark.

When we were in school, he recognized the Blackhawks needed someone who could protect his teammates considering the stars they had at the time: Bobby Hull, Stan Mikita, Pit Martin, Jim Pappin, and Dennis Hull. The Blackhawks needed some toughness on that team, and that's what enabled Keith to make an impact.

In the first preseason game that he played, he went up to the toughest guy on the opposition and tried to start a fight. He got his butt kicked, but Keith just kept coming after him. That incident showed that he was going to stand up for his teammates no matter what.

With his level of dedication to the team and to the Blackhawks, it was really only a matter of time before Keith became captain, and he was great at that as well. He was vocal when the opportunity presented itself. He'd stand up and single people out if he needed a little extra from them, but on a day-to-day, game-to-game basis, he was pretty low key.

When Keith was done playing, he became the Blackhawks head coach and I joined his coaching staff. It was easy for both of us to work together because of the closeness that we shared. We were closer to each other than we were to our own brothers. I understood fully what my role was as an assistant coach, and what his was as the head coach. He was the enforcer and I was there to support him as much as possible.

Though it was easy for us to work together, it was a different situation in the locker room. One year we were playing with the guys, having a beer with them and socializing with them; the next year we were their bosses and telling them *not* to have a few beers. So that was an uncomfortable situation for both of us.

After Keith's coaching days ended, he still wanted to be a part of the game, but his larger desire was to help people within the community. He probably had the biggest heart of any individual I've ever known. I very seldom saw him say no to a charity function. That's something that was taught to us by Bobby and Stan. That's the kind of thing you have to do as a professional hockey player in the city of Chicago, and Keith really embraced that. A lot of times, he would ask me to go with him to visit kids in the hospital; he continually did that.

He's touched so many people. He was able to balance his work life, his charity work, and his family. I don't know how he did as much as he did, but I think people remember him most for how much he gave back to the community.

But what I think Maggie would most want to be known for is the Blackhawk Alumni Association, which is his greatest lasting legacy with the team. Twenty-five years ago, there was a need to help players make the transition to life after hockey. Not all players were fortunate enough to have college degrees like we did, so our motto back then was "players helping players."

There were eight of us at that first meeting, including Stan and Dennis, and we put the wheels in motion. We started raising money, and we decided that education was important because of what it did for Maggie and me. So we set up a scholarship program for high school hockey players in the state of Illinois. Keith was the president and he led the organization for the rest of his life. With the groundwork that the few of us laid, we have given out 78 scholarships and millions of dollars based on grades and community involvement, and that scholarship now bears Keith's name.

That his number is now in the rafters at the United Center is a tribute to Maggie as a player, but even more so to him as a person. He wasn't the greatest player ever to hit the ice, though he certainly served his purpose and showed his hard work and dedication. It's the off-the-ice stuff—all the people he touched, from little kids to senior citizens—that's the thing most people remember about him.

—Cliff Koroll

Preface

I have four distinct sports memories from my childhood.

As a four-year-old I heard Jack Buck's voice describing a St. Louis Cardinals baseball game for the first time, as my family drove through southern Illinois on a steamy July night.

As a five-year-old I saw Soldier Field, the home of the Chicago Bears, for the first time passing it as my kindergarten's bus was on its way to the circus at the International Amphitheatre.

As a six-year-old I saw Wrigley Field for the first time, coming up the stairs to the seating area from the concourse while seeing the famous placard attached to the wall, which alerted me to Watch out for Foul Balls!

And as a nine-year-old, riding through Chicago's near west side on our way to a Blackhawks game, I saw Chicago Stadium for the first time.

As our car skidded on the slick exit ramp from the Kennedy Expressway and started to inch its way down Madison Street, there were no bright lights to lead the way, as there are in New York when one heads to a Rangers game. Instead, all I saw was the deep, lonely night of the late Chicago winter, with tired buildings and tired faces shuttered from the wind. As our vehicle moved along, just a few hearty souls were seen ducking in and out of the Palace Grill for hot coffee and sandwiches. The white radiance of snow draped around the endless string of the city's ancient structures. To me, there was always a strange, solemn stillness with snow—whether in my little town outside of Chicago or in the chaos of the big city—as if the mounds of white powder combined with the cape of the early dusk to provide extra layers of tranquility, which was then muffling the urban traffic.

As our car crossed Ashland Avenue, the PEOPLE'S STADIUM PARKING sign came into view, luring drivers with illuminated arrows as invitations.

And in the next instant, through the winter's darkness and with no fanfare or warning, the stark, aging hulk of Chicago Stadium itself suddenly came into view.

Essentially miniature in comparison to today's sports venues—yet at one time the largest indoor arena in the world—the Stadium may just as well have been the Roman Coliseum upon my first glimpse. While I had seen Soldier Field and Wrigley Field on television (and then in person), few sporting events were televised from the Stadium around the Chicago vicinity in that era. Thus, like a person attending a game in the days prior to television, my initial view of the building had an imposing effect. With tales of historic feats echoing from the very cracks in the Stadium's foundation, we parked the car as I took my father's hand, striding reverently toward the gate.

It was immediately clear to me that no ordinary men worked in this place.

"Playing there was like the gladiator movies," former Hawks defenseman Chris Chelios confirmed when I described this memory to him years later. "Coming up the stairs from the locker room, it was the setting for a battle or a war."

Once inside, the labyrinth of dark stairwells, cavelike concourses, peeling paint, dim lighting, and leaking pipes gave it the feel of a dungeon, as if any beast could be lurking around the corner near the popcorn machine.

Squeezing through the entrance tunnels that seemed constrictive even for my third-grade frame, we took our spots in the second balcony, in the old wooden chairs. The date was March 14, 1979.

Scratched that night from the Hawks lineup was a 32-year-old defenseman named Keith Magnuson, the team's captain. Magnuson had been sidelined since December after an operation on his right knee, his third surgery on the joint since he entered the National Hockey League in 1969.

I was disappointed by his absence, as Magnuson's facial expression always made me pause when I flipped through my stack of hockey cards back home; his fiery red hair and his determined countenance always struck me as magnificent. I asked my father about Magnuson, and he explained that the player was fighting through a variety of injuries and was temporarily unable to perform at his previous level of excellence. I was then immediately reminded of a moment five years earlier when, at the age of four, I saw my first Cardinals game. A "washed-up" old pitcher named Bob Gibson was on the mound that day. Like Magnuson at the time of my Stadium visit, it was Gibson's second-to-last season of play. Gibson soon drew my toddler's wrath because of his poor outing, permitting 14 hits and five runs in a loss to the San Francisco Giants. Over the course of the game, I apparently began complaining to a stranger sitting next to me. Before I embarrassed myself any further, my father then quickly and curtly informed me that Gibson had posted much better statistics in previous seasons, and, like Magnuson, was doing his best to hang on. Both Magnuson and Gibson, he added, fought through immense pain to help their teams in any manner they could.

But Magnuson, in fact, had already spent an entire decade fighting uphill battles with the Hawks. He first had to convince his coach and teammates that college players such as him and his buddy Cliff Koroll were NHL-worthy; he next had to deal with talented veterans leaving the team, which put the club in disarray; then with a never-ending litany of young players replacing the veterans in an attempt to rebuild; then with the Philadelphia Flyers becoming the league bullies; and then with the Montreal Canadiens and the New York Islanders dominating everyone.

And all the while, Magnuson was determined to ignore myriad injuries that were usually the result of his selfless sacrifice for the team. In addition to blocking shots with all parts of his body while others on the team assumed the glory of scoring goals, Magnuson would nightly "volunteer" to do battle with the aggressors of other teams, aggressors whom other Hawks were unwilling to confront. Like a wounded soldier helping a comrade along, Magnuson always did the small, nearly unnoticeable things that galvanized morale.

He carried this spirit and devotion into his great success off the ice as well—in business and in charity, but most of all to those with whom he came into personal contact each day. As far back as anyone could remember, Magnuson's teammates, friends, family, and even strangers depended upon him 100,000 times—and 100,000 times, he came through. He was there if someone needed something, without any fanfare, applause, or payment required for his autograph. He was, in a word, *dependable*.

"Whether you win or lose," Magnuson would often say, "it's all about showing up."

1

From Wadena to Saskatoon

"A person's toughness must come from somewhere, and in my case I believe it came from where I was born. Gothic, *I learned in school, was something stark and unadorned, medieval, perhaps even primitive. My rural beginnings were somewhat like this."*

—Keith Magnuson, 1973

The driving distance from Chicago, Illinois, to Wadena, Saskatchewan, is exactly 2,000 kilometers, or 1,243 miles, to the northwest. The path cuts across some of the most unforgiving landscapes in North America—a vast, endless expanse of prairie and plains, with each gaze at the horizon more barren than the last. Endlessly in front of the traveler is a true northern frontier, through which fewer and fewer will pass in going further north.

For generations, many of the greatest players in the sport of ice hockey have been carved out of this frontier, individuals crafted in a region where the frigid arctic air is whipped up in thick, hearty slices that oppress creatures in its way. With temperatures plummeting lower than 30 degrees below zero for weeks at a time, young hockey players in western Canada nonetheless are happy to scratch their skates across the countless frozen ponds and lakes, battling against the cold—and each other. These are not the climate-controlled, suburban indoor rinks that hide players and their parents from the wind. They are raw places of war, where a deep commitment to the game is a prime requisite for survival. Ill-fitting skates, passed down from one brother to another, serve as little defense against frost-bitten toes in these parts, toes which need to be thawed near a fire as darkness falls at the end of a day's play. And with no "pro shop" nearby for proper equipment, curled-up magazines serve as shin guards and hunting trousers make do as hockey pants.

This has been the Canadian rite of passage for many decades. But still today, as they always have, the ponds and lakes around Wadena—like those in Parry Sound and Point Anne over in Ontario, and so many other Canadian villages like them—remain the frosted proving grounds for hockey's future legends, similar to the sun-baked rural and urban sandlots in the United States that have traditionally produced baseball's next superstars.

A small hamlet of about 500 people halfway between Edmonton and Winnipeg, Wadena is perhaps as honorably nondescript as any such place that one could examine. It was here where a red-haired boy named Keith Arlen Magnuson was born on April 27, 1947, the youngest of four children to Joe and Birdie Magnuson.

Joe ran a hardware store in town, a large asphalt building which stood distinctly on the one major street in the community. That one major street was part of the scenery that made Wadena resemble something out of the Old West, a place where one could walk down to that street's end and stare off into an eternity of open land, making one wonder what lay beyond. Fittingly known as "Big Swede" around Wadena (as he was a full-blooded Swede; Birdie was half Swedish and half Norwegian), the multiskilled Joe would compile a long list of occupations that including being a penitentiary guard in Alberta as well as a deacon at the local Baptist church. He was a strong man with "fists that resembled a bunch of bananas," according to one who knew him.

As younger men, Joe and his brother Mac would stroll to a local gathering place, where they were known to challenge other men to arm-wrestling matches at any time; if an impromptu tournament was suddenly arranged, the two Magnusons usually wound up in the final round against one another after defeating everyone else.

Keith mentioned about his childhood in watching the scene from a safe distance down the street, "On Saturday nights there, I remember, they would go to a hotel lobby and set up a ring to see who was the strongest guy. They wouldn't drink. None of that; they were too religious. It was just good, clean fun."

The practice of religion was paramount in the Magnuson household. Smoking, drinking, or hanging out at the local pool hall were not acceptable activities for Keith and his siblings, but regular attendance at Sunday services certainly was. And in addition to churchgoing, the Sabbath was expected to be a day of rest on which no activity whatsoever was permitted. This even included hockey—a true sacrifice on one out of every seven days for a boy like Keith.

"I loved morning Sunday school," he admitted, "but I fell asleep in church. To stay awake, I'd write down on the church calendar the hockey routine that I'd practice on Monday. On Sunday nights, I wanted to play hockey instead of going to church, so I'd have to sneak out."

Once Sunday obligations were over and the work week returned, hockey was a prime focus at the Magnuson home. There were only six teams in the National Hockey League at that time, and Joe's favorite of those was the Chicago Black Hawks[1]. His favorite player on the Hawks was Reggie "the Ruffian" Fleming, a player in the true Canadian tradition who deftly combined athletic skill with a resilient toughness and a willingness to fight all comers. As in most homes fortunate enough to have televisions, all other attention stopped at the Magnuson house when the Hawks were televised nationally on *Hockey Night in Canada*, the fanatical equivalent to the show launched in the United States in 1970 known as *Monday Night Football.*

Despite the outward displays of bravado with pond hockey and arm-wrestling matches, the family also valued the finer things in life. This included a great enjoyment of music, with household songs popping up just as often as challenges of physical prowess. And while Keith admitted an inability to carry a tune, he would do his best as a youngster to bellow along with his mother, father, and brother Dale, while his brother Wayne piped out notes on the trumpet and his sister, Meridel, joined in on the piano.

Their house was a two-story structure near the center of Wadena, across the street from the church—making any excuses for not attending those Sunday services hard to come by. A variety of flowers surrounded the lot, and a large elm tree stood in the front yard and supported an old tire swing. With no indoor plumbing in the house, it soon became young Keith's distasteful job to carry a bucket to the cesspool at the back edge of the family's property "where the rats hung out," as he remembered. "I hated facing those huge, well-fed, evil-looking animals that were always there."

This inconvenience was suggestive of the practicality and resourcefulness of the Magnusons and most people in the area, who did what was necessary to advance their well-being. Wayne was an excellent

1 Until 1986, the team was known as the "Black Hawks," at which time the name was shortened to one word as "Blackhawks." Thus, to correspond with the timeframe covered, "Black Hawks" will be used in this book.

trapper and hunter, and helped provide meat in the wintertime when he would score a deer or two, or perhaps some mallards in the summer. He also liked to pick crows off the power lines and had a keen shooting eye. Once while riding in the back seat of the family car, Wayne spied a blackbird perched above the highway. Not wanting to first alert Joe or Birdie, he reached for his pump-action shotgun in the hope they would stop the car for a shot, but he mishandled the rifle. The safety off, the gun discharged and blew out the back window. Despite thc surprise, the Magnusons were reported to have hardly flinched, and escaped the situation unscathed—just another raw episode from living in the country. "A person's toughness must come from somewhere, and in my case I believe it came from where I was born," Keith stated.

For the sub-arctic Saskatchewan days that were simply too brutal for hockey on the ponds and lakes out in the open lands, Wadena (which actually fell within the official definition of "subarctic" at 51 degrees latitude) did offer a makeshift facility for hockey and public skating in town, as primitive as it may have been.

"There was a potbellied stove in the middle of the dressing room and rough boards on the floor," recalled Dale. "The ice was natural. The hits were cold. That's where Keith got his start."

From the Magnuson home, Keith would sprint down a back alley as a shortcut to the rink—often with his skates already on, so that he would waste no time. (This would cause damage to his blades, of course; a local man would sharpen his skates for 50 cents, but Joe would permit only one sharpening per year. Keith would be careful to remember this, and made the annual repair count.)

And thus, as he would do many years later with another group of friends, Keith would always be the first among his teammates to leap onto the ice.

He sprung right into organized hockey in Wadena at the age of five, playing in the "Tom Thumb" level for beginners. For additional practice, he also regularly joined boys of all ages for pickup games at the rink and on the ponds. Whether it was a league game or a quickly assembled pickup contest, Keith would recall being in a bad mood—even to the point of tears—if his team lost.

Always an admirer of his older siblings, Keith immediately began playing defenseman because that was the position Wayne played. Likewise, in the springtime, he would emulate Wayne as a catcher in baseball. Soon everyone noticed that, even at a young age, Keith was a perfectionist on the ice, carefully monitoring every detail in the advancement of his skills. He continued to jot down his practice routine on the church calendar during services.

"Keith always had a checklist and was very systematic," said Herb Pinder, a childhood acquaintance. "Every night when we didn't play, or even sometimes on days when we practiced, he would write a list of what he needed to work on and then go out on the outdoor neighborhood rink and follow that list. He was very disciplined that way."

Developing his physical traits early, Keith later in life claimed that the only time he was naturally good at sports was in the first grade, when he was big for his age and the fastest runner in his class.

At the age of seven, he received an autographed photo in the mail from one of his favorite players in the NHL, a young star with the Detroit Red Wings. The writing on the photo read:

To my little friend, Keith... Best always, Gordie.

Gordie Howe, at age 26 that year, had already won four league scoring titles, in the previous four seasons (1951–54), and was yet another player formed out of those rough Saskatchewan winters.

And just as had happened to Gordie in his childhood, Keith's father grabbed an opportunity to move the family to the province's central city of Saskatoon for better fortunes. When Keith was eight years old, Joe got an offer to sell insurance and run a wholesale hardware business in the municipality of 100,000 people that lay 130 miles to the west—and it was too good to refuse. Keith had earlier told his dad that he never wanted to live in the city, but he understood why his father took the job.

As the family was packing up to depart for Saskatoon, one thing the pensive Keith wanted to leave behind in Wadena was what he considered his reputation as a "bully" among other kids, despite his young age. "Because I was big when I was little, I'd usually beat up my peers," he once wrote of his time in the early grades. "Of course, it didn't get me anywhere. Sure, at the time I might win a point. But then I began to realize that kids didn't want to play with me. This hurt."

Unfortunately, he was unable to avoid confrontation in his new surroundings. In his very first day at Churchill Elementary School in Saskatoon, he was taunted by another youngster who told him that "we don't want any farm boys" when Keith tried to take part in a schoolyard game. While many joined in the jeering, one new friend who did stand up for Keith was Tim Gould, who ultimately would be by Keith's side often—including on the ice—in the years to come.

In spite of the kind gesture, Keith did not need Tim's help. Instead, the young Magnuson felt compelled to at least momentarily go back to his physical ways. And after a thorough whipping, the main aggravator—along with the others at Churchill School—did not ever challenge the new red-haired kid again.

Most elementary schools in Canada had their own hockey teams, and this was particularly true in larger cities like Saskatoon. And much to his own surprise, by the sixth grade, Keith's demeanor had improved so much from those earlier "bullying" days in Wadena that he won the award for "Most Gentlemanly Player" that year (although the recognition would not necessarily forecast a Lady Byng Trophy for him in the future).

On the other side of the city, the same award had been won by a seventh-grade student at Princess Alexandria School, Cliff Koroll. The two went head to head on the ice on several occasions. Years later, someone asked Magnuson what he remembered about Koroll from those childhood days; after thinking for a moment to summon a distinctive quality, he offered that Koroll's "ears stuck way out from his helmet."

As for Cliff, he would later describe his own first impressions of Magnuson. "I remember this little redhead comes off the farm, skinny, arms down below his knees, bowlegs," Koroll said. The two would have many youth-league battles as opponents before joining forces on the same side years later. "He would always try to hit me in the corners," Koroll added, "and [he] would always bounce off me, as I was much bigger than he was. He would get up and run at me again."

The two quickly became friends through other sports; some of their more notable meetings took place on the baseball diamond. "When our coach gave the signal to steal, it was not to steal second but to go to third because he [Magnuson] would end up throwing the ball into center field," Koroll chuckled. "He was a small kid between [ages] 10 and 15 but he always had those long arms and huge hands." And oftentimes it was Gould, playing third base, who would get the final throw on the play from the center fielder who had retrieved Keith's errant throw to second.

Magnuson and Koroll—like many of the most promising young Canadian players—had their hockey futures essentially mapped out for them by the time they reached their early teens. The youth hockey clubs in Saskatoon and most other places were, in effect, an extension of the Canadian Juniors system, the tradition-rich "minor leagues" of the sport from whence the vast majority of the players in the NHL had come, with few high school age players considering collegiate play as an option. Teams around the city such as the Saskatoon Blades and the Midget Red Wings were fully sponsored by NHL clubs—making the teenagers on their rosters de facto possessions of those teams.

"I was the Blades' [the Los Angeles forerunner of the Kings] property at 10 years old," Magnuson recalled. "By the time I'd reached 16, however, Chicago and L.A. had worked a deal transferring Cliff Koroll and me to the Black Hawks... It's like being a product on the exchange—a negotiable item among high-powered businessmen. Even at 12, I recall having to sign a professional sponsor's form" (along with his parents).

While only a teenager, Keith was nonetheless always looking for an edge to increase his strength and performance. Starting in junior high school, he began to spend a portion of his summers working at Boychuk Lumber Yard in Saskatoon, where he was paid $1.50 an hour.

"I'd cut two-by-fours or load 80-pound cement bags, and go out on deliveries or work construction projects, such as building a granary," he remembered.

Despite the strenuous labor, he also dedicated himself to rigorous athletic training upon coming home at night, regardless of his level of fatigue from the lumber yard. Despite the hard work, Keith's growth had slowed heading into high school, as he started his freshman year at only 5'6" and 140 pounds—not much bigger from when he was admittedly pushing kids around in his first grade class back in Wadena. However, with one more summer working at Boychuk after his first year in high school, he "zoomed up" to 160 as his efforts finally paid off. His sports skills now took off as well, as he twice won the Saskatchewan province title in the javelin throw as a track-and-field competitor and was a city champion in football while leading his team at quarterback.

But hockey, of course, remained his true love. And naturally, Keith marveled at the idea of pursuing a regular spot in the prestigious-but-rugged Juniors system. However, he and his parents also recognized the challenging lifestyle of the Juniors for a teenager, and took this fact into careful consideration as he began his time with the Blades.

Players in the Juniors roomed together all season long with teammates from their same communities. Most would never finish high school, dubbed "hockey dropouts" when they would wind up short of their NHL dream and with no education on which to fall back. A player named Dave Schultz, with whom Magnuson would have much contact down the road, revealed the off-the-books education that the system otherwise provided.

"If nothing else," Schultz said after his playing days were finished, "Juniors taught me the hard facts of life about hockey...up until then, hockey to me had been a pretty game of skating, shooting, stickhandling, and playmaking. When a stick was rammed into my stomach, a butt end massaged my ribs, and a thick leather gauntlet was pushed in my face, I got a different impression of what organized hockey was all about."

Keith acknowledged that, in his last year of high school while playing for the Blades, he was flunking half his courses because all his attention turned to hockey. Through the winter of 1963–64, he would play in 54 games for the Blades as a defenseman, scoring two goals and collecting nine assists, with two more assists in five playoff contests.

At about this time, the University of Denver head hockey coach Murray Armstrong was on a recruiting trip to Saskatoon, which was one of his favorite places to mine talent and take it back to the States. Koroll was already at DU as a freshman after fighting off the temptation to go full-bore into the Juniors, and Armstrong now returned to offer new scholarships to six other city residents: Magnuson, Gould, Don Thiessen, Neil McQueen, Bob Sutcliffe, and Dale Zeman.

Despite several familiar faces heading to Denver, Keith was reluctant to go, and it was a reluctance that was somewhat shared by his parents. He had never spent much time away from home. But

Armstrong—frank, fair, and honest with the parents and guardians of the players whom he recruited—assured Joe and Birdie that he would take excellent care of their son. Keith would have the opportunity to further his education in addition to his hockey career.

"There was no letter of intent or anything like that," Denver player Jim Wiste said of Armstrong's sales pitch. Wiste and Magnuson would soon become great friends as well as teammates. "Murray would come to your home and would tell your mom and dad, 'I would want my own son to go to Denver.' And when a player complained that there was no signed piece of paper that stated he had a scholarship, Murray would simply reply, 'You have my word—that is better than a piece of paper.'"

Armstrong's sincerity won over the Magnuson family, and Keith worked hard to improve his grades in the final months of his high school career. He also continued to fine-tune his hockey skills into the late hours of the night at a Saskatoon rink, where his siblings would help him.

He was formally accepted into Denver a week before classes began in the fall of 1965. Right at that time, a couple of National Football League rookies named Butkus and Sayers were departing their first professional training camp to join the Bears in Chicago, and the sports scene in that city was about to enter a new era.

2

A Pioneer in America

"I wanted to become a hockey player, and there's no better place than Denver for that."

—Keith Magnuson, 1970

Murray Armstrong was definitely part of the "old guard" of hockey, having played in the NHL for the Toronto Maple Leafs, the New York/Brooklyn Americans, and the Detroit Red Wings from 1938 to 1946, with a brief interruption for military service during World War II. After a few years of coaching in the top level of the Juniors system, he took on a new challenge in 1956 in what some might have considered the hockey coaches' graveyard—becoming the head man at an American college.

The University of Denver Pioneers had long been an exception in this regard, however—and Armstrong was a perfect fit to take over for departing coach Neil Celley. Armstrong quickly advanced the program to new heights, claiming the school's first national championships in 1958, 1960, and 1961. And in 1965, Keith Magnuson and his friends from Saskatoon were being relied upon to carry the flag onward as the new batch of talent.

On the first day he set foot on the ice at DU, Magnuson was paired on defense with Tim Gould—the one who had stood up for Keith on the playground on his first day of elementary school in Saskatoon. Both young men noticed immediately that Armstrong ran very creative practices that kept the players' attention, interest, and conditioning at an optimal level. "A hockey game is won or lost in the corners!" the coach would holler—if Magnuson heard Armstrong utter this phrase once, he heard it a thousand times.

In addition to lengthy drills in physical training, Armstrong also utilized competitive games to motivate the players—such as one of Magnuson's favorites, Oranges and Lemons. Occasionally at the end of a practice, Armstrong would have the players split into two teams and attempt breakaway shots on the goaltenders at each end of the ice. As this occurred, Armstrong could be seen shuffling along the edge of the rink, lining the top of the boards with one row of oranges and one row of lemons; the team that scored more goals was permitted to eat the oranges after practice, while the side with fewer goals had to suck the lemons.

The coach also took a very professional approach during workouts with his players—in a literal sense.

"Armstrong ran practices under NHL rules," Magnuson said of the overarching environment. "We hit all over the ice…we got more experience with a hitting style than you might expect [from a typical college program]."

In further preparing his players for the possibility of playing at the next level, Armstrong also had them match up at practice and "spar"—a simulation of a fight that, instead of throwing punches, involved learning the skills necessary to gain leverage on the opponent's jersey, maintaining balance on one's skates, and the multitude of other factors involved in hockey self-defense in addition to simply letting one's fists fly.

"We often practiced from 1:00 to 4:30 PM for several days at a time," Jim Wiste recalled. "The amount of time we were on the ice might well be considered illegal today by the NCAA."

Armstrong had indeed been hardened through the tough ranks of the game in the raw, Canadian way. And with Magnuson, Gould, and the others from Saskatoon as examples, the coach made it clear that he preferred recruiting Canadian players almost exclusively—and Keith readily agreed that this approach led to DU's relative dominance in American collegiate play.

"I remember our freshman games against [the University of] Colorado," Magnuson stated about his very first year of skating in the States. "CU was a team of Americans who had simply not grown up in the rough, tough Canadian tradition. We soon let them know we were on the ice by running at them every chance we got. And if an American came out for the Denver team, we'd give him a hard time, too. Nothing dirty, mind you, just good, hard checks. And if he couldn't hack the hitting, he'd leave. Quite a few did."

But it was not only Armstrong who made an instant impact on Magnuson's game and life; so did Armstrong's assistant coach, Harry Ottenbreit, who at the time was also going through law school at DU. Ottenbreit complemented Armstrong's knowledge by impacting Keith's development in hockey from an intellectual standpoint.

Since freshmen were ineligible for varsity play, much of Magnuson's first year at Denver was spent working and learning, learning and working, until Armstrong's system had been fully ingrained in his mind. Ottenbreit would stay on the ice with Keith long after the regular team practice was over and work one-on-one with Magnuson on the weaker points of his game. Ottenbreit noticed that the young Keith was often running at players wildly and out of control, so the coach introduced Magnuson to the value of the hip check as a more controlled and effective physical option, and modeled the technique for him until the defenseman mastered it.

In addition to following the advice of their coaches, Magnuson and his fellow freshmen also made it their task to emulate the characteristics of the upperclassmen who made the program successful. During his initial year in Denver, Keith was rooming with four of the other plebes from Saskatoon (Gould, Neil McQueen, Bob Sutcliffe, and Dale Zeman). They helped each other adjust to life in college as well as life in America. Also among the freshmen in 1965 was Craig Patrick, the son of former NHL player Lynn Patrick (and grandson of hockey legend Lester Patrick) who himself had already played three years in the Juniors.

While much knowledge was gained, there were also considerable challenges. In battling players in practice a few years older while juggling a first semester at college far away from family—Keith had struggled to attain a modest report card in his initial term—the first few months at Denver had taken their toll on Magnuson. Thus, Keith enjoyed a much-needed rest over Christmas 1965 back home in Saskatoon, catching up with local news from his parents, siblings, and friends. It was just the refreshment he needed; and upon leaving town, he was grateful to receive a car from his father to take back to Colorado and use on the Denver campus.

Naturally, the likable Magnuson's popularity with his college friends increased even further after he returned to a school with a car of his own. One night, he offered to transport some friends out to the local bowling alley to roll a few frames. But when they returned to the parking lot later that evening, the car was missing. Thinking it had been stolen, Keith called the police while hoping the situation could be resolved—in one way or another—before he had to inform his father of what had happened.

As Magnuson stood talking to the officer in the previously occupied parking space, a man suddenly came running up the street, screaming in a frenzied state that a car had crashed into the living room of his home—and was still sitting there—and also claiming the car had a license plate displaying a "state" that he never heard of, and could not even pronounce. Keith then suddenly realized that he had forgotten to set the parking brake. The car subsequently had rolled down a long hill—completely unscathed, amazingly, through three busy intersections—before coming to rest inside the man's home (at which point the car and the man's home was certainly scathed). Fortunately, the victim was also a big fan of DU hockey, like most everyone near the campus, and forgave Magnuson and his friends, even offering to call a towing company for them.

A week or so later, the phone rang at the Magnuson house back in Saskatoon. It was the family's insurance man, who happened to be calling about another matter—but who also inadvertently gave Keith's dad his first inkling of the accident: "By the way, Joe, the car's almost fixed."

After the mishap, Keith returned his focus to his hockey and academic work, and his growth continued through the end of his first year of college. He and his freshman classmates continued to labor against the sophomores, juniors, and seniors in practice, helping the older players ready themselves for play in the tough Western Collegiate Hockey Association while improving themselves at the same time. That season, the varsity finished with a solid 18–11–3 record, but everyone could sense that greater things were ahead with Magnuson and his promising fellow youngsters in the pipeline. And as Keith soon learned, Armstrong and Ottenbreit would suddenly be expecting much more of him.

Perhaps one reason Keith was a popular driver among his friends was that he did not drink alcohol during his freshman year at Denver.

It was a practice he brought with him through high school, which had made him a safe choice behind the wheel. Nonetheless, he admitted his habits changed in his sophomore campaign—first for the slightly worse in the short term, and then for the much better in the long run.

He endured a rough beginning to his initial season on the varsity in the fall of 1966; the team lost its first two games in the third week of November by scores of 2–1 and 3–2 at Michigan Tech University. Denver struggled to score against the home team's formidable senior goalie, Tony Esposito. Esposito, two years earlier, had led MTU to the national championship back in his own sophomore year in 1965.

Armstrong was not only enraged to start the season 0–2; he was even more disgusted by the team's lackadaisical play in doing so. Knowing that leaders had to emerge from the new cadre of players, he openly challenged Magnuson and the rest of the team after the opening loss. Things came to head after the second defeat, when the team went on a consolatory drinking binge—after which Keith could barely make his way back onto the Pioneers bus. Now finished with his anger and sensing a teachable moment, Armstrong gently sat down next to Magnuson for the ride to the airport, as well as on the plane to Denver.

"You know, if you play it right, you can have quite a future in hockey," he said to Keith. "You've got all the credentials: desire, determination, you want to learn, and you don't mind working hard.

"But just look at yourself right now. I don't mind my players enjoying themselves, letting off steam, and having a few beers once in a while, but you're running around half-cocked. And the point is, there's a great pro future waiting for you, if you'll but work for it."

Keith was so embarrassed that he decided, then and there, that no distractions would get in the way of his development ever again. He worked harder in the classroom, and his grades improved. He spent even more time on his hockey skills after practice with Ottenbreit, staying at the rink to work until dinnertime and beyond, often missing the meal altogether. But most of all, he became obsessed with making Armstrong proud of him.

Magnuson could feel the camaraderie among the rest of his teammates growing. On the day of home games at DU, the team started gathering for steak dinners at the Writers Manor Hotel in Denver in the early afternoon—and left the heavier partying to its appropriate time, as their experience had taught them. The result was a very strong year with a final record of 22–8. The season ended with a loss to the powerful North Dakota squad in the NCAA playoffs. (Despite the team's alleged abstinence, Armstrong believed one reason for the loss was a spring break trip to Mexico that was being planned by several Pioneers players upon season's end.)

Magnuson's work ethic had not wavered, however, just as he had promised. And it had paid off, as he was named (along with co-winner Bob Munro) the WCHA Rookie of the Year, an honor annually given to the sophomore who makes the greatest impact in the league. Magnuson was confident he could carry his club even further; great things were expected of the DU team entering the fall of 1967, as the tremendous recruiting class of which Magnuson was a part was expected to blossom after a year of varsity play under its belt.

The captain of the 1967–68 DU team was Cliff Koroll, Magnuson's former youth league opponent back in Saskatoon, now a senior. It would also be the second straight year that the two young men would be roommates, their first living off campus. They were joined by Wiste, yet another pro prospect on the Pioneers from Saskatchewan, who had gained valuable experience playing for his hometown of Moose Jaw in the Juniors. Now settling comfortably into the college milieu, Magnuson began exhibiting several entertaining personal habits and routines for which Koroll and Wiste would tease him for the rest of their lives.

"Maggie was very gullible at times and usually the brunt of our jokes," Koroll revealed about the living arrangement. "It was all in good fun and he took it well. Keith would incessantly write reminders to himself on little pieces of paper, which were found all over the apartment." The practice would follow Magnuson for years to come. "He would always screw up the punchline of jokes," Koroll added about his friend, "which was funnier than the jokes themselves. That's why we gave him nickname 'the Riddler.'" In an effort to relieve stress from classes or hockey workouts—and perhaps as a form of superstition in the midst of a winning streak (a characteristic that would also follow Keith in later years)—the guys attempted to relax in the apartment by listening to Tchaikovsky's *Swan Lake* over and over again.

As another form of entertainment—as well as an opportunity to earn a few dollars—Magnuson, Wiste, and some of the other players had found jobs at the local horse racing track. Wiste parked cars as a valet (wearing leg weights while running back and forth from the parking lot to build his strength) while Magnuson took bets at the ticket window. Not long after being employed there, Magnuson stunned Wiste with some news.

"Jimmy," Magnuson said, "I've just hit six races in a row, and I have a system for picking the winners."

"Tell me the system!" Wiste replied.

"Well, I look through the program for each race, I see the weights of each of the horses, and I simply pick the lightest one—that one has to be the fastest, right?"

"Maggie," Wiste told Keith, "the weight listed is the *jockey's*—not the horse's."

Wiste also recalled an incident from the summer of 1967, during which time Magnuson was especially admiring Paul Newman's character from the movie *Cool Hand Luke*, which had just hit the theatres. It gave Wiste an idea.

"Maggie, can you eat 25 hard-boiled eggs?" he asked his friend. Magnuson replied in the affirmative, and Wiste and others began taking bets—just as the cellblock leader Dragline had done in the movie. And the red-haired kid from Saskatchewan did not disappoint anyone, downing the 25 eggs without hardly batting an eye.

But time for such jocularity was rare; there was much work for the young men to do, both on and off the ice. With sights on NHL careers further down the road, the three could more often be seen running up the stairs of the DU football stadium, again and again, challenging themselves to push their physical limits.

Unlike the Christmas season during his freshman year when Keith returned home to Canada, Joe and Birdie instead returned the favor to their youngest son in December 1967 and drove down to visit him over the holidays. Unfortunately, they were involved in an auto accident on the way; and when they finally met up with Keith, Joe displayed a black eye and Birdie had a sore back. They saw him get his first taste of international hockey in the Broadmoor World Tournament in Colorado Springs, in which DU competed against the Finnish, Italian, American, and Russian national teams.

Denver began their portion of the schedule on December 26 by playing Finland to a 2–2 tie, followed by a 5–4 loss to the American national team before beating the Italians 5–2. Next were the vaunted Russians on December 30, the mysterious and powerful opponent whom everyone in international hockey feared. Getting a glimpse of their training methods, even Armstrong and Ottenbreit were stunned by the unmatched intensity with which the Soviets went about their work. For example, Magnuson himself noticed that on the day of their game with the Russians, the Soviet players not only did an hour of calisthenics and runs around the mountains but also held a full practice session, including seemingly endless skating drills with no pucks (suddenly the football stadium stairs on campus did not seem so bad to Magnuson, Wiste, and Koroll after all). The Russians then capped their busy day with an 8–1 thrashing of DU, providing Magnuson another lesson about the lengths to which a hockey player could drive himself to improve.

Keith and the entire Denver team took the defeat as instructive—they did not lose again that year. After departing Colorado Springs, Armstrong's men ran off 22 straight wins to finish the season, capped by a 4–0 shutout of North Dakota in the 1968 NCAA championship game that vindicated the Pioneers' ousting from the previous year's WCHA tournament by UND.

After experiencing the thrill of the national title, Magnuson was determined to leave Denver on just as high a note after his senior campaign the following fall. As a senior, he once again chose to live off-campus—along with Patrick and other teammates Cab Stitt, Jerry Powers, and Jeff Jennings. Koroll and Wiste had moved on; both men were now in the farm system of the Black Hawks, playing at Dallas in the Central League and preparing for their first taste of training camp in Chicago with the big-league team in September. It was now Magnuson's turn to be captain, as he gratefully took the *C* from the sweaters of Koroll and Wiste (which Magnuson would also share for the season with Patrick and fellow teammate Tom Miller).

Not resting on his laurels, Magnuson's intensity during Denver practice sessions actually heightened in his final season. In the summer before the start of school his senior year, he had also begun studying karate at nights (while earning money by collecting rent for a Denver real estate firm during the day), believing that training in the martial arts would be extra preparation for professional hockey down the road. While he did not care much for other aspects of the karate classes, Magnuson instead much preferred the free-sparring segments of his training sessions. Seeking physical activity wherever he could, in the previous year he had even joined the DU lacrosse team with Koroll,

Wiste, and Patrick—and the hockey players took to the sport naturally. Magnuson's burning desire for victory, not surprisingly, was not checked at the door.

"In a game against Air Force Academy, the first fight ever in Colorado lacrosse took place," Koroll revealed with a chuckle. "Guess who started it."

While still unrelenting in his dedication to his sport and teammates, Keith knew that leadership also involved the wisdom to know when a little levity was in order to keep the team loose. In addition to the Writers Manor Hotel, the players would also hang out at the Ninth Hole bar in Denver, where the owner had already put large pictures of local heroes Magnuson, Koroll, and Wiste on his wall. While there relaxing one day—in sandals—Keith bet his friends that he could make the three-mile run back to campus in 20 minutes or less. Popping off his flip-flops and sprinting barefooted, he bolted off and soon phoned the rest of them from his friend's apartment on campus—exactly 18 and a half minutes after leaving the bar. Not coincidentally, Magnuson was the "patient" the next day in his athletic training class, taught by team trainer Gene Bradshaw, who demonstrated the proper technique for treating foot blisters while Keith yelped in pain.

By this time, an easy confidence was bursting from every part of the Pioneers roster. As Magnuson and his classmates had done as freshmen, a new crop of hungry recruits challenged the varsity in practice. Following their 22 straight wins to close out the 1968 championship, the upperclassmen lost the first two games to North Dakota in November 1968 before winning 15 of their next 17 games with Magnuson at the helm as captain. An eight-game winning streak then closed the season in the spring of 1969, which not only included a two-game sweep of the Canadian National Team but a defeat of Cornell University in the NCAA finals as well, bringing DU its second straight national championship. To get by Cornell, Denver had to contend with another outstanding goaltender—a young man named Ken Dryden, who two years earlier had led the Big Red to the NCAA title and who had compiled a career record at Cornell of 76–4–1 in goal. (A year later in 1970, after Dryden's departure, Cornell would reclaim the NCAA title from DU with a perfect 29–0 record, the only college team to finish a season undefeated while Denver, without Magnuson, slipped to a 21–10–1 mark and bowed out to Wisconsin in the playoffs.)

In addition to excelling on defense, Magnuson also outscored all the forwards in the 1969 NCAA tournament in total points (goals and assists combined), and was named the Most Valuable Player as he prepared for the next step of his hockey career—the largest one of all.

Few players had ever jumped from the college ranks to the NHL while bypassing the Juniors system, but Magnuson looked to be one of them. He had also finally proven himself in the classroom, earning his degree in business administration. Just as Keith's family had done back home in Saskatoon, Armstrong had carefully prepared him for life after college, and the coach always knew that Magnuson would be able to take care of himself.

"You never, ever worried about Keith being ready to play or doing the right things," Armstrong would say in 2003 at the age of 87. "He was our captain. He was the heart and soul of our team, and one of the most outstanding young men I ever had the privilege to be around."

As for Magnuson himself, he had no doubt he had made the right choice in coming to the Mile High City. "I wanted to become a hockey player," Keith would say in 1970, a year after he finished his work at the campus. "And there's no better place than Denver for that. You play a good, long schedule and you get all the practice time you want. And Murray Armstrong is really an excellent coach for a guy who wants to play in the NHL."

• • •

Sensing that Wiste and Koroll would need business-related representation in negotiations with the Black Hawks, Ottenbreit had offered to be their legal adviser and business manager in 1968; in 1969, he assumed the same role with Magnuson. They were his very first clients.

Not 20 minutes after DU had won the national title against Cornell—and just 10 minutes after learning of his selection as tournament MVP—Magnuson was approached by Black Hawks general manager Tommy Ivan to discuss a contract with Chicago. Ivan had already been with the Hawks for 15 years, after a successful run with the Detroit Red Wings that included being the first professional coach for Gordie Howe just as World War II was ending.

Ivan was under the employ of Arthur M. Wirtz, the owner of the Black Hawks who graduated from the University of Michigan in 1922 and was the son of a Chicago policeman. Few people gobbled up more Midwestern real estate during and after the years of the Great Depression than did Wirtz, who had quickly launched his own real estate firm in Chicago in 1927 after leaving Ann Arbor.

Surviving the pitfalls of the Depression when others in his field could not, Wirtz continued to acquire disbanded properties as competitors took losses. Along the way he would meet a man named James Norris, who would kindle his interest in hockey and with whom Wirtz would partner on many business ventures in banking and real estate. In 1929 the two men took over the Detroit professional hockey franchise, and, in turn, invested in the future growth of the NHL as a major league sports operation to compete with baseball (and the fledgling National Football League) in the United States. Wirtz also assumed controlling in interest in the Olympia arena in Detroit and the Chicago Stadium soon after. In time, Wirtz would control the St. Louis Arena as well, which had been finished in 1929 and would become the home of the St. Louis Blues upon their first season of play in the NHL in 1967. (Until the Blues entered the league, the arena was used by a Hawks farm team in the Central Hockey League before being purchased by St. Louis businessman Sid Salomon Jr.)

Wirtz and Norris struck again in 1946, taking ownership control of the Black Hawks, and five years later, Wirtz left behind his Detroit ventures to devote his attention to his Chicago matters. Norris passed away the following year in 1952, leaving Wirtz in complete charge of the franchise. In 1954 he hired Ivan as general manager, and by 1966 had installed his son, Bill Wirtz, as president of the Black Hawks, to handle most of the team's business and hockey operations.

After a quick word in the corridors of the Broadmoor Arena in Colorado Springs (which, in addition to the world tournament in which DU played, also hosted the NCAA finals in 1969 for the first time after a 12-year hiatus), Ivan, Ottenbreit, and Magnuson took their meeting to a local hotel room a short time later. Sitting stoically across from Magnuson and Ottenbreit, Ivan pushed a piece of paper across the table that contained a $15,000, one-year contract offer. To Ivan's shrewd pleasure, Magnuson was noticeably excited and was only a split-second away from leaping from his chair to extend Ivan an accepting handshake. But Ottenbreit grabbed Magnuson's knee under the table just in time and stopped him. Instead, Ottenbreit countered Ivan with a multiyear deal at $25,000 per season. Irate, Ivan stormed out of the room as he snapped at the two men back over his shoulder.

"It appears, Magnuson, that you don't want to play for the Chicago Black Hawks," Ivan concluded simply.

Once again, Keith felt compelled to jump up from the table—but this time, it was to stop Ivan from leaving the room, to drop down to his knees, to beg Ivan for forgiveness, and to sign the contract for *any* amount. But Ottenbreit stopped him again. He had a plan, he assured

Keith with a calm nod. Ivan left the building; and despite Ottenbreit's assurances, Magnuson was beside himself with worry.

Ottenbreit convinced Keith that the Black Hawks did not have a "policeman" on their roster at the time—that is, one man to whom the team can turn to be a defender—or if need be, a fighter—against another team's toughest players. The Hawks had long been in need of a more physical roster, since their home rink—the Stadium—was 12 feet shorter than the standard NHL arena, providing a more compacted playing area with less skating room in the neutral zone. (The Stadium ice was 188 feet long, as opposed to the regulation length of 200 feet—a rule which the NHL had put into force after the Stadium was built.) Fighting, while a controlled tradition in professional hockey, was not part of the college game; Magnuson, most of his teammates, and most of his opponents had little formal experience with it on the ice, unless they had previously played in the Juniors. Ottenbreit, however, told Magnuson that if he stepped up his fighting skills and general physical play, there would be a place for him in Chicago—at a much better price than what Ivan was offering.

As a result, Ottenrbreit and Ivan retreated to their calculators after their initial picket-line volleys, and subsequently dug in for contract negotiations during the summer of 1969. Magnuson, meanwhile, was given one job to do, and he did it: ramping up his already intense physical training while integrating some new pugilistic skills.

"Sure, it got monotonous and was pretty lonely as well, running up and down those stairs in that big empty stadium," he said of once again traversing the steps of the DU football complex, sometimes with Wiste and Koroll, who had returned to work out with him, and sometimes by himself. "But now I felt driven…by pretending I was in the Chicago Stadium with the noise of the crowd echoing in my ears, I could psych myself up beyond description."

For further lower-body training, Magnuson also began strapping five-pound weights to his skates when he hit the ice—just as Wiste had done during his valet job—all while continuing his karate practice in addition to still working 8:00 AM to 5:00 PM most days for the Denver realty firm. And each time Keith would come into the office for work, Ottenbreit (who was an advisor for the firm) would instruct someone to take a jab at him—to see if Keith could block or avoid the punch. For extra pay in advance of looking forward to his first professional contract, Magnuson even supplemented his income by washing dishes at a sorority house on campus.

"That really bugged me," Magnuson would say a couple years later about one aspect of that job. "For two years in a row I was named All-American, helped my team to two national championships, and those girls still laughed at me."

And despite being an All-American, he was by no means getting wealthy at the job.

"A lot of times I'd be down to my last quarter...sometimes I'd write checks for a dollar or two, because that's all I had. On weekends when the sorority house closed, I'd walk over to a restaurant called Pat and Lucy's with a hungry look on my face. They were good friends and they knew what the problem was. They would see me and say, 'Come on in, Maggie. We have some stuff in the back that we're not using.' I was really grateful. I only got about $40 a month in expenses for playing hockey, and that didn't go very far."

Koroll and Wiste had spent the past year furthering their own hockey education in the Central League, and Ottenbreit sensed another opportunity with them back in town, covertly instructing them to give Magnuson an advanced taste of the pro game.

"Harry still felt that one hole remained in my training: growing accustomed to being hit behind my own net and in the corners, something that hadn't happened since my Canadian hockey days in Saskatoon," Magnuson recalled.

Koroll, a strong, physical forward in addition to being a scoring threat, started to beat on Keith at Ottenbreit's command in a way his friend was not familiar. At one point, they even got into a heated shoving match at the boards before Ottenbreit blew the whistle. Just as the whistle sounded, Magnuson and Koroll had grabbed each other by the jersey and were ready to throw punches at each other. They happened to look over at Ottenbreit and saw him smiling—his point had been made, as he believed that Keith had now graduated into the pro ranks. Later, after getting two cracked ribs as a result of his efforts to tangle with Koroll, Magnuson even thanked Cliff for the lesson.

"Wait 'til you get to Chicago," Koroll replied with an ominous chuckle.

Magnuson left no stone unturned in his preparation for the next step in his career, and he also used unconventional methods to steel his body. As an example, he convinced Denver friend Hawley Chester to join him on the ice and fire slap shots at him—with Keith trying to block them with his body.

"We'd get a bucket of pucks," Chester would recall, "and Maggie would say, 'Come on.' It used to hurt *me* just to shoot at him. I hit him in the head once or twice. After we were finished, I'd look at him in the dressing room and his arms and chest were black and blue."

The persistence paid off. Perhaps learning of how hard Magnuson was working, Ivan made another call to Ottenbreit later in the summer with a $20,000 contract offer, plus an additional signing bonus. Ottenbreit and his client agreed to the terms, with the contract to be signed after Magnuson joined the team in Chicago. A few days later, with Wiste close behind them, Magnuson and Koroll jumped into a car and headed east to Illinois for Keith's first major league training camp.

Upon arriving in the city, the boys from western Canada stared in awe at the massive skyscrapers along Michigan Avenue and marveled at the fancy stores (while Koroll and Wiste had been in camp with the Hawks the previous year, it was the first visit to Chicago for Magnuson). Before checking into the Bismarck Hotel where all the players would be staying during training camp, Koroll decided to drive Magnuson by the home of the Hawks—the massive Chicago Stadium, the largest indoor arena in the world at the time of its construction in the 1920s. Entering through the famous players' portal on the north end of the building which adjoined the larger Gate 3 (an entrance for buses and service vehicles), Magnuson gazed upwards in amazement as they reached the open expanse of the Stadium's interior.

"We walked in Gate 3½ and stood by the opening where the Zamboni was," Koroll said. "Keith looked up and said, 'Look at all the seats...this place even has its own smell.'

"I looked at him and said, 'The circus was in town last week.'"

On September 15, 1969, Magnuson would set foot on the Stadium ice for the first time in his initial practice session at the Black Hawks training camp. That same evening, the talent-laden Chicago Cubs had just rung the death knell in their infamous 1969 collapse. After dropping an 8–2 decision in Montreal on the 15th, the Cubs had lost 11 of their last 12 contests, and in that span had seen their five-game lead in the Eastern Division transform into a four-and-a-half game deficit behind the hard-charging New York Mets, who had won four of every five games since the end of July.

The Hawks training camp would be a grueling two-week stretch of two-a-day practices in advance of their exhibition schedule. On the morning of the first workout, Keith was up out of bed at 4:00 AM at the Bismarck, unable to sleep due to his excitement. He dressed quickly in the Stadium locker room; and just like back in his boyhood days in Wadena and Saskatoon, he leapt onto the ice with boundless energy before the rest of the players, undaunted by the lack of rest the night before.

"Keith Magnuson is a defenseman from Denver University [sic]," Ted Damata informed his readers in the *Chicago Tribune*, as he was checking out the team's first skating session from the stands. "He is a towhead, is boyish-faced, and has the same strong happy-skating action of Boston's famous Bobby Orr."

In responding to Damata's assessment of him, Magnuson's first interaction with the Chicago press was as polite as he could make it, as he instead was trying to focus on his work.

"He was surprised when told he looked like the great one," Damata continued about Magnuson's response to the allusion to the Bruins defenseman. "No one had mentioned it before. 'They don't see Orr in Denver,' he [Magnuson] suggested, but was pleased with the comparison."

Another nervous rookie on the ice for his first practice was Esposito, the goalie from Michigan Tech whom Magnuson had faced in collegiate play. Esposito had appeared in 13 games for the Montreal Canadiens the season prior, but was claimed for $25,000 by the Black Hawks in June (as part of the intraleague draft of unprotected players on teams' rosters—later to be known as "waivers") and would be vying for the starting position in the nets with returnees Dennis DeJordy and Dave Dryden. Dave was the older brother of Ken Dryden, whom Magnuson had also faced in the 1969 collegiate finals. (Dave, unable to take a spot from Esposito or DeJordy, would be suspended by the Chicago organization in October for refusing an assignment to the minor league team at Dallas.) The team had not experienced a steady force in goal since the departure of Glenn Hall to St. Louis, who was left unprotected in the expansion draft in 1967 after winning the Vezina Trophy as the league's top netminder.

Yet another individual making his debut at that first workout in 1969 was Gary Hull, the 26-year-old brother of more famous siblings

Bobby and Dennis, and whom their father had claimed four years earlier would "be the best of them all." While Bobby Hull had elevated himself to among the best the sport had ever seen (evidenced by his scoring a league-record 58 goals the past year)—and with Dennis not far behind—Gary had been in a brief hiatus in his hockey career while assisting Dennis on his cattle ranch before deciding to jump back into the game.

No one would match Magnuson's energy from his very first day with the Hawks. He credited the physical training he did in the thin mountain air in Denver his advantage in his initial interaction with the big-leaguers in Chicago. "Though I was still a naïve, gullible, red-haired western Canadian kid, and sure as hell scared at my first pro camp, I nevertheless felt in better shape than anyone there... Right then I determined that if I didn't make this team on my ability, I'd make it on my desire."

Back in Denver, Ottenbreit had suggested to Magnuson that, at some early point in camp, he should pick a fight with someone to establish himself (but to stay away from the stars in doing so, such as the Hulls and fellow headliner, Stan Mikita). Afraid to make a bad impression, however, Keith instead chose not to fight anyone—except for one minor scrap in the corner with veteran Eric Nesterenko, which amounted to little more than an exchange of forearms. But at Magnuson's gametime debut in a preseason contest in Toronto, that first fight came. Wiste had noticed that, in the locker room before each exhibition game that autumn, Magnuson would keep asking him or Koroll to name the toughest player on the opposing team. Regardless of which city in which the Hawks happened to be playing, Magnuson would make it a point to search that player out. In Toronto, the first fight was with Mike Walton, a veteran of the 1967 Stanley Cup–champion Maple Leafs. Walton was one of the Leafs' top scorers, having finished 1968 just ahead of his linemate Bob Pulford on the team's point list. Magnuson jumped on Walton early, on a play near the boards, but Walton got the best of him by unleashing several hard punches.

Magnuson was able to recover from the beating and tap a goal into the net in his first NHL game, and his presence that evening garnered him the "First Star" award in a 4–0 Hawks win. Greeting the rookie in the hallway outside the visitors' locker room at Maple Leaf Gardens was none other than Tommy Ivan, just as he had greeted Magnuson after the NCAA championship. Ivan was ready and smiling with the contract he had promised, and the perspiration from Magnuson's jersey dripped onto the page as he signed it.

Later that night, Magnuson, Ottenbreit, Wiste, and Koroll quietly celebrated Keith's finalized contract and first pro game with a couple of beers at (what they figured to be) a discreet, out-of-the-way Toronto tavern. While leaving the place, however, they just happened to bump into a man named Billy Reay on the sidewalk. The Black Hawks head coach since 1963, he previously had been the head man of Toronto, and thus was well aware of the local establishments in the city that players enjoyed frequenting. As a player himself with a 10-year career with Montreal and Detroit in the 1940s and '50s, Reay had won two Stanley Cup championships, but he was still searching for a title as the man behind the bench, having reached the final round as the leader of the Hawks in 1965 only to lose at the very end. The bitter defeat to the Montreal Canadiens in the seven-game series meant Chicago's last Stanley Cup championship had come in 1961 under coach Rudy Pilous, who, like Reay, was a Winnipeg native.

When the men encountered each other on the sidewalk, Reay took one second to study and register the familiar faces, and then became incensed with Ottenbreit for having the players out on the town (even though the players immediately attempted—unsuccessfully—to head in the opposite direction upon seeing their coach). Magnuson was afraid all over again, just as he had been in the Colorado Springs hotel room when Ivan stormed out—fearing that his NHL career was in jeopardy before it even began. But Ottenbreit quickly explained to the coach that Keith had just inked his first deal, so the low-key outing was justified. Reay relented and even laughed a little bit with the men after hearing the news. All was forgiven.

As the group headed back to the team hotel, Magnuson realized that his boyhood dream was now upon him.

"Dad always said that if you work for something hard enough, with God's help you'll attain it," he said.

Even so, he would have to work even harder, every day, to keep that dream alive—and to earn the respect of his peers in the rugged world of the NHL.

3

Rookie at the Madhouse

"'Here Come the Hawks!' is a punchline to most people today, but that song still gives us the chills because it reminds one of better days, a rockin' Stadium, and always, always, of Keith Magnuson."
—Sportswriter Barry Rozner, 2003

When the team arrived back in Chicago after the preseason game in Toronto, and put on the home sweater, Keith Magnuson could not wait to please the local crowd.

"Right from our first exhibition game," Stan Mikita recalled of Keith's first appearance at the Chicago Stadium for the 1969–70 season, "he climbed the stairs from our locker room and hit the ice in full stride."

Mikita, who had already led the league in scoring four times when Magnuson entered the NHL, knew that the rookie would soon become a team leader.

"Most guys skate rather easily at the start of practice or for a pregame warmup, but Maggie looked like he was in a race. A lot of times, you find that players with that attitude are doing it for affect. Not Maggie. He was the real thing."

Yet again, Keith wanted to waste no time in leaping onto the ice before all of his friends.

"After watching him for two days in his first training camp," Mikita added, "I said to the other players, 'This guy has heart.'"

Magnuson's youthful enthusiasm, in fact, reminded some observers of a rookie who made his debut in Major League Baseball six years earlier. During a spring training game in Florida, a smirking kid from the west side of Cincinnati ran out every play as hard as he could—much to the jealous derision of some veterans watching him from the opponents' dugout. "Look at Charlie Hustle there," they said. New York Yankees legends Mickey Mantle and Whitey Ford snickered at the Cincinnati Reds rookie named Pete Rose. The nonstop, all-out hustle of Rose, however, would become one of the hallmarks of his supreme career on the diamond over the next 24 years.

Magnuson would do the same for hockey in Chicago. "Talk about spirit. Have you watched that Magnuson before the game, when they play the national anthem?" Bobby Hull asked a writer just after the regular season began. "He looks like he'd take on the whole North Vietnamese army, doesn't he? And when we come out to warm up for the game, he has skated three revolutions of the ice before the rest of us have done one. He gets that psyched up."

Magnuson, however, had yet to encounter the wear and tear of a full NHL regular season, which at the time was 76 games; it was for this reason that Billy Reay asked Keith to "tone it down" and save some energy, not wanting his rookie defenseman to exhaust himself in the course of the marathon. But Reay discovered that his request was in vain. When the coach ordered wind sprints at the end of a Hawks practice, Magnuson would always lead the charge—even though he was not considered to be among the faster skaters on the team.

So in that very first home exhibition game in the fall of 1969, Magnuson made his way up the 21 treacherous steps from the Hawks locker room in the basement of the Stadium, a building which later gained the nickname "the Madhouse on Madison" for being one of the loudest arenas in the NHL.

Modeled in part after the old Olympia Stadium in Detroit (which had opened two years earlier), the Stadium was completed in March 1929. In many respects, it took much longer for the Stadium to enter the modern age of NHL-caliber venues. Like the Olympia and the Boston Garden, the Chicago Stadium still featured an old-fashioned, analog-dial clock, in use since 1943, which kept the game time and the penalty time for hockey games; Boston and Detroit ditched their antiques in favor of more modern, easier-to-read digital timepieces before the end of the 1960s.

By the close of that decade, the Stadium was showing its age. "Some of our best friends were the cockroaches that would scurry when the lights were first turned on," Cliff Koroll would say of the locker room. Peter Marsh would confirm their presence when he arrived to play for the Hawks in the early 1980s. "When we hung our elbow pads and shin pads up in our stalls overnight," he recalled, "we had to check them for cockroaches the next morning. There were also cats scattered everywhere in the basement of the Stadium—I don't know if they were there on accident, or placed there to handle the bug problem." Another creature, however, was certainly there on purpose. "When I was a rookie with Vancouver, it was an intimidating place to play," Dale Tallon said. "Near the visitors' locker room, there was a large German shepherd dog named Bruno that was caged up, and he would growl at you." Bruno's job was to roam the inner hallways of the Stadium at night, checking for prowlers.

The Stadium did have some amenities, however, as Koroll revealed. "Adjacent to the dressing room was a lounge with a TV and pool table. We would relax in this room before games," he said.

It would be fair to say that, at least until the dawn of the 1960s, the Stadium got little attention for its hockey productions; for as local sportscaster Chet Coppock put it, Chicago was a "hockey graveyard" before the Hull and Mikita era, with chicken wire surrounding the ice instead of Plexiglas.

What the players perhaps dreaded the most were those last few steps before reaching the rink, which each time proved to be a difficult path to navigate.

"The road to the ice was an interesting one," Koroll said. "We had to go through the lounge area, turn right, go about five yards, go up three stairs, turn right, and then make our way up to the 'gladiator pit'—a total of 21 stairs. Over the years, several players fell down those stairs, especially trying to get down them."

Keith, however, navigated them happily and quickly each day, as the entrance to the ice led to the grandest of all spectacles. "As soon as we came up the stairs, everything changed. The place was definitely to our advantage," Marsh said.

Whether it was for a practice or a game, Magnuson was always first in line behind the goaltender in breaking into a full sprint upon reaching the gate, "with his fire engine–red hair flapping in the breeze," as noted by hockey writer Chuck O'Donnell. "He had an unusual skating stride," is how O'Donnell described Magnuson's gait in accelerating around the boards, "almost as if he was sitting in a chair." A Canadian writer watching the Hawks depicted his style another way: "His weight is forward, stance wide for balance, knees locked and slightly bent. Those short, choppy, deceptively awkward-looking strides of his suggest an extra surge of power coming from his thighs."

As Magnuson made his dash through the gate and onto the ice in front of the Chicago crowd, the now-long-forgotten tune of "Here Come the Hawks!" would begin blaring from the Stadium's speakers; it was a staple at every Hawks game through the 1990s. "We all file up that long, dark basement stairwell from the dressing room to the rink," Magnuson remembered of the pregame ritual for the team. "Al Melgard on that giant organ right above us starts to play the team's music as 20,000 fans roared. For me, this is one of the biggest moments of every hockey encounter."

For anyone who attended a Hawks game at the Stadium, the song was part of the exciting anticipation that rose every evening:

Here come the Hawks, the mighty Black-hawks!
Take the attack, yeah, and, we'll back you Black-hawks!
You're flyin' high now, so, let's wrap it up
Let's go you Hawks, move off!
Now all look out!
Here come the Hawks!

The Stadium had acoustics all its own, as noted by broadcaster Pat Foley. "That building was a small structure with brick walls that went straight up, so the place had a special noise," Foley said. "The sound really bounced around in there. We just hung one crowd microphone from the booth. That's all we needed." To compare the decibels in the Stadium to the arena with which modern Hawks fans are accustomed, Foley pointed out that when the United Center took the Stadium's place across the street in 1994, it housed two-and-a-half times the square footage of the Stadium—but held but only 3,000 more seats.

"Our broadcast booth was a small, separate balcony which hung off of the first balcony and over center ice behind the player benches," Foley recalled about his perch above the Stadium ice. "It was a great perspective from which to call the game. The Stadium had a spirit, an atmosphere, and a life we will never see again."

Bobby Hull reacted the same way when asked about his memories of the old building. "I have been all over North America and Europe," Hull said, "but the Chicago Stadium was the greatest sphere of action and energy of any building I've ever played in." The energy in the building was Magnuson's fuel, the very jolt that got his adrenaline going each night.

Nonetheless, it took more than fight songs and the youthful enthusiasm of the Denver rookies to improve the team's fortunes in the 1969–70 NHL season. Hull exercised an early fall holdout over his contract, which contributed to the Hawks' last-place finish in the old Eastern Division; the Hawks allowed the most goals (246) in the division. It was undoubtedly the tougher division; a 1967 expansion brought six new teams into the league—St. Louis, Philadelphia, Oakland, Los Angeles, Minnesota, and Pittsburgh—all of which were placed in the West. The "Original Six," meanwhile, comprised the East (Chicago, New York, Boston, Montreal, Toronto, and Detroit). Thus, the Hawks found themselves ending the season in the cellar of the Eastern Division in the spring of 1969 despite having a winning record. (The St. Louis Blues, meanwhile, were the only team in the Western Division with a winning mark.)

So the Hawks missed the playoffs for the first time in 10 years, and changes were to come. In much the same way that Cubs manager Leo Durocher had wanted to "back up the truck," as he put it, and overhaul the roster upon his arrival in Chicago in the mid-1960s, Reay was also looking for new leaders to revive his own moribund club. As had Armstong, Magnuson noticed that Reay did very little yelling as a coach; the cold stare of each man sent his messages for him. Reay was encouraged by the prospect of talented youngsters like Magnuson, Koroll, Jim Wiste, Tony Esposito, Gerry Pinder, and others coming to the fore, but like most all NHL coaches and front office personnel at the time, he wasn't sold on players coming from the college ranks.

"You can never be sure about players who pass up a chance to develop on Canadian Junior teams to attend college," Reay would assert. "You have to wonder if they really are serious about making hockey a career. Because no matter how much college hockey has improved—and it has, plenty—it still hasn't reached the class of hockey played by the Juniors in Canada. And unless a player is really something, he's going to take a year or so in the minors before making it to the majors if he goes to college. On the other hand, plenty of players have come right out of Juniors and starred in the NHL."

Reay could tell early on, however, that Magnuson and his Denver teammates were exceptions to the "softness" that some pro coaches perceived in the college player of that era. Those mentored by Armstrong had a special toughness, Reay thought, a special desire. This was proven to the Hawks coach when he witnessed Magnuson staying behind to work further on his game, all by himself, after one of those first team practices in September—just as he had with Harry Ottenbreit back in Denver. Walking to his office, Reay saw Magnuson shadow-boxing all alone on the ice, practicing the blows he planned to impart on opposing players.

In fact, at various points during the 1969–70 season, there would be as many as seven college men on the Hawks roster—including Magnuson, Koroll, Esposito, Eric Nesterenko, Wiste (who would be sidelined with a broken hand halfway through his first NHL season), Pinder (a 21-year-old who had been in his third year at the University of Manitoba), and Lou Angotti (who had been at Michigan Tech nearly a full 10 years before Esposito). While many college players were once considered second-tier in terms of possessing hockey "instincts," several significant athletes from the NHL scene of the 1970s—including Magnuson, Koroll, Angotti, Red Berenson, and Lou

Nanne, among others—also became coaches or front office employees in the NHL and the college ranks themselves once their playing days were finished.

• • •

As the 1970s dawned, Mikita and Hull were the unquestioned leaders of the team. Both were among the most physically gifted players in the sport to that time, and they did not waste those gifts. Hull, in particular, was not only perhaps the fastest skater in the game, but his peerless, legendary slap shot was reputed to travel at speeds in excess of 115 miles per hour.

"All of a sudden the puck became invisible," said former NHL goalie Les Binkley of having the experience firsthand. "When Bobby Hull shot one at me, it started off looking like a small pea and then it disappeared altogether."

On March 12, 1966, Hull became the first player in league history to score more than 50 goals in a season, and eventually posted a season total of 54. By the end of the 1968–69 campaign he had shattered his own mark, putting 58 pucks in the net. But as the new season began, Hull sat out of training camp once again over a sticking point in his existing contract. Rumored to revolve on how the club permitted him to invest some of his money in other ventures, the disagreement had carried over from a brief holdout by Hull at the start of the previous year. By the third week of October 1969, word was even circulating that Hull—nicknamed "the Golden Jet" for his unmatched skills—was planning to retire from hockey.

Without him, the Hawks were winless in their first six regular season games, managing only a 1–1 tie with the Rangers in New York as Koroll—now being called a Johnny Bench look-alike for his resemblance to the up-and-coming Cincinnati Reds catcher—got his first

NHL goal. The Hawks had even been outscored by three expansion teams—the St. Louis Blues, the Oakland Seals, and the Minnesota North Stars—by an aggregate score of 13–4. Hull was sorely missed, and *Sports Illustrated* called the spat between him and Arthur Wirtz "one of the bitterest cases of player-management friction in hockey history." Bill Wirtz had decided to fine Hull $1,500 for each game he missed, and simply stated that "Hull has a contract with us and we expect him to live up to it."

Koroll's tally in New York must have inspired the team. Despite the continued absence of Hull, the Hawks went on to win seven of their next eight games. Keeping the Hawks loose during Hull's absence was Mikita's sense of humor, in addition to that of Magnuson's—the latter of whom did not go through the typical hazing and isolation that most rookies experience. This was because Magnuson's teammates not only respected him immediately but liked him as well; they were comfortable giving him the same teasing he had endured from Koroll and Wiste in college. A couple of months into his rookie season, Magnuson approached the veteran Mikita for advice. "He asked me if there was anything he could be doing better," Mikita recalled. "I told him, 'You're doing great, but there's one thing I would suggest: When you take on a guy in a fight, lead with your left or your right—not your chin.'"

There was one brief, minor tussle with Marc Tardif of the Canadiens in the Montreal Forum on October 25, 1969 (during the first of what would be a remarkable number of shutouts for Esposito in his rookie year, a 5–0 win over the Canadiens). Magnuson engaged in his first real NHL combat a month later on November 21, when the despised Boston Bruins came to Chicago Stadium.

"Magnuson, the young pugnacious Hawks defenseman fought with [Bobby] Orr, Derek Sanderson, and challenged the entire Boston club," noted Ted Damata. "The Bruins, earlier, had been taking runs at him and Keith ended up pouncing on anything that looked like a Boston uniform."

This season would be the first dominant year in the league for the young phenom Orr, who at the age of 21 already had three NHL campaigns under his belt. In an incident that would provoke hard feelings between the Hawks and the Bruins throughout the next few seasons, Magnuson took offense to Sanderson—the NHL's Rookie of the Year in 1968 who was back in the Boston lineup for his first game in nearly seven weeks after a knee injury—hitting Chicago winger Jim Pappin after the whistle. Magnuson, in an effort to cement his role as the team's on-ice protector, leveled Sanderson near the boards—at which point Orr, underrated as a checker and a fighter because of his gaudy statistics on offense, flew in from behind with a hit of his own that sent Keith sprawling to the ice. As the battle played itself out, Magnuson was held punchless while Orr got in several right hands. Magnuson certainly got the worse end of the fight; as Boston goaltender Gerry Cheevers reflected, "I must say it was the worst beating I ever saw a player get. It was the biggest pool of blood I ever saw on the ice, too."

Magnuson and Sanderson squared off once again later in the game, when Keith leapt out of the penalty box prematurely (good for a $100 fine) and assisted teammate Ray McKay, who at the time was fighting Sanderson himself. McKay would only play in 28 games in his three years with the Black Hawks, but he got the best of Sanderson that night thanks to several vicious blows.

A new era in Chicago hockey was born. The season was only six weeks old, but Keith Magnuson was indeed the new enforcer for the Black Hawks. Magnuson's courage spoke volumes to the Hawks—no one, not even Orr, would be allowed to intimidate his team, especially on Stadium ice. Like an offensive lineman in football, Magnuson knew he would find little glory in his role but that his sacrifices would benefit the team as a whole.

Magnuson's status as a policeman took full flight in a December 19 game against the Seals in Oakland as he gained his first fighting "victory." He was challenged three separate times that evening by Carol Vadnais, considered one of the new tough guys in the league and rumored never to have lost a fight in the Juniors.

Vadnais had the upper hand in the first round, in which he clotheslined Magnuson near the boards, and was on top of him before he could respond. In the second round, with a faceoff occurring in the Hawks zone, Magnuson was not caught by surprise again—he squared off immediately with Vadnais after they jostled their sticks outside the circle. But the linesmen jumped in quickly and separated the men before any real punches could be thrown. The third bout between the two, however, proved to be the decisive one, once again occurring in front of the Chicago net, and two minutes into the third period.

Gloves and sticks dropped, Magnuson began to hover around his prey in a slow, backward circle. He then gave a quick shrug of the shoulders—showing his opponent that he was loosening his guns for the impending fracas. It was a move which would become a trademark of Magnuson's fighting stance in the years to come. As the punches flew, Vadnais had the initial advantage, but Magnuson got in three solid, unreturned blows—each one collapsing the staggering Oakland player closer and closer to the ice. The final right cross caught Vadnais squarely on the nose, breaking it, and sending him down in a crumpled heap.

Despite the reputation that Vadnais had carried with him from the Juniors, the 1969–70 season would be the only one in his lengthy NHL career in which he compiled an excessively large number of penalty minutes (212, which was one fewer at season's end than Magnuson's league-leading 213). In the locker room after the game, Magnuson admitted to a couple of teammates that it was one of the first times he had experimented with his karate skills on the ice—in practice or a game situation—since leaving Denver. The knockout galvanized the Hawks and Esposito, who got his fifth shutout that night as the defense permitted only 23 shots against him in the Hawks' 4–0 win over the Seals. Chicago had previously struggled with the expansion franchise on Oakland's home ice, as this was their first win in the Bay Area since Dave Dryden shut them out in February 1968.[2]

• • •

With the help of Armstrong, Ottenbreit, Reay, and his careful observance of veteran players, Magnuson—more adroitly and more quickly than most rookies—developed a deep understanding of what is known as "the Code." The Code is a tradition in hockey, similar to those seen in other professional sports—an unspoken, unwritten policy manual, followed among the fighters as well as nonfighters in the NHL, with consequences for each type of player if it is broken.

For those outside of hockey who may wonder why fighting is somewhat permitted in the NHL, the Code gives an explanation as to its purpose. Hockey, being a highly physical contact sport, involves aggressive interaction between opponents. But in the process of being a properly aggressive player, there are things that are permissible to do and things that are not. The term "policeman" began to emerge in the 1960s (whereas its role, without the name, existed even earlier). The policeman, as the moniker implies, keeps order; he is an unofficially appointed individual (or perhaps two or more) on a given team whose job is to make certain that his team's nonfighters—typically the faster-skating but less-intimidating goal scorers—are freed up to manage the puck. If another team's tough guy takes an intimidating

2 The following season, the team changed its name to the "California Seals," and then soon to the "California Golden Seals."

run at a team's scorer, it is the policeman's job to retaliate with either a punishing body check or a full-blown fistic assault. The deterrent that provides peace, ironically, is a show of strength.

"Fighters are there to keep the peace and protect their skill players," as author Ross Bernstein put it. Bernstein wrote specifically about the role of fighting in the modern NHL in his book *The Code*. "In order for the skill players to do their jobs effectively, they must be allowed the freedom to skate, pass, and shoot without the fear of being run over by a bigger player who is out to intimidate them."

The Code also contains the codicil, or at least the notion, that "justice is best served cold." It is a concept best understood by veteran players—often at a rookie's expense—as noted by former NHL goalie Darren Pang.

"If a guy like Gordie Howe ever got disrespected out on the ice," Pang said, "he took that guy's number down and saved it for later. He didn't tell anybody about it, he just locked it in his memory."

An example of Howe's patience in meting out justice came after an incident involving a young Stan Mikita. Mikita recalled the time early in his career when he elbowed Howe in the face in the corner, part of Stan's effort to establish his presence on the ice. When he returned to the Black Hawks bench, Mikita's older teammates warned him to watch out, as Howe would be sure to get even at some point.

Several matchups between the two teams came and went without incident, so the inexperienced Mikita assumed that Howe a) did not care about the elbow, b) had forgiven him, or c) had forgotten about it altogether. A couple of months later, however, Howe found Mikita in the perfect situation, and returned an elbow directly to Mikita's mouth. It was part of an amazing (and self-admitted) transformation that changed Mikita's career.

"I stopped mouthing off to referees," he said. "Another thing I did was make an honest assessment of my behavior on the ice. I studied the score sheets after each game to break down what kind of penalties I was taking." The result was two Lady Byng Trophies, given to the most gentlemanly player in the league, in 1967 and 1968. "I guarantee you, if you had placed a wager during my first few seasons in the NHL that I would someday be hailed for sportsmanship and gentlemanly conduct, you would have gotten some really long odds."

Magnuson, during his rookie year in the fall of 1969, would be the latest NHL youngster to feel Howe's wrath. In a November game at Detroit, Magnuson tried to push his boyhood idol out from in front of the net. The 41-year-old Howe—whose picture still sat on the Magnuson family mantle back in Saskatoon—quickly disposed of the rookie with a single right forearm to the head, skillfully landed while the referee was otherwise occupied.

"Howe cuffed Magnuson's ears and turned away," reported *Sports Illustrated* about the momentary clash after which Howe skated by the Chicago bench, "muttering to Doug Jarrett, Keith's partner on defense, 'He's a tough kid, but he'll learn.'"

Howe would not soften with age. Ten years later in October 1979 at the age of *51*—in his final season, and with the Hartford Whalers, Howe was unceremoniously slammed into the boards at the Chicago Stadium by rookie Hawks defenseman Keith Brown, a 19-year-old playing in only his third NHL game. When the Hawks visited the Whalers in Hartford a month later, the patient Howe once again found the right place and time to get retribution.

"Right in my face," Brown would say years later to *Chicago Tribune* writer Bob Verdi about where Howe's vengeance had landed. "I come out of the corner bleeding, he comes out of the corner and scores. Howe is the same age as my dad... Naturally, I'm upset, so I start yapping. I yell at Howe, 'I'm gonna get you!' Finally, [fellow Chicago defenseman] Greg Fox, who knew better, told me to go sit down on the bench and shut up."

Unlike some other fighters in the league in 1969, Magnuson honored and obeyed the Code, abstaining from cheap shots and going after anybody who did not want to fight. "I just can't hit a guy if he's turned sideways to me or hasn't got his dukes up," he said. He also had the wisdom and mercy to know when to back off a beaten opponent. "If a man goes down when I'm fighting him, I simply can't hit him again," he continued. "If he wants to keep going, fine. But I'll drop it the moment he stops responding. By then he knows he's made a mistake, and that's all a good policeman is trying to prove. So that's where it ends for me. Anyone who can't exercise such controls on himself has to be a little sick in the head."

"Keith was not a bully," Bobby Hull said. "He minded his own business, but he also made sure nobody on the Hawks was bullied."

Like Howe, Manguson developed his own way of settling scores as he became a veteran himself. He would look closely at himself in the mirror and see a scar from a particular opponent's fist or stick from a past game—"Twelve stitches owed Ferguson, 15 for you, Fleming…"—and would then note the "amount" owed in his mental ledger.

But for Keith, fighting in hockey was not about the physical marks left behind on an opponent, but rather the mental ones. "To me, blood doesn't mean anything," he explained. "What counts is what you've done to the guy *inside*, what he'll be thinking about next time."

Thus, with every night in an NHL arena, Magnuson was increasing his understanding of the psychology behind the pro game. He used his intelligence to his advantage and carefully crafted a long-term strategy for each opponent.

• • •

Magnuson, Koroll, Esposito, and the other young Hawks watched their experienced teammates and tried to make good first impressions as the veterans showed them the ropes. To start the season, Magnuson was paired on defense with Pat Stapleton, a crafty player who stood only 5'8" but used his quickness as his main weapon—whether moving the puck or disrupting an opponent with his stick.

Coming off his second NHL All-Star Game appearance, Stapleton—nicknamed "Whitey" for his brilliantly blond hair—had been named the captain of the team after Pierre Pilote left for Toronto a year earlier. (Pilote was the captain of the Black Hawks from 1961 to 1968; the team had gone without a first captain for the 1968–69 season.) And while Magnuson was fully aware that he was being thrust into an important role with the team, he also figured he would have time to make some adjustments. In reality, little time passed before Reay asked him to take on a heavier burden.

In February 1970, Stapleton went down with a serious knee injury after playing in only 49 games, which put Magnuson in a defense pairing with new partner Jarrett and which necessitated the summons of another young defenseman from the minors in Paul Shmyr. To further shore up the back line, Tommy Ivan also swung a deal on February 20 to obtain the highly regarded Bill White from Los Angeles, along with center Bryan Campbell and goalie Gerry Desjardins, in exchange for goalie Dennis DeJordy, defenseman Gilles Marotte, and forward Jim Stanfield. Naturally, this move also cemented Esposito as the undisputed No. 1 goaltender in the Chicago nets.

Jarrett had been with the Black Hawks since 1964 and was a product of their farm system. His nickname was "Chairman of the Boards," as he was the biggest of the Hawks defensemen at the time at 6'3" and 205 pounds and used his frame to physically pound on opponents. "There's nobody who can quite hit like him," Magnuson observed. "He just splatters guys, sometimes even two at a time. And that's a beautiful sight. Like homemade apple pie, my favorite dessert." Dennis Hull confirmed Magnuson's assessment: "He could skate backward like the wind," he once claimed of Jarrett, "and would line a guy up and jump in his face and smash him with a hip check."

Jarrett was also sometimes called "Tuna" by his teammates because he dreamed of being a big-shot owner of boats and cars and driving them around Chicago like Tony "Big Tuna" Accardo, one of the mob bosses of the city. But the one peccadillo that would constantly annoy Reay was Jarrett's tardiness for team practice sessions.

"Practice was at 10:00 AM, and Billy used to close the door to the rink right on the hour," Dennis Hull recalled. "Doug would always just make it as Billy was closing the door. But Doug has these wonderful excuses. It finally got to the point where Billy would call everyone to center ice just to hear the excuses. 'Okay, Dougie,' Billy said, 'what is it today?' 'Well, the dog ate my keys.' 'Both sets?'"

Stapleton had been with the Hawks nearly as long as Jarrett (coming from Boston in 1965) but was only slightly more adept at arriving at practices on time. According to Magnuson, Stapleton was the team's fastest dresser, and would sometimes get to the Stadium 10 minutes before practice began. If a player was late getting on the ice, he would usually try to sneak quietly into whatever drill or talk was going on to avoid Reay's glare; unfortunately for the tardy player, his teammates would good-naturedly smack their sticks on the ice to let Reay know of his transgression. Magnuson and the rest of the Hawks were always amazed with the timing with which Stapleton made his appearance, which was always mere moments before the clock struck 10:00—a skill which seemed to elude Jarrett. "Whitey always steps on the ice with just a few seconds left. And we all give him a big hand," Keith recalled with a laugh.

Along with Mikita, Stapleton was unquestionably the team's top prankster. "Without out a doubt he was the No. 1 practical joker on [the Hawks]," affirmed Dennis Hull, "and he may have been the best in the league. He was unbelievable."

One of the gags Stapleton frequently liked to pull was hiding the microphones of the broadcast crews—not just those of the Chicago television (WGN) and radio (WMAQ) stations covering the Hawks, but even those of the national CBS broadcasts. Once, he even located the luggage of NHL referee Bill Friday, who was on the same flight as the Hawks to an out-of-town game, and stole Friday's skates. "At least Bill got his skates back just before the game," Stapleton's linemate and accomplice Bill White told Verdi. "That's one rule Pat and I always had. We never kept anything."

Then, addressing Verdi directly, White added, "You should know. You got your typewriter back after we stole it from you on the plane to Vancouver, didn't you?"

But Stapleton's main target was Magnuson, and much like his friends in college, none of Magnuson's teammates could figure out if he was really being fooled or deftly playing along. Stapleton regularly liked to tell Keith that, while walking by Tommy Ivan's office, he overheard talk of a deal being struck that would send Magnuson out of town. "I can't count the number of times Stapleton convinced Maggie that he was about to be traded," recalled Mikita. Others confirmed the ploy. "Once a week [Stapleton] would tell Magnuson he was traded," added Verdi, "and once a week Magnuson would believe him. Or pretend to."

Magnuson was also a victim of a "snipe hunt" prank in his rookie year, courtesy of Mikita and Stapleton. One night, Magnuson and fellow rookie Terry Caffery were convinced by the two veterans to head out into the countryside beyond Chicago's western suburbs, along with a couple of ropes and a canvas sack, and were told to be on the lookout for the dreaded creature known as a "snipe." Incredibly, in the next 10 minutes, the pair was picked up by the playfully complicit Elmhurst Police Department and booked into custody for the charge of "snipe hunting without a license." Stapleton and Mikita let their teammates sweat it out for a few hours before arriving to post their "bail."

While Jarrett relied on his checking and Stapleton on his skating speed, Bill White relied more on the skillful use of his stick to thwart opponents. By the time he came to the Black Hawks, White had nearly spent more seasons in the Juniors than in the NHL, toiling for a long duration under the notorious watch of Eddie Shore at Springfield of the American Hockey League. (White, a Toronto native, started in the Juniors at age 17 in 1956 and did not reach the NHL until 1967.) Jarrett and Magnuson would soon be established as partners for the long term; the same would hold true for White and Stapleton.

"Pat and I just seemed to click right away," White said once in an interview. "I was more of a stay-at-home type, and Pat liked to rush the puck. It was like we always knew what each other was thinking and was going to do." White, like Stapleton, had been selected as a league All-Star in the 1968–69 season and would proceed to make six straight All-Star Games from 1969 to 1974.

Jarrett, Magnuson, Stapleton, and White would ultimately make up one of the best defensive foursomes ever seen in the NHL. And the newest player among the group was impressing Chicago's foes as much as any of them.

"He was tall and he had long arms which made it tough to get around him," veteran Rangers forward Pete Stemkowski said in remembering his first one-on-one battle with Magnuson. "He would take two or three strides and he'd catch up with you."

Soon, the defensemen were often heard yelling "None against!" to each other before faceoffs in the defensive zone, a phrase started by Keith and a sacred pact to do whatever was necessary to keep the puck out of the net.

They began doing so at an unprecedented rate.

The Hawks, after a slow start to the season, were firing on all cylinders as the winter progressed. On the last day of January 1970—with three months still remaining in the regular season—Esposito garnered his 11th shutout of the season, in Philadelphia, one short of the Hawks record set by Chuck Gardiner in 1933–34 and just two shy of the league mark held by Toronto's Harry Lumley (1953–54). During the 5–0 win over the Flyers, Magnuson went toe-to-toe in a fight with Reggie Fleming, a favorite of Keith's father, Joe. The salty veteran Fleming gave Magnuson some fighting tips, just as Big Swede had done back home; he lowered Keith's body toward the ice and pulled his jersey up over his head, then proceeded to pound Magnuson with a couple of uppercuts, leaving a severe cut over Keith's left eye.

After the shaky start to the season and having to rely on so many young players, the Hawks were nearly unbeatable in the second half of the season. Just three weeks after Magnuson's fight with Fleming, Bobby Hull scored the 500th goal of his career; the roar was so loud at the Stadium that public address announcer Harvey Wittenberg had to wait several minutes before he could even give the official summary of the score. The team lost only seven times in their final 41 games, and their swelling confidence was palpable as they sprinted toward the playoffs.

"You could feel it starting to build," said Magnuson, who in his quickly growing role would play in every Hawks game as a rookie. "The whole team [was] jelling, coming together as a unit, every single guy contributing something."

On March 29, 1970, Esposito notched his 15th shutout of the season in a 4–0 blanking of Toronto at the Stadium, a season standard that no goalie has equaled since. One of the Hawks' goals had been set up on a beautiful pass by Magnuson, on which he found Pappin near center ice, who in turn slid the puck to Pinder for a breakaway in on the Maple Leafs goal. Bobby Hull also scored twice in the win, which moved the Hawks into a first-place tie with Boston.

When the final buzzer sounded, the Hawks pounced on the puck that was in play to ensure that Esposito got it for his trophy case to commemorate the record-setting shutout. Magnuson retreated from the celebrating pack on the ice, skating over to the boards to take a moment just to catch his breath.

"Usually I'm one of the first to congratulate Tony," Magnuson said of Hawks victories, "but tonight I was one of the last. I was just limp. The pressure of that game was unbelievable."

The game was also payback for the Hawks' lackluster performance the night before in Toronto, a 1–1 tie during which Magnuson was flattened by Toronto's Bob Pulford in the corner, his face slammed against the glass.

"Really, all that hurts is my lips," Magnuson revealed to an inquirer in the locker room.

"If anyone's got tough lips," offered Koroll from a few seats away, "it's you."

Meanwhile, across the room, Bobby Hull broke out in a Frank Sinatra song.

"When I was 21, it was a very good year..."

Hull was referring to being a 21-year-old in 1961–62, the season in which the Hawks won their last Stanley Cup.

"Maggie," Hull halted his singing and yelled to the rookie defenseman, "this *could* be a very good year."

After his 15th shutout, Esposito had allowed only one goal in his last 260 minutes of play. With the playoffs ahead, Ted Damata wrote in the *Chicago Tribune* that "the battle for the Cup returns to Chicago after a one-year absence; a year in which 'the best team that ever finished last' is emerging swanlike from the ugly-duckling status.... Big Tony now has a 14-goal cushion in the quest for the Vezina Trophy.

He has a stranglehold on the Calder Trophy [for league rookie of the year]; and, if the Hawks succeed in finishing in first place, the Hart Cup [the most valuable player trophy] has to be stolen from him. It would be an unprecedented sweep in the annals of hockey."

Yet despite Esposito's unmatched number of shutouts, there was talk of Magnuson being more deserving of the Calder Trophy, in consideration of the physical pounding Keith was taking in front of the net on a nightly basis.

Magnuson had been able to find respite from the brutality of the NHL thanks in part to having a comfortable place to live. During the season, Keith shared an apartment with Koroll, his former roommate at Denver. Cliff was seen by Bob Verdi to be "the perfect cerebral and grounded half to this odd couple arrangement."

"We'd never yell at each other," Magnuson said of his living situation with Koroll, one which would last another three and a half years—until Koroll got married. "Not that we never had differences. It's just that we're so competitive most of the time that if there's anything bothering us we try to settle it on the ice. So sometimes during practice we'd really belt each other, usually over some stupid little thing that had started back at the apartment."

Keith claimed to do all the cleaning, while Cliff handled the cooking. And when Koroll finally did get married, he permitted Magnuson to live with the newlywed couple for another three months "until I finally kicked him out," Cliff said with a laugh.

Koroll also noticed that Magnuson continued to write short notes to himself, just as he had done in Denver and much to the amusement of his friend. "If you looked around, you'd see those lists," Koroll said. "When we roomed together in college, we [Wiste and other roommates] used to mess with him all the time and shuffle his notes. We used to get a kick out of reading his notes, which were as simple as 'Wake up,' 'Wash face,' 'Comb hair,' and 'Brush teeth.'"

One time, Magnuson wrote "Phone Bill" as reminder to make a payment—but then misplaced the piece of paper, and soon it was forgotten. Upon finding it months later, Keith agonized in straining to remember just who "Bill" was.

• • •

By April it was clear that one of the most exciting finishes in NHL history would take place in the stretch run to the playoffs. The Hawks, Canadiens, Rangers, Red Wings, and Bruins all had a shot at first place in the Eastern Division going into the schedule's final week. As Magnuson remembered, "It was as if we had to win every night just to keep pace." Ultimately, it came down to Orr's Bruins against Magnuson's Black Hawks for the top spot in the standings on the last day of the season.

While hockey had not yet reached widespread popularity in the United States as the 1960s closed, the race for the 1970 Stanley Cup had captured the interest of the nation, seeking a fresh sports story after the "Miracle Mets" had overtaken the Cubs on their way to baseball's World Series in the past October. In recognition of the riveting sprint for the championship, the new face of Chicago hockey was displayed for the whole world to see on the cover of *Sports Illustrated* during the first week of April. The cover showed a sweaty, red-haired, grinning battler with one missing tooth, clutching his stick defensively but seemingly without a care in the world. It was Keith Magnuson, posing next to a caption that read, "Chicago and Boston in Hockey's Hottest Race." In the coming years, Magnuson would also appear on the cover of *The Sporting News*, *Hockey Illustrated*, and *Hockey Digest*, as well as *Weekend* magazine, one of the top publications in Canada, as his celebrity status grew. But this was the first true national exposure for the new tough guy in Chicago.

On the final day of the season, the Hawks completed their "worst to first" resurgence by drubbing Montreal 10–2 at the Stadium. The lopsided score was made possible when the Canadiens pulled their goalie midway through the third period, as Montreal needed to score a certain number of goals to overtake the Rangers for fourth place in the East, and thus claim the final playoff spot. (With a loss to Chicago, Montreal finished with the exact same record as New York at 38–22–16. The tiebreaker at the time deferred to total goals scored, and the Canadiens would have to muster at least five in the game against Esposito.) The Canadiens did not score at all during their nine minutes with the extra attacker—and thus missed the playoffs for the only time in a 47-year period from 1948 until 1995.

With the Hawks firmly in control of the game and having fun firing at an empty net in the last half of the final stanza, Magnuson realized his teammates were trying to get him his first NHL goal, as he was passed the puck as often as possible. It was not meant to be, but Magnuson and the Hawks celebrated the victory with their acceptance of the Prince of Wales Trophy for the best record in the NHL regular season. Chicago and Boston actually wound up tied in the standings with 99 total points (during those days in the NHL, two points were given for a win and one for a tie), but the Eastern Division title was given to Chicago by virtue of the Hawks' 45 wins to the Bruins' 40.

After the cheers simmered down in the Chicago locker room, there was silence as Mikita suggested a moment of prayer. During the reflection, Magnuson admitted to shedding a tear in the midst of the powerful scene, knowing that he had played a large part in the team's turnaround.

Red Wings coach Sid Abel had recently absorbed much criticism from the local and national media—and from the Bruins—after resting several of his best players on the April 4 regular season finale against the Rangers. The Wings' postseason spot had already been assured, but many of the playoff seedings for the other teams were still to be determined.

The playoffs opened with the Hawks taking two straight from the Red Wings in the Stadium before the series shifted to Detroit. That city—like Chicago—had been primed for a return to success on the ice.

"Fans, starved for hockey as they used to know it in the glory days of the 1950s, snapped up all the standing-room tickets by early afternoon," reported Mark Mulvoy outside the Olympia before the game and shortly after the first drop of the puck. "And not even the oldest Howe-Lindsay-Abel worshippers could remember the last time that happened…traffic on Grand River Avenue was so jammed, many fans missed the first 10 minutes."

Before the team boarded the bus at the hotel for the trip to the arena, Magnuson and Koroll had attempted to pass the time—as well as the jitters about their first NHL playoff game on the road—by going shopping. Keith soon put his nervousness to rest, helping to direct the Hawks to victory twice more in Detroit for a sweep of the Red Wings. Detroit dropped all four games by the same 4–2 score.

"Magnuson was playing spirited, flawless hockey," continued Mulvoy, "the kind that in just one season has made him the Hawks' chief fire-lighter."

With the Red Wings out of the way, it was on to the semifinals and a more formidable opponent—the vaunted Bruins.

• • •

Despite nearly matching the Hawks' regular season record, skeptics believed the Bruins might not get past New York in the first round. Until March 25 of that year, Boston had not beaten an Eastern Division team on the road. Like many teams in the East, they had fattened up on the expansion teams in the West, and therefore, many doubted they could handle the Rangers in a seven-game series.

While Orr was generally regarded as the best fighter on the Bruins, a case for the team's chief antagonist on the road could easily have been made for Sanderson, who was an overwhelming fan favorite at home in the Boston Garden.

"It is interesting that in a hockey town like Boston, where Bobby Orr is both prime minister and chairman of the board," observed Phil Elderkin of *The Sporting News*, "there is no shortage of fans for Derek. You would need an applause meter to measure his popularity."

Always looking to drum up publicity, Sanderson suffered no shortage of self-promotion. His license plate read BRUINS16; he liked to hang out with Joe Namath (he was reputed to be part-owner of a nightclub with the football star, and like Namath's famous shoes, Sanderson once tried to order a pair of white skates for further showmanship); and he also liked to keep a wide assortment of girls around.

After the regular season had concluded, Bruins coach Harry Sinden scheduled a practice session at Watson Rink on the campus of Harvard University. Sinden told his players after the workout that they would be flying out of Boston that night instead of in the morning to avert an impending strike by air traffic controllers. Sanderson was annoyed by the change of travel plans, as it meant that he would have to rearrange his social calendar—or at least, that is what he wanted his teammates to believe.

"I had a date with Jackie tonight," *Sports Illustrated* reported him as saying. "No, with Susan; I forgot, Jackie was the backup."

While certainly unwelcome with the fans in Chicago, Sanderson was so despised in New York that extra police officers were dispatched to the area of the penalty box when Sanderson received an infraction in Madison Square Garden.

Dave Schultz, the Philadelphia fighter who had about as many battles with Sanderson as he did with Magnuson, sounded as if he felt sorry for Sanderson.

"Sanderson was a classic example of a professional athlete who became a victim of his overnight wealth," Schultz wrote in his autobiography. "Derek was a troubled personality...the distractions of big money disturbed his concentration. He became fat—both literally and figuratively—and he was never the same quality hockey player after that."

Cheevers, however, believed that there were many misconceptions about Sanderson. "You have to know Derek," the Boston goaltender suggested. "There are only 18 or 19 guys in hockey who really know him, and they're all Bruins."

After Boston took a 2–0 lead at home in their series against the Rangers, the games shifted to Madison Square Garden. There, the arrival of Sinden's men on the ice resembled the moments seen in the movie *Slap Shot* after the Hanson brothers joined the Charlestown Chiefs. From the moment they emerged from the locker room, the Bruins were subjected to numerous missiles such as batteries, eggs, and rubber balls being hurled their way, as well as a steady stream of insults. To some witnesses, the tension between two NHL teams had never seemed so high.

After dropping the next two games in New York, Sinden's men took care of business and dispatched the Rangers in six. Next, they would look to exact revenge upon the Hawks for sneaking past them in the regular season standings.

The series began in front of a raucous crowd at the Stadium on April 19, with some expecting to see more fireworks from Magnuson, Sanderson, and Orr in a carryover from the fight back in November. Given the importance of the series, however, all three showed restraint, with no major fighting penalties being issued in any of the games.

Unfortunately, the 6–3 decision for Boston in the opener was a harbinger of things to come. The Bruins' high-octane offense blitzed Esposito, scoring an average of five goals per game in achieving a four-game sweep. Magnuson broke up a 2–0 Bruins lead in Game 4 at Boston with his first NHL goal, but the onslaught continued thereafter. Boston had become so hockey crazy, in fact, that when Game 2 was sent via television back to the city on WSBK, the station got the highest-ever rating for any show on the old UHF band.

"Every day the Bruins are Page One stuff," said Leo Monahan of *The Sporting News*. "Politicians angle for seats...autograph hounds surround players...practice sessions have to be put off-limits because of the humanity crush."

Thus, the 1969–70 regular season and the playoffs had become Orr's first, and what would be his brightest personal showcase—the first time in many years that Bobby Hull, after returning to the Chicago lineup after his early-season holdout, took a backseat to someone else in the sport.

"The Golden Jet has seemed to have lost his zip and fire," opined hockey writer Stan Fischler. "It could be a result of Chicago's new defensive style or it could be Hull's age—or both. But Orr is hockey's king of the '70s."

Orr swept the major individual awards by winning the Hart, Norris (top defenseman), Conn Smythe (playoff MVP), and Art Ross (scoring title) trophies, the last the first ever claimed by a defenseman. And as a finishing touch, Orr ended the postseason with perhaps the most dramatic goal in hockey history. In front of the home fans in Boston against the St. Louis Blues in Game 4 of the Finals, he launched a beautiful give-and-go play with Sanderson. Charging to the front of the goal mouth, he positioned himself to easily tap-in the game-winner as Sanderson centered the puck from behind the net. A Blues player tripped Orr the moment he scored, sending him flying parallel to the ice in his famous celebratory pose. (Despite the dramatics and Orr's general dominance during the season, it could be argued that Cheevers equally carried the Bruins to the Finals, logging at least twice as many minutes as any other goalie in the 1970 playoffs.)

In addition to being Orr's breakout season (and the first in his four initial NHL years in which he was able to stave off injuries and play in every game), the 1969–70 schedule was also the last outstanding season for Gordie Howe. For a record 21st time, he finished in the top 10 in the league in scoring.

• • •

With rushes into the offensive zone rarely seen by a defenseman in the game's history, Orr was singlehandedly changing the way hockey was played—much the way Babe Ruth helped change baseball with his unprecedented home-run hitting in the 1920s. While Magnuson was well aware of his role with the Hawks and was not looking to become a "puck-moving" defenseman, he nonetheless was impressed enough by Orr to continue working on his own game, not taking his successful first year in the NHL for granted.

Seeking to gain any advantage he could find, Magnuson looked to new resources and techniques in the summer of 1970—in particular, the boxing ring. Having gotten his first basic boxing lessons as a boy from his father back in Saskatoon and later from Ottenbreit while in college, Magnuson would now be coached in the sweet science by Johnny Coulon. Born in Canada but raised in Chicago, Coulon—81 years old in 1970—had been the bantamweight champion of the world from 1910 to 1914 and had spent his whole life in the sport, even serving as a pallbearer at the funeral of former heavyweight champion Jack Johnson. In his eighties, he continued to run his gym on Chicago's south side, where Magnuson would train—a place at which such notable figures from Ernest Hemingway to Muhammad Ali were said to have practiced as well. And no one, including Keith, pitied Coulon's advanced age when they saw his level of fitness; he could still leap over the top rope of a boxing ring from a standing position and walk across an entire gym floor on his hands.

While the team's performance against the high-powered Bruins in the playoffs was a disappointment, the Hawks had served notice to the NHL that they were back. And with youngsters Magnuson, Koroll, and others having gained valuable experience, Chicago boasted a lineup which figured to soar to great heights in the coming years—particularly with the team's move to the Western Division for the 1970–71 schedule, one of a few switches made by the league to provide a better mixture of competitive balance between divisions. Verdi, from his desk at the *Tribune*, expected the Hawks to begin a powerful run through the league. "If you were lucky enough to be a rookie writer for the big newspaper in town," Verdi would pen in 2003, "you figured it always would be like this."

4

One Win Away

"If you're going to play in this league—and that's all I've ever wanted to do—you just have to be able to take care of yourself. If you can't, the established players will run you out."

—Keith Magnuson, 1970

While Keith Magnuson felt that his league-leading 213 penalty minutes in his rookie year helped establish him as the team's enforcer, coach Billy Reay felt that some of those penalty minutes, in addition to some of those fights, were unnecessary. The coach did not hold this against Keith, trusting that it was simply the result of a lack of experience and that he would learn to better choose his battles in later seasons.

After a brief rest in Canada following his training at Johnny Coulon's gym, Magnuson returned to Chicago for his second camp with the Black Hawks in September 1970. Whether it was from witnessing Bobby Orr's spectacular rushes with the puck or some other reason, Keith was suddenly worried that other parts of his game were beginning to suffer. He thought he needed to be more of an offensive-minded player instead of relying on brute force all the time. When he experimented in displaying this new persona at the team's first few workouts, one of his veteran teammates on defense had a different and simpler idea for him.

"Pat Stapleton came up to me and said, 'Maggie, we need you to hit,'" Keith recalled. Magnuson never looked back from this directive, now finally convinced of not only what his role should be, but that his teammates had confidence in him to fulfill it.

And as the 1970–71 season began, it did not take long for Magnuson to author a signature statement in his fighting career, announcing in no uncertain terms that he was *the* policeman for the team in the Indian-head sweater.

On November 7, 1970, the Hawks had played the Flyers to a 1–1 tie in Philadelphia in what became a chippy contest of late hits and cheap shots (even though Philadelphia coach Vic Stasiuk would call it "our best game of the season" to date). The prime culprit on the Philly side was a player named Earl Heiskala, who was one of the original tough guys on the Flyers' expansion outfit several seasons before the team's "Broad Street Bullies" reputation came into being. Early in the game, on a play near the boards, Heiskala momentarily distracted Magnuson by chopping at his legs with his stick. As Keith's mind was temporarily focused on the lower half of his body, Heiskala then struck with an elbow to his face, sending the Hawks defenseman sprawling downward and loosening a couple of his teeth (the "chop-and-elbow" technique, as it was called, was one that other Hawks said was actually more typical of Derek Sanderson, John McKenzie, and few other Bruins).

Keith fell to the ice in a daze and then reached out to try and grab hold of Heiskala, but the linesmen already had the two separated. Magnuson yearned for revenge, but composed himself for the rest of the game as he again took heed of the lesson taught by his childhood hero, Gordie Howe—to wait for the right moment to strike, a cold dish to be served at the opportune time for the best effect.

He found the right moment just 96 hours later.

Four days after the incident, the Flyers came to the Stadium for a game that would simply become known later as "Heiskala Night"—not in reference to anything noteworthy in the Philadelphia player's performance but instead because of the show put on by the red-haired Chicago defenseman. "The hero of the masses was Keith Magnuson," reported Ted Damata about the game for the *Tribune*. Indeed, the moment for which Magnuson had been waiting came quite early in the game.

Immediately after the opening faceoff, the puck scooted down the boards and into the Hawks' zone on Magnuson's side of the ice. Just as they had in Philadelphia, he and Heiskala once again met at the glass.

Putting his practice from Coulon's gym to the test, Keith immediately landed a right fist to Heiskala's face. "No one could believe it when my first punch landed exactly seven seconds after the opening whistle," Magnuson recounted. "I was pretty surprised myself."

His opponent returned his own right cross to Magnuson's head. After a wild swing by each man, the third clean punch of the melee—a square shot to the mouth by Magnuson—dropped Heiskala to the ice like a marionette whose strings had snapped, and he lost two teeth in the process. The final strike was "a dynamite six-inch jab that was reminiscent of Sugar Ray Robinson in his prime," reported Stan Fischler for *The Sporting News*. After later seeing a film of the punch, one veteran NHL defenseman added, "You don't see many like it… Earl's knees buckled like a pillar in an earthquake."

Heiskala staggered off to the dressing room with assistance, missing the remainder of the first period in addition to his teeth, plus needing 12 stitches for his lip. "Never before or since have I really injured a player this seriously in a fight," Magnuson would state a couple years later. Just 13 seconds after the scrap, Dennis Hull took immediate advantage of the momentum swing and scored to give Chicago a 1–0 lead.

But the fireworks for Magnuson were not over. Around the 12:00 mark of the first period, Bobby Hull raced with the puck into the Philadelphia zone on the left wing. Circling the net, he found his center, Bryan Campbell, who then quickly slid the puck over to Magnuson at the right point. Keith let loose with a 40-foot slap shot that carried high into the net past Flyers goalie Bernie Parent, as Magnuson deposited his first regular season goal in the NHL. It was one of four tallies the Hawks would blitz upon Parent in opening frame (with goals coming later from Chico Maki and Bill White as well). Magnuson's first foray into the goals column was ultimately the game-winner as the Hawks piled three more on Parent in the second period, who was then replaced by Doug Favell, as Chicago won going away 7–1.

After being held scoreless in his rookie season (except for the goal in the playoffs against Boston), the game capped a watershed evening for the young man from Saskatchewan. "Maggie's goal brought out a volume of cheers," noted Damata. When the puck went in and the Stadium goal light came on, Magnuson threw his arms above his head with such excitement that his gloves actually flew right off his hands—the opposite direction from which they normally flew off, which was dropping toward the ice before a fight. The next day, his teammates teased him by doing the same thing in unison when Keith came onto the ice for practice.

In perhaps the most moving tribute for Magnuson, the considerate Bobby Hull thought quickly and was able to recover one of Heiskala's teeth from the ice right after the fight, as well as the puck from Keith's first goal. Hull mounted the tooth on top of the puck in a gold-plated leaf and presented the sculpture to Magnuson as a memento of the occasion.

Magnuson and other Hawks players later noticed that Heiskala, once a truly physical force in the sport, was never quite the same player again, becoming more submissive in the corners and playing with less aggressiveness. Heiskala would never challenge Magnuson to fight again, nor would any other Flyers for the remainder of the season. Heiskala finished his career a couple of seasons later, his only significant fight taking place in an upstart professional league, the World Hockey Association, with Paul Shmyr.

"Heiskala's career as an enforcer lasted as long as it took Magnuson to reach back and waste him with one punch," marveled Dave Schultz, who would soon step into Heiskala's role for the Flyers.

After the Heiskala fight, the national media once again took notice of Magnuson in the wake of his appearance on the cover of *Sports Illustrated* the prior spring. "Off the ice, Magnuson's bridgework gleams in a smile of childlike innocence, and bromides fall from his lips like gentle rain," as *Time* magazine described him a few weeks after the battle with Philadelphia. "On the ice, beware. The angelic face twists into a toothless snarl, while the bromides give way to threats of mayhem." Added Dan Moulton of *The Sporting News*, "Magnuson [has] set about establishing himself as the policeman the Black Hawks had needed since the departure of Reg Fleming a few seasons ago." (Interestingly, Fleming—long ago the Magnuson family favorite back in Wadena and Saskatoon—would square off with Magnuson once again on December 9, a rematch after the pummeling Keith took from Fleming in his rookie season.)

As expected, the Hawks had rocketed to the top of the standings in the weaker Western Division by early December, with a 14–4–5 record. On the second of the month, the East-leading Bruins arrived at the Stadium with a sparkling 14–4–4 mark of their own. The Bruins' focus was now firmly on the eye-catching, second-year Chicago defenseman. "For the first time in memory, the pregame talk isn't about Bobby Hull," wrote John Ahern of the *Boston Globe*. "This time the subject was Keith Magnuson, the sophomore defenseman, who has become the Black Hawk leader despite his youth and newness to the league."

A week earlier, the two teams had played in Boston, where Sanderson and Magnuson had dropped the gloves when once again Keith was compelled to come to the rescue of a teammate who had been hit from behind by Sanderson along the boards. In looking back on Magnuson's career, Chicago announcer Pat Foley noted that most of Keith's scraps did not originate from his actions. "Many of the fights he had were not the result of something done to him by an opposing player," Foley said. "If someone took a cheap shot on any one of the Hawks, that person would have to deal with Magnuson."

The Bruins certainly seemed obsessed with knowing the whereabouts of Chicago's No. 3 when he was on the ice. "Last week the Bruins won 3–2," Ahern continued, "probably because Magnuson was banished with 13 minutes [of penalty time], making the work a little easier." Boston defenseman Don Awrey agreed. "He does a lot. He leads that club. He's a guy who can beat you." Added Bruins forward Ken Hodge, "He likes to play it rough and he provides a spark...this kid is something."

Near the end of the first period of the December 2 contest, a bench-clearing brawl had ignited between the two rivals. It began with a scrap between Jim Pappin and Awrey, and later directly involved Sanderson, McKenzie, Hodge, Ted Green, Rick Smith, Ace Bailey, Bill Speer, and Wayne Cashman from the Bruins side and Pappin, Magnuson, Wayne Carleton, Dan Maloney, Pit Martin, and Bobby Hull of the Hawks. (The only one not on the ice was backup goalie Gerry Desjardins for the Hawks, who attempted to do his part by tugging at the jersey of a Boston player when the melee drifted over to the Chicago bench.)

Things had appeared to have calmed down after a few minutes, at which point Magnuson skated away from the combat. When one of the Boston players said something—the origin of which Keith could not decipher as it came from the middle of a group of seven or eight Bruins who had circled around him—Magnuson charged back into the pack single-handedly, throwing a few more right hands until he was separated from the Boston roster. One of the players in the Boston pack was Orr, who had taken exception to Magnuson getting a final punch in on him before the linesmen pulled them apart. The protection of Orr had been the Bruins' focal point all evening, and they felt Magnuson had been out to get him since the opening whistle. As Orr and Magnuson were making their way off the ice, eyeballing and jeering at each other all the way, Cheevers—once again in the nets for Boston as the goaltender that night—overhead Orr saying to Magnuson, "With 10 seconds left, no matter who's ahead, I'm gonna get you." Magnuson, meanwhile, did not care who it was challenging him. To him, Bobby Orr was the same as any other threat, and had to be dealt with accordingly. "If you're going to play in this league—and that's all I've ever wanted to do—you just have to be able to take care of yourself," he once wrote. "If you can't, the established players will run you out."

True to his word, Orr found Maggie in the game's final minute. After a few right hands from Orr, the two went down to the ice like a pair of wrestlers, with extra punches flying thereafter. Even though Magnuson was badly bloodied, he was so incensed that referee John Ashley had to jump in and assist the linesmen in restraining him further. With Orr heading down to the ice and both men's sweaters in a tangled mess, Magnuson descended one final blow to the Boston star.

Orr's attack was of no consequence, as Magnuson's energy had spurred the Hawks in front of the electric Stadium crowd. They pulled out a 4–3 win in the fierce battle with the Bruins, part of a stretch from late November 1970 to early January 1971 during which the team went 15–3, a run that would be capped by yet another victory over the Bruins in the Stadium on January 9 (in which Magnuson got his second goal of the season). By the end of March, the Hawks had posted a 26–2–2 record at home, including 18 straight games at the Stadium without a loss since the start of the regular season—a club record. The streak began with an opening night home win over the California Golden Seals, the team formerly known as the Oakland Seals, whose title had been changed by their new owner Charles Finley, the franchise's third CEO in four years. In October 1972, Finley would be able to convince his fellow owner Wirtz to move a game between the Seals and Hawks four days later on the calendar, in order to accommodate Finley's desire for attention to be placed on his other team, the Oakland A's, which was playing in the World Series. "We insisted that our players get World Series tickets while they were in Oakland," Bill Wirtz would say. "Not free ones, either. We'll pay." And as with the A's, Finley ordered his newly acquired hockey team to begin donning bright-colored uniforms as well.

• • •

Magnuson's play had earned him his first trip to the NHL All-Star Game in 1971, joining seven other Black Hawks—at the time, the most ever elected from one team for the event. How much he would enjoy the honor, however, remained to be seen—the 1971 version was scheduled for the Boston Garden, and the fans in Beantown were in no mood to set aside their animosities for their favorite persona non grata, in spite of the special occasion.

"Keith Magnuson, the robust Chicago defenseman, must know he has arrived," wrote Fischler in covering the event for *The Sporting News*. "The rampaging redhead was the only West Division skater consistently booed by the Boston Garden fans during the All-Star Game. There is a lot of hockey player in that young man."

Despite their vocal displeasure with Magnuson and his teammates from Chicago, the Boston fans witnessed a 2–1 victory by the West, powered by goals by Maki (only 36 seconds into the game) as well as Bobby Hull. Maggie, meanwhile, gave the local throng some pleasure by going to the penalty box halfway through the third period, and the Garden security kept a close eye on the spectators nearest him. He jokingly suggested to Maki that the next time they come to the East Coast for a road trip, Chico should bring along some fireman's helmets for extra protection (in an era before helmets were worn by most players in the NHL, Maki worked as a part-time firefighter in the Chicago area).

Kevin Walsh was on the scene at the All-Star Game for the *Boston Globe* and was impressed with Magnuson's performance in the hostile environment. "Magnuson, who was greeted by a loud round of boos during the introduction, certainly ranked as one of the stars in the West victory," Walsh wrote. "The defenseman who made the jump from the college ranks to the NHL look easy was able to keep the East attack off balance while he was on the ice." But Maggie, using his stick more than his body this particular night, sounded disappointed with what transpired over the course of the evening. "There wasn't much hitting out there," he said.

While Magnuson continued to pile up the penalty minutes along with the fights, it had appeared that some help might be on the way to shoulder the load of policing the Chicago ice. The 1970–71 season was the rookie campaign for 22-year-old Hawks defenseman Jerry Korab, an imposing figure who stood 6'3" and checked in at 220 pounds.

Korab had posted an impressive log of time in the penalty box himself, including 284 minutes for the Port Huron Flags of the International Hockey League in 1968–69. In 46 games in his rookie NHL season, Korab would find time as a third- and fourth-pair defenseman, putting up 152 minutes in the box while adding four goals and 14 assists. Magnuson would always feel that Korab, however, had actually been at a disadvantage because of his height; it often appeared that the tall Korab led with his elbows when running into an opponent when in fact he was not, precipitating undeserved penalties.

Even with Korab's assistance, it was Magnuson who continued as the team's unquestioned enforcer. On March 6, he once again took on multiple opponents in the same game, which was also evidence of Magnuson's remarkable stamina and conditioning. "It is important to remember about Keith," Jim Wiste pointed out, "that he often had to fight more than just once a game. Toward the end of the third period, Maggie might be having his third bout of the game, while the guy he is now fighting is fresh and maybe jumping on the ice for the first time that night."

Just two minutes into the contest against Toronto, Magnuson knocked Brian Spencer into the boards at Maple Leaf Gardens, after which Spencer sprung to his skates and exchanged blows with him. Next up was Garry Monahan, who tangled with Keith a minute into the second period. By the end of the evening, Magnuson had added 14 more penalty minutes for a season total of 267, just six short of the NHL record. Soon the mark would be his; he finished the league schedule with 291 minutes in penalties, the most ever, as the Hawks also secured a team-record 49 wins to easily claim the Western Division title.

"I sure can't complain about most of the fights and penalties Keith has," Reay said. "When a player is being goaded into fights and tested, it generally means that he's playing effectively and causing a lot of trouble for the other teams. What coach could ever be unhappy with a player like that?"

Magnuson felt that the fights meant little if they did not help the team succeed, and he desperately wanted to lead his team to greater heights in the 1971 postseason than he had in his rookie year. After easily disposing of the Flyers in a four-game sweep in the opening round, the Hawks engaged in two epic battles with two Original Six teams for the rights to the Cup—two series which would be remembered for decades to come.

First up were the New York Rangers in the league semifinals, a team filled with veteran, battle-tested talent, much like Chicago. Unfortunately for the Hawks, they saw their promising young scorer Gerry Pinder leave the team temporarily after a heated argument with Reay early in the series. Pinder had missed a team practice and then did not even show up for Game 2 at the Stadium. The player had complained about the amount of ice time he was getting, which was less than what he thought he should be getting. "I know I haven't played well this season," Pinder admitted, "but I don't see how I could ever lace my skates again for that man [Reay]. The coach has lied to me this season. He says there's nothing personal, but it must be. He's hardly said hello to me in two years."

The team, however, remained cohesive enough to give the Rangers all they could handle. With Black Hawk Fever reaching its zenith in Chicago, Reay's men won Game 5 in overtime at the Stadium as Bobby Hull scored on a one-timer off the draw from Martin in the New York zone. The team had been fired up after comments in the newspapers by New York's Vic Hadfield, who had boasted after his team took two of the first three games in the series that "we had let them win one." After the Rangers won Game 6 back in New York in a contest that lasted three overtime periods, the two teams collided in a decisive Game 7 at the Stadium on Sunday, May 2.

Laboring to hold on to a 3–2 lead late in the game, Magnuson, Tony Esposito, and the rest of the defense scrambled against an extra Rangers attacker as a barrage of shots were fired toward the Chicago goal. Maki was able to work his way to the puck, however, and slide it down the ice for an empty-net goal, an effort that clinched the game and the series. Upon Maki's tally, CBS announcer Dan Kelly noted that the press box had suddenly started shaking as the old structure concussed with a deafening roar. The Black Hawks were now one series victory away from their first Stanley Cup in 10 years.

In the final round they would face the Montreal Canadiens, also known as the Habs in reference to *les habitants*, the nickname given to French settlers in Quebec in the 1600s. The Canadiens had acquired the unfamiliar role of being underdogs all season long, after their first playoff absence in 22 years the season prior. Comparisons of their aged roster were now being made to George Allen's "Over-the-Hill Gang," the NFL's Washington Redskins of the same era, as Canadiens coach Al MacNeil utilized a roster of veterans. Greats such as Jean Beliveau, Frank Mahovlich, John Ferguson, Henri Richard, and others were well into their thirties, and the current season's sunset was expected to be the last for many of them. But it also marked the first postseason for rookie goalie Ken Dryden—the same netminder Magnuson had faced in the NCAA championship game versus Cornell just two years earlier.

Originally drafted by the Bruins in 1964, Dryden was unlike most any goaltender to enter the league for some time. At 6'4", he not only played with a lanky, unorthodox style but also presented himself with distinctive articulation and engaged in cerebral pursuits off the ice. Dryden was concurrently enjoying an impressive start to a career outside of hockey as well, having already gained his bachelor's degree in history at Cornell. By 1971 he was working on a law degree from McGill University, asking friends to take notes for him in classes while the Canadiens were out of town. (In later years, Dryden would be elected as a member of the Canadian Parliament.) Like Magnuson, Dryden had bypassed the Juniors after college and instead came straight to the NHL. Playing in only six games for the Canadiens in the spring of 1971, he had won all six and thus had wrestled the starting job away from Rogie Vachon for the playoffs.

"Chicago isn't an easy rink for a visiting goaltender, especially a rookie just starting," observed Montreal general manager Sam Pollock after Dryden had beaten the Hawks 2–1 in the Stadium back in March, one of Dryden's first appearances in the league. "Anyone who was there couldn't have been surprised at him starting the first playoff game... Our other goalies, [Phil] Myre and Vachon, had been inconsistent."

The decision to go with the rookie Dryden as the man in the nets was another bold move for MacNeil, a former Hawks player under Reay in the mid-1960s (and at that time, a roommate of 1971 Hawks center Lou Angotti) who had replaced Claude Ruel as the Montreal coach just 23 games into the season. Heading into the series with the Black Hawks, MacNeil had rejuvenated his roster of older players, leading them to play like inspired rookies. They had been on a recent tear across the league to end the regular season, winning two-thirds of their games in the final weeks of the schedule before ousting the Bruins and then the Minnesota North Stars in the first two rounds of the playoffs.

The Hawks looked like a team of destiny as the Finals commenced against the Canadiens, dashing toward the Cup with two rousing victories at the Stadium to open the championship round. The first contest was a 2–1 overtime thriller on May 4, followed by a more conventional 5–3 win two days later. With the series moving to the Forum in Montreal for Game 3, Chicago showed no signs of relenting, building a 2–0 lead in the first period thanks to goals from Cliff Koroll and Bobby Hull. "For 20 minutes this afternoon it was a team with championship poise," Damata penned ominously in the *Tribune*, "a finely-tuned machine geared for a third victory in a row in the World Series of professional hockey.

"It looked at the time as if Chicago's Black Hawks might, just might, do the seemingly impossible: make a four-game sweep of the Montreal Canadiens. That was a wishful dream, a fantasy that evaporated before the winds of reality."

The team's fortunes changed, in the minds of many of the Hawks, when the highly regarded referee Ashley—the man in the middle of the Chicago-Boston brawl back in December—began blowing his whistle with great regularity. Fourteen infractions were called during the second period alone, and a total of 27 throughout the contest. Sixteen of them were against the Black Hawks, which nearly matched the meager number of 18 shots they could muster on Dryden. Damata noted that in that middle period, Stan Mikita, Martin, Pappin, Angotti, White, and Bobby Hull all spent time in the box, which in his words "destroyed the rhythm" that had led to Chicago victories in the first two games.

On one even-strength shift, Pete Mahovlich beat Magnuson to a puck in the corner in the Chicago zone. Mahovlich, who at 6'5" towered over most of his opponents, slashed at Magnuson's legs, an illegal move which permitted him to gain control of the puck. He then wheeled around quickly and fired a low-angle shot at Esposito that crept past him for the Canadiens' first goal. Ordinarily, Magnuson would respond to such a slash with a drop of his gloves; but he did not do so this time, for fear of getting a fighting-major and thus putting his team in a deeper hole. "If Magnuson had retaliated," Reay said afterward, "he probably would have drawn a double penalty."

Pete's brother, Frank Mahovlich, soon tied things up at 2–2, and later added another goal after Montreal had already grabbed the lead for a 4–2 victory. The final tally for Frank was his 13th goal of the playoffs, which matched the record set by Boston's Phil Esposito the previous year.

While the Canadiens appeared to take the physical toll of the season and playoffs in stride, the Hawks were showing signs of infirmity by Game 4. Mikita and Esposito were both nursing leg injuries, and Stapleton still had over 100 stitches in his face thanks to an extensive laceration from the blade of a Canadiens skate four days earlier. While the origin of Mikita's soreness was a mystery, Esposito suffered his blow when Canadiens defenseman Guy Lapointe—who would bump into Magnuson for a brief bout in the fourth contest—knocked him down when Esposito and Lapointe both raced after a loose puck in Game 3. The Hawks played like the tired team they were, dropping another contest in the Forum 5–2 to even the series at 2–2.

The Hawks responded in fine fashion before their home crowd, with Esposito gaining his second shutout of the playoffs in blanking the Canadiens 2–0. The win put Chicago one win away from the championship. In a confrontation many were anticipating, Magnuson was finally challenged to a fight by Montreal strongman John Ferguson, who like Beliveau was at the very end of his career. But even in his record-breaking season of penalty minutes, Magnuson once again backed away from a fight—not out of fear of throwing fists with Ferguson, but to avoid spending time in the penalty box in such a critical game.

Even so, it was evident that the Hawks were trying to ramp up their physical play in the series, especially at the Stadium. Inserted into the lineup for four of the games in the Finals—despite playing only two regular season games during the year—was Rick Foley. Foley was another young defenseman in the Korab mold, big and strong at 6'4" and 225 pounds, and a player who, it was assumed, would also take some of the checking duties away from Magnuson and Doug Jarrett.

Much to the dismay of Montreal's fans and players, as well as general hockey onlookers, Canadiens star forward Henri Richard inexplicably "spent most of the game anchored to the bench" in Game 5, according to writer Todd Denault. Consequently, Richard—who, along with Beliveau, had spent more time in a Montreal uniform than anyone on the current roster, and who would play in as many games in the Stanley Cup Finals as anyone who has worn skates—blasted MacNeil publicly in the locker room afterward, as Ferguson had similarly done earlier in the series. Richard called his young coach "the worst he ever had," adding tension to an already edgy team environment with the Canadiens one loss away from elimination. The story even took a cultural turn in the press "with the French-speaking Henri, the younger brother of the still-worshipped [Maurice] 'Rocket' Richard, on one side and his English-speaking coach, Al MacNeil, on the other."

When the two teams returned to Montreal in preparation for Game 6, MacNeil—who originally had intentions of becoming a priest instead of a hockey coach—received death threats at his office at the Forum. Montreal police officers stood by MacNeil's side as he took his place behind the bench. Somehow, the coach and his team remained focused on the task at hand as the Canadiens took a 4–3 victory to force a winner-take-all seventh game back in Chicago.

• • •

The sports darlings of Chicago in the past few years had been Leo Durocher's Cubs, a talent-laden roster of friendly players that nonetheless disappointed the city by losing a large divisional lead in 1969. On the afternoon of May 18, 1971, at Wrigley Field, the Cubs and pitcher Milt Pappas fell to the San Francisco Giants 7–3, thanks to a couple of hits by Willie Mays and a home run by Bobby Bonds. The loss dropped the Cubs to a 19–18 record, and the end of Durocher's tenure seemed to be imminent. A meager crowd of just more than 12,000 had witnessed the event; while such a figure was perhaps typical for a Tuesday afternoon at Wrigley at the time, the city was that day focused on another event.

For that evening, almost twice that number would cram into Chicago Stadium.

The structure on Madison Street began gradually filling with patrons as the gates opened around 5:00 PM. Heading into the 7:00 hour, regular programming on the CBS television network was preempted for live coverage of the decisive game, just as it was on national television in Canada; the game ultimately reached an estimated 27 million households. For those milling around Chicago that evening with errands to run or for those otherwise unable to watch, their game coverage was also on WMAQ radio, in its first season as the Hawks' flagship station after the team had been on the airwaves of WGN for several years. Greeting the listeners as always was Lloyd Pettit, the voice of the team since 1964. Pettit began his remarks that night by mentioning how, in his memory, the excitement of the semifinal series with the Rangers was matched only by this final round with the Canadiens. He was joined in his opening comments to the audience by his sidekick Harvey Wittenberg, who had covered the Black Hawks in the local media since 1961 and who also served as the Stadium's public address announcer (in the latter role, Wittenberg became famous for his alert three times a night of "One minute to play in the period," as well as his other regular lines).

Pettit and Wittenberg gave the pertinent pregame information to the fans on WMAQ as the drop of the puck neared at the top of the hour. As the tension mounted for the imminent action, the first to appear out of the gate and onto the ice was referee John Ashley. He was booed loudly by the Stadium crowd as a result of the multitude of penalties he had called on the Hawks in Game 3 in Montreal. And despite the fact that linesmen do not issue penalties, Ashley's colleagues, Matt Pavelich and John D'Amico, would get the same response as well. (All three men would one day be elected to the Hockey Hall of Fame.)

A rhythmic cry began to rain down from the first and second balconies of the old barn: *"Ash-ley's a bum! Ash-ley's a bum!"*

Then the Canadiens took the ice, knowing that their season, as well as the career of one of their storied icons, would end that night. News had leaked out in the Montreal press earlier that day that, win or lose, this would be Beliveau's last game. The hockey giant was the first NHL player to appear on the cover of *Sports Illustrated*—15 years earlier—and like Orr and Hull, seemed to be encircled with a halo while dashing around on his skates. He was a regal, larger-than-life presence in the sport.

After a few seconds of silence with the Stadium noise in the background, Pettit suddenly broke in again to inform the listeners that the local heroes had arrived: "A standing ovation at the Chicago Stadium...as the Chicago Black Hawks come on the ice before the 20,000 people jammed in this edifice."

As Magnuson led the team out—as he did every game—the view and sound that the players experienced was like none other. The fight song "Here Come the Hawks!" once again bellowed out of the speakers on cue, and the overflow crowd was, almost in a literal sense, hanging from the rafters at nearly the highest reaches of the building. As Pettit estimated, there were indeed more than 20,000 spectators present, but compliance with the fire code required the Hawks to list the official attendance for each sold-out home game at the Stadium as "16,666."

The fans were there for a coronation, not a game; this was the Hawks' year. It was to be a May crowning to which they were entitled, a splendid moment for the franchise, and it was only a couple of hours away after 10 years of waiting. It was to be a special gift for the strong-willed Magnuson, who had led the team as a youngster with his blood, sweat, and fighting spirit; a gift to Reay, who had been eluded by the Cup for so long; a gift to Mikita, the deft playmaker and loyal subject of the team for a decade; and a gift to Bobby Hull and his underrated brother, Dennis, the former of whom had passed Maurice Richard for second place behind Howe on the NHL's all-time goals list back in February with his 545th. (A week after passing Richard, Hull would get his 27th hat trick, also surpassing Richard in this category.)

It would be fair to say that at that time, there had never been such an air of expectation at one Chicago sporting event. The Bears had taken the NFL championship eight years earlier over the New York Giants at a frozen Wrigley Field, but that was a hard-fought battle with uncertainty going in; this, however, was to be the Hawks' night for sure. All knew it.

While pandemonium reigned inside, no one in the Stadium gave much thought to the conditions outside. A turbulent late-spring day in the Midwest had produced an unstable atmosphere, with temperatures reaching the 90s in the afternoon and forecasters calling for the possibility of severe storms in the area into the night hours during and after the game. Even though it was claimed to be the first indoor arena with a comprehensive air conditioning system, the Stadium had absorbed the cumulative effects of the outside conditions over the past several hours. By faceoff, a stifling heat began to rise inside. "The temperature outside the Stadium read 85 degrees at game time," reported Damata. "And the massed humanity inside sent the thermometer soaring." Later that night, Damata would amend his remarks in describing the worsening conditions: "By the third period it seemed it wasn't a matter of temperature but of steam pressure." On the WMAQ airwaves, Pettit would periodically make mention of the growing warmth. His broadcast was being sent worldwide on Armed Forces Radio, which included the war-torn area of southeast

Asia known as Vietnam. By May 1971, the 10-year war raged on despite the fact that U.S. troops in the region had been reduced to fewer than 200,000 soldiers.

Beliveau and Mikita, two of the great centermen in the game, glided to the dot at the red line for the drop of the puck. Just before the start, Wittenberg chimed in with one of his various plugs of WMAQ sponsors: *"Get power to clean and power to burn with STP."*

For the first portion of the game, Reay placed the team's fate in the hands of his best players, including Magnuson, the Hull brothers, Mikita, Pappin, Maki, Martin, White, Stapleton, Jarrett, and Koroll. According to writer Gare Joyce, Bobby Hull "was on the ice for seven of the first 10 minutes of the first period, more than four minutes in one stretch." The Hawks immediately took the play directly to the Canadiens, and forced a holding penalty on Montreal's Terry Harper within the first two minutes when he illegally restrained Maki's rush up the ice. The power play resulted in no shots; even so, the crowd remained as raucous as any Pettit could recall at the Stadium. He felt compelled to apologize to his listeners on WMAQ for continuing to describe the play on several occasions after an offside infraction had been called seconds earlier by linesmen Pavelich and D'Amico—Pettit could not hear their whistles.

As much as anyone else, Magnuson fed off the enthusiasm of the crowd. He was playing in tremendous pain, the result of a gradually worsening right knee injury which would require surgery in the off-season. But for now, his teammates needed him. And near the 5:00 mark of the first period, he announced his presence. After Esposito gloved a Montreal shot and held on, Magnuson nudged Canadiens center Jacques Lemaire in front of the crease. Lemaire turned and shoved Magnuson back but no punches were thrown, as Magnuson displayed the same restraint he had offered earlier in the series in the run-ins with Ferguson and Pete Mahovlich. But Ashley sought to maintain a tightly controlled game—at least as opined by Pettit and Wittenberg—and he gave both players minor penalties for roughing at 4:09. The fans once again booed Ashley vociferously, this time in direct support of Magnuson, as Wittenberg struggled through the crowd noise to get in another advertiser's message with the break in the action.

"Why buy a dull car when a full-sized Pontiac is only 57 dollars more than America's most popular lightweight car?"

The first period played out with few scoring chances for either side. With seven minutes to go, Mikita fed Eric Nesterenko on a dazzling pass into the Montreal zone on the right side, and he fired a low shot that seemed destined for the inner half of the right post—but Dryden stretched out his left leg as far as he could and barely nicked the puck with his skate to send it dribbling harmlessly past the pipe.

Bobby Hull was still playing heavy minutes on the ice toward the end of the first period, and midway through the opening frame he had missed on a tremendous scoring chance when he rushed past Montreal defenseman J.C. Tremblay and charged in on Dryden. Unfortunately for Chicago, the puck hit a rough patch of ice as Hull carried it, and as a result, he was able to only push a soft shot on goal which Dryden stopped easily. Hot on Hull's tail at every turn was Canadiens rookie forward Rejean Houle, assigned by MacNeil as the defensive stopper on the Hawks legend during the series.

After Hull's thwarted breakaway, Pettit again commented on the heat of the building: *"A moment ago I thought I saw some steam coming from the ice."*

Five years earlier, Houle had been in his first season as a rising star in the Quebec Juniors when he attended a game between the Hawks and the Canadiens at the Forum. Outside the arena after the game, the teenaged Houle walked over to the Hawks bus, climbed right up the stairs past the confused driver, and directly addressed the

Golden Jet as the rest of the team stopped, fell silent, and stared at Houle. "Mr. Hull, one day I'll play against you," he said simply, and then walked back out of the bus as Hull politely smiled and nodded encouragingly to the youngster. Not long thereafter, Houle was being hailed as his franchise's next superstar, scoring 53 goals in 54 games for the Montreal Junior Canadiens in 1969.

Now, Hull was working hard to shake free of the pesky Houle. Hull never liked when people compared him to Orr; he said that unlike a defenseman, a forward does not have as much room to work on the ice. While Orr might have as much as 70 feet of ice with which to work up speed, a forward may only go 10 feet before a defender is on him. Houle, despite his inexperience, had done a yeoman's job in the series and was not letting up on Hull in the seventh game.

With two minutes left in the first period, Hull finally found an opportunity to return Houle's original greeting on the bus five years earlier. He drilled Houle with a hard body check, as the rookie—understandably frustrated with the monumental and futile task of trying to halt the seasoned Chicago star all series long—retaliated by holding Hull as Bobby tried to skate away from the scene, and Houle was sent to the penalty box for two minutes by Ashley.

The Hawks took advantage. Manning the point near the blue line on the power play where he could unload his deadly slap shot, Hull received the draw in the Canadiens' zone and triggered his howitzer on Dryden. The goalie got a solid piece of the puck, but it caromed into a favorable position near Dennis Hull at the left faceoff circle. Hull poked it into the back of the net off Dryden's glove for a 1–0 Chicago lead with 48 seconds remaining in the period. The Hawks had not been shut out during the 1970–71 season, and the goal by Dennis—who, provided the Hawks would win this evening, would likely have been on his way to the Conn Smythe Trophy as playoff MVP—assured that it would stay that way.

As the first period ended, the play had been largely in the Hawks' favor, with Chicago outshooting Montreal 12–6 and the majority of the Canadiens' chances having come from beyond 50 feet.

At the horn, Wittenberg got in another commercial statement: *"When your goal is pleasing everyone, set the table with Leon's Polish Sausage."*

Shortly into the second period, Magnuson was called for a tripping penalty on Pete Mahovlich, leaving him and other Hawks players concerned that the momentum might shift. But the penalty-killing unit, led by surprise special-teams appearances by Angotti and Nesterenko, was able to stave off the Montreal attack. Mahovlich later tried to induce Nesterenko to fight while Magnuson was in the box, but the veteran did not take the bait. As gritty, old-school, defensive-minded players, Nesterenko and Angotti were two men in whom Reay had confidence in shutting down the Canadiens scorers. Angotti, in a story told by Wittenberg, once told his Hawks teammates that he was so tough he could eat broken glass—and showed them so by punching out a window in the Mayfair Bar in Detroit and subsequently chewing on the shards.

Despite the successful ending of Magnuson's penalty time, observers wondered why Bobby Hull and Mikita were seeing less ice time as the second period wore on, particularly in penalty situations. The Hawks received another penalty at 4:14 for too many men on the ice, but once again, Hull and Mikita were not part of the shorthanded unit. Nonetheless, this infraction was successfully endured as well, and at the 7:00 mark Chicago forward Danny O'Shea was sent free with the puck into the Montreal zone on Dryden for another scoring chance. He hit the post on a rocket blast from the slot, but Martin gathered the puck moments later on the same shift, wheeled in behind the net, and slid it out in front to give O'Shea another opportunity. Danny gathered the puck in his skates, fired, and the shot got past

Dryden for a 2–0 lead. It was O'Shea's first goal in the playoffs since the opening round with Philadelphia, and delirious fans scattered debris all over the ice as another nail was seemingly hammered into the Montreal coffin.

"I remember looking over to the Canadiens bench after that goal and their heads were hanging down," Koroll said. "I thought right there that we had them."

Pettit, however, warned his listeners not to be too optimistic. He pointed out the Montreal club had rebounded from a two-goal deficit in the past, and had overcome a 3–2 Hawks lead in the third period in Game 6 in Montreal. Perhaps to inject comfort, Wittenberg then interrupted with another mention of a local sponsor: *"It's Su Casa for exciting Mexican food."*

One minute after O'Shea's goal, Bobby Hull hit the crossbar on a blazing wrist shot in front of the Montreal net which would have made the score 3–0. The puck bounced straight back out toward Hull but in a slightly downward angle from the lower half of the bar, suggesting that the Hawks had been within a fraction of an inch of taking a commanding lead.

Some hockey historians, such as Joyce, questioned why Reay continued to take most of his stars off the ice after the halfway point of the second period, and instead gave more ice time to Chicago's third and fourth lines. In any event, it was hard to keep track of the ice time for each player with any precision, as line shifts were held to under a minute by both coaches because of the searing heat in the building, and thus, the exacerbated fatigue of the skaters.

Even so, the play seemed to accelerate through the second period. Koroll was bumped hard after the whistle by Houle at the 12:00 mark. As the two started jawing at each other, over wandered the two cops, Magnuson and Ferguson, to see what was going on; more shoving ensued before they also had to be separated. The scene led, however, to Magnuson being given another minor penalty 30 seconds later for a hard check on Ferguson. A Montreal penalty a moment later produced a four-on-four situation, which presumably would open up the ice to both teams' top skaters—but once again, Hull and Mikita were not sent into the game.

At the other end of the ice, Esposito was noticeably tired. He had been the exclusive goalie down the stretch and all the way through the playoffs. The only other goaltender currently available on the roster was Ken Brown, who had played only one period in one game during the regular season. Now, it was apparent that the Stadium heat was affecting Esposito as well, as he hung an arm on the crossbar for extra rest at every opportunity.

As the second period was nearing its close, Lemaire dumped the puck into the Hawks' end so his team could make a line change. As players occasionally do in such circumstances, Lemaire decided at the last moment to send the puck on goal, even though he was near center ice and there was virtually no chance of scoring from that distance. Lemaire wound up and "uncorked a booming slapshot," according to Denault, and then, "turning toward the bench, he soon heard a commotion from the crowd and turned to see that the puck had ended up in the Chicago net behind a dejected Tony Esposito."

As Lemaire's shot was en route, the fatigued Esposito's knees had buckled momentarily, which caused the puck to graze only a portion of his glove before it flew past him. The puck had traveled a long way "through a humid haze which hung over the ice," according to Verdi, and "carried high into the net beyond Esposito's belated right-hand reach." A few minutes earlier on the radio, Pettit himself had used the word "hazy" to describe the deteriorating, heated conditions inside the Stadium.

Lemaire knew that he had immediately lifted his team with his inadvertent score. "It was the strangest goal I have ever scored that was so important," he said. "We started to skate better and play better. They [the Black Hawks] dropped. It was a matter of time after that. It turned the game."

Mere moments after Lemaire's goal, listeners on WMAQ had their broadcast of the game suddenly interrupted by an emergency weather message. A tornado watch had been issued for all of the northern Illinois area until 4:00 the following morning.

As the broadcast returned to Pettit at the Stadium, Lemaire was already in the process of striking again. He found Richard in front of the Hawks goal and Henri poked it past Esposito at the 18:20 mark. Once again it had been a four-on-four situation, and yet again, Hull and Mikita were not on the ice.

The tally evened the score 2–2, and suddenly made the third period a winner-take-all, tension-heightened, 20-minute segment of hockey.

"I spent both intermissions praying," Magnuson would later admit.

Two and a half minutes into the third period, Houle—now playing like a veteran—spotted Richard jumping over the boards near the Hawks' blue line, coming on a line shift. Reacting instinctively, Houle pounced on the opportunity and slid him a pass. In his haste to do so, however, Houle somewhat misfired. "When Rejean got the puck to me," Richard would later describe, "the puck was in my skates, and was in the skates all the way in."

Magnuson reacted late to the play and dug his legs back into a retreat, his bad knee flashing with pain as he scrambled as best he could to get back into a defensive position. Worried he was about to get beaten, Magnuson then turned and sprinted with Richard stride-for-stride, much as a football defender would do against a pass receiver going deep. Richard gathered the puck into his stick blade and found a burst of speed, turning the corner on the defenseman at the faceoff circle in the Chicago zone, and zoomed in directly on Esposito. In a final attempt to stop him, Magnuson stretched out his body in a full-length dive. Straining for all he was worth, he lunged out his stick with his belly on the ice in a frantic attempt to send the attacker off course. "I didn't see Richard," Keith would explain later about the moment the Montreal veteran had hopped onto the ice from the Montreal bench. "Then when I did, I thought I had him poke-checked away from the puck. I should have tripped him or something."

Richard eventually got around Magnuson and put one fake on Esposito. "I made a move toward Esposito with the stick," Richard said, "then I pulled the puck back and got it over him after he went down." The red light behind the glass went on, signaling the score that gave the Canadiens their first lead in the game at 3–2 as the crowd was instantly hushed.

"A comparatively quiet Chicago Stadium..." Pettit uttered a moment later.

Mikita, who according to Dennis Hull had an extreme dislike of Richard, went after the Montreal winger in the final minutes with every chance he got. "Stan was as good as Wayne Gretzky with the puck," Hull stated, "but in order to get an image of what Stan was like as a player, you also have to imagine Gretzky hacking and spearing opponents...when they [Mikita and Richard] were both sitting in the penalty box, I liked to go over to hear them scream at each other. It was the worst stuff you could imagine."

Suddenly in desperation mode, Reay now ordered more forecheckers into the Montreal zone to increase the pressure on their defensemen and Dryden. Opportunities abounded, with Harper and Pete Mahovlich both called for hooking penalties at 5:36 and 7:27, respectively. But despite several golden chances, the Hawks could not even the score in those power-play situations.

Near the 11:00 mark, Pinder made his first appearance of the game. Still in Reay's doghouse since his absence during the semifinal series against the Rangers and the public comments he made about the coach, Pinder was still considered by Reay to be a top scoring threat and thus was given several important minutes in the final half of the third period. He, like several other Hawks forwards, bombarded Dryden with everything he could muster. The rookie goaltender held firm, however, turning away every assault. "The Canadiens clung to their slender lead while the final minutes were ticking off on the big clock suspended over center ice," wrote Bill Brennan of *The Sporting News* in watching the analog hands of the Stadium's ancient time-keeping piece dissipate, much to the Chicago players' and fans' anxiety.

Dryden, withstanding 33 Chicago shots compared to the mere 25 his club had put on Esposito, would hold on for the 3–2 win, and he was mobbed by his teammates at the final horn. It was only the second time the visiting team had won a seventh game in Stanley Cup Finals history, and the result kept Chicago from claiming its first sports championship since the Bears had taken the NFL title in 1963.

When the Stanley Cup was presented to the Canadiens moments later at center ice, many noticed that MacNeil was not smiling. Beliveau, the longtime captain and legend, having now completed his final game, proudly hoisted the revered trophy over his head and began the traditional team skate. The fans in the Stadium gave him, the Canadiens, and their Black Hawks—despite having already disappeared into the home dressing room—a standing ovation.

In Montreal's saunalike locker room, there were handshakes all around. Decided Henri Richard, it was "the best of the 10 Stanley Cups I've won. This one was the best because we were so much the underdogs." Frank Mahovlich, basking in his NHL-record 14 playoff goals, agreed wholcheartedly with a smile and nod from a few feet away. And, in an abrupt change of tune, the Canadiens were now apparently behind their head coach. "We played with confidence because he had confidence in us," Guy Lapointe said of MacNeil. MacNeil, in fact, had been unofficially named the game's "first star" by broadcaster

Howie Meeker of *Hockey Night in Canada*, in respect to the coach's pushing all the right buttons. And while there was now speculation that MacNeil was suddenly popular in Montreal and would remain the team's leader, GM Sam Pollock instead installed Scotty Bowman as Canadiens coach for the following season. Thus ended the mysteriously brief yet successful run for MacNeil in Montreal; he would return to a head coaching role with the Atlanta and Calgary Flames in the 1980s, and then briefly for Calgary once again as a 67-year-old in 2002.

Dryden, having been summoned to the NHL for the first time only a couple of months earlier, had played in all 20 playoff games for the Canadiens. He took home the Conn Smythe Trophy as the top man in the postseason—although, ironically, he could still qualify for Calder Trophy in the following season, as he did not play in the requisite 25 regular season games. In admiration of Dryden's performance and style, Scott Young of the *Toronto Telegram* wrote, "I never saw a goaltender before who, when the play becomes ultra-confusing in front of him, stretched out across the goal like a lady on a chaise lounge. Low shots plunked into his pads and the high ones he caught." Esposito had a better overall record in the 1971 playoffs than Dryden (11–7 with a 2.19 goals-against average and two shutouts versus Dryden's 12–8, 3.00 GAA, and no shutouts), but in the ultimate battle of the two magnificent goalies, Dryden was able to give his team the deciding, final nudge at the wire.

Over in the Black Hawks' own steam bath of a dressing room, the atmosphere was naturally the polar opposite.

"They gave everything they had," Reay said simply of his charges. The coach chose not to bury his outfit, but rather to praise it. "I'm mighty proud of this team. We had a great season, and it's too bad we couldn't have won it. We have nothing to be ashamed of. You just couldn't play in two tougher series than the ones we were in against New York and the Canadiens."

The local writers, meanwhile, were mournful about what could have been. "The Hawks lost this game and the Cup by inches," penned Damata for the *Tribune*. "And those inches meant the difference between a water shower and a champagne dousing. Those tiny bubbles poured like Niagara Falls in the Canadiens clubhouse, mixing with perspiration that ran down the faces of the giggling champions and spattering onto the already sopping red uniforms. It was honest sweat, for the Canadiens, too, gave all they had."

The Chicago players felt the pain most of all.

"I still wake up at night, wishing it was a nightmare," Cliff would say years later about Game 7. "That one really hurt."

In much the same way that baseball's World Series winner's share was coveted before big salaries came into the picture, the 1971 matchup between Montreal and Chicago was one of the last true, heroic, old-time standoffs in the Stanley Cup Finals. It was reported after Game 7 that Montreal defenseman Jacques Laperriere had played since Game 2 with a broken arm. Nearly half the roster on each side was enduring some sort of significant ailment, such as Magnuson's knee and Stapleton's lacerated face, but all of them fought through it. As Joe Falls of *The Sporting News* said, "You come across something like that seventh game of the Stanley Cup playoffs in the cauldron of the Chicago Stadium and suddenly everything becomes worthwhile... You are experiencing high emotions...You sit there and you're so nervous it is almost painful. And yet, it is a sweet, excruciating pain."

But the laurels of bravery do not dress the wounds of defeat. Magnuson sat in a forlorn stare in front of his locker when he got off the ice after Game 7, just like when he went into a foul mood back in Wadena or Saskatoon as a boy when his team lost a simple pick-up game. He had no desire to remove his equipment. Capturing the emotional moment was a photographer; later, local artist Rosa Lee would use the photo to compose a portrait of Magnuson with his face in his hands, with only his red hair and his white No. 3 home jersey visible.

Naturally, he was stewing over the Richard goal in the third period. "A play," Verdi recounted, "which brought from Keith Magnuson some regretful, almost tearful, words, a bit too harsh: 'I lost the game for us.'" Magnuson then began to wonder about other turning points in the series in which he was involved—would things have turned out differently in Game 6 if he had fought with Ferguson? Would his team have raised the Cup if he had done battle with Pete Mahovlich, perhaps giving his team some spirit as his bouts had done during the regular season?

Right then and there, in the basement of the Chicago Stadium, Magnuson considered quitting the game. He would never be welcome in Chicago again, he figured, and would have to move out of the area—whether he decided to continue with hockey as a career or not, he reasoned.

However, as it always does, time would give him perspective.

As the Hawks and their fans headed out onto Madison Street, they would have to ponder the defeat while driving through the impending storms belting the Chicago area.

When Magnuson showed up inside the Stadium the next day to gather a few personal items, it was a stark example of how the atmosphere in a place can change within a matter of hours.

"You get to know all its moods, its lights and shadows," Magnuson said of the vast, expansive building which had so moved him when Koroll brought him inside the first time in September 1969. "There's the game mood that's a lot like a giant party, with 20,000 celebrants roaring...but practice the next day is like the morning after. No one's there at all. The rink is a cold and solitary place then, echoing any number of moods I may be feeling."

• • •

Magnuson knew that a majority of his summer would be spent rehabilitating from the requisite surgery that was to be done on his right knee. He was still uncertain about his place in hockey, Chicago, and on the Black Hawks—but he was not about to give up.

After a successful operation, Keith attempted some basic exercises to build strength, both with the knee and with his confidence. In an effort to have a little fun in the midst of the recovery, he and Koroll decided to spend an evening out at a Chicago bar. While at the establishment, an inebriated patron—a critic who likely had never been in the arena with his face marred with blood or sweat—stumbled over to their table. He started giving the immobilized Magnuson a hard time about the Richard goal (this occurred only when the man had waited in cowardly fashion for Koroll to leave the table and go the restroom). Completely helpless from his knee surgery, Magnuson could not even get up and walk away from the man, so he sat there and tried to look in another direction as the verbal abuse continued.

The man left after a couple of minutes, whereupon Magnuson paused, took a deep breath, and struggled to his feet. He got up onto his crutches, hobbled out of the place, and stepped into the rainy night in tears—not because of the man's message, but from the memory that by not stopping the Richard goal, he surely had let his team down. When Koroll returned from the restroom, he had no idea where Magnuson was and was greatly concerned. Sprinting out into the street, he found Magnuson in a rain-soaked alley a few blocks away, still distraught and banging his fist in frustration against the bricks of an old building. Koroll put his arm around his buddy and guided him into a taxi. They went back home to their apartment, where Koroll had to carry Magnuson—who was now completely immobile from traumatizing his knee during his hastened limp out of the bar—up the stairs to their unit. Now a bit more calm, Maggie sprawled out on his bed and stared up at the ceiling, once again wondering if he could still play hockey at the level to which he was accustomed—or if he even wanted to.

Then, Koroll put an old favorite song of theirs from college on the stereo, and Magnuson felt a sense of comfort cover him like a blanket. He began to believe that everything would be all right, and it was thanks to his best friend. Keith came to grips with the fact that failure was a part of life and part of being an athlete. He also knew then that he could deal with it.

"I suddenly realized that part of being a true professional," Magnuson would reflect years later on that watershed moment, "is learning to leave all your karma and guilt behind and not to carry your losses around like an enormous bag of yesterdays."

He was forgiven, even if he did not know it—and even if he did not think he deserved it.

He had given all he had in that seventh game against the Canadiens, just as his teammates had. As they slumped into their lockers in the basement of the Stadium, they were all physically spent. And even though they came up short, Magnuson and the Hawks knew they had left every bit of themselves on the ice. Their effort was echoed the words of Sir Walter Scott:

> *One hour of life, crowded to the full with glorious action, and filled with noble risks, is worth whole years of those mean observances of paltry decorum, in which men steal through existence, like sluggish waters through a marsh, without either honor or observation.*

5

Life without the Jet

"Magnuson is just so busy all the time. He gets the hell beat out of him, but he keeps coming back for more. You have to like a kid like that."

—Philadelphia Flyers coach
Vic Stasiuk, 1970

His knee stronger after a summer filled with intense workouts similar to his days in Denver, Keith Magnuson settled into a comfortable routine as a Chicagoan in the summer of 1971. He started making more personal appearances around the city, often stopping for a lunch of "milk, a bowl of clam chowder, a hamburger steak, and a vanilla sundae" at Bruno's downtown before heading to the Stadium. On other occasions, he would meet his teammates in the suburb of Hillside, where many of them lived and frequented a local restaurant called Stimac's. The bitter taste of the loss to Montreal still lingered, however, through the hot July and August days of picnics, parades, and ballgames. The Hawks eagerly awaited the start of training camp—dedicated to making the 1971–72 season the one in which they would not fall short again.

They indeed started the new campaign with a vengeance, sprinting out of the gate with seven victories in their first eight games. And just as they had in the previous year, the Hawks became virtually unbeatable in the Stadium the entire season. By Christmas they had not lost in Chicago, going 15–0–2 in their first 17 home games; they didn't lose on Madison Street until the Bruins came to town on December 29. Lloyd Pettit and Harvey Wittenberg, meanwhile, had their WMAQ broadcasts moved to the north side of the Stadium, near the outer edge of the first balcony, which finally placed the announcers closer to center ice as opposed to the awkward angle in the corner from which they previously called the games.

Among the consistent home triumphs was a contest on October 13 against St. Louis, in which the Hawks beat the Blues for the second time in four days in a 1–0 shutout. (In fact, the Hawks would proceed to shut out the Blues all three times in the Stadium in this particular season.) Shortly into the second period, in a play behind the Chicago net, Magnuson collided with George Morrison, a teammate at the University of Denver and at whose wedding Magnuson had even been a groomsman. Magnuson dropped the gloves on a surprised Morrison and proceeded to inflict a savage beating upon him, despite the fact there was no known negative history between the two players. There were reports in the St. Louis papers the following day that the Blues should have retaliated on Magnuson, but they never did. As for Magnuson, he simply felt he had a job to do, part of an overall strategic plan in helping his team gain an edge toward victory—no matter the opponent.

Keith had recently noted, "If you leave your label on a guy convincingly enough, you'll later see him skating around watching for you, either worrying about getting hit again or getting you back. He's stopped thinking about the game itself."

Two days later—and obviously confident that Magnuson could stand apart as the lone regular fighter on the roster—the Hawks unloaded their tough young defenseman, Rick Foley, to the Philadelphia Flyers, acquiring promising center Andre Lacroix in the process. Magnuson and Foley would do battle in the Stadium three weeks later as a full house turned out in hopes of seeing the one-on-one matchup; perhaps seeking desperately to prove himself, Foley had publicly questioned Magnuson's ability in the Philadelphia papers after leaving Chicago.

But the date the Hawks and their fans truly had marked on their calendars was November 24, 1971. It was the date when the Montreal Canadiens would return to the Stadium, their first visit since downing Chicago in the epic seventh game of the previous year's final round. (The two teams had played three weeks earlier at the Forum in Montreal, resulting in a hard-fought 2–1 Canadiens win).

In particular, Magnuson had been looking for Pete Mahovlich. Back in Game 3 of the 1971 Finals, it was Mahovlich who had slashed Magnuson in the corner at the Forum and stolen the puck, subsequently turning and firing on Esposito to score a crucial goal. Now, six months later and near the end of the first period, the two men's paths crossed again, with their forearms high up in the air. Magnuson absorbed a couple of early right-hand blows from the taller Mahovlich and then went to work in "windmilling" his fists on him, in Ted Damata's description, as the Montreal player "slumped leeward and was saved from complete collapse by intervening officials." Mahovlich emerged from the fight "with cuts over both eyes that bridged the nose" in a clear triumph for Magnuson. "Keith even won the debate in the penalty box," Damata footnoted, "but the dialogue has been censored." The two great teams skated on, extending their evenness from the past spring, battled to a 3–3 tie—Chicago's first deadlock of the year.

It was only a matter of time before the Hawks would match up with their other great rival. They returned to Boston on January 15 to face the Bruins in Bobby Hull's 1,000th regular season game. Magnuson was still Public Enemy No. 1 in Boston for having the audacity to take on local beloveds Derek Sanderson, Bobby Orr, John McKenzie, and others. During this contest, however, Bruins forward Wayne Cashman was Magnuson's particular target of choice. He was a player who was a respectable scorer and a decent fighter but, like Mahovlich, also liked to raise his stick in opponents' faces—something which Magnuson and most all of the league's other pure fighters despised as dirty play. After Magnuson checked Cashman into the glass, the two dropped the gloves immediately and exchanged a flurry of punches in one of the better fights the league would witness during the year. It was also one of the few times that the Bruins seemed to allow one of their own to take on an opposing player one-on-one—especially in their friendly surroundings of the Boston Garden.

Later in the season, in another game in Boston, Magnuson would dispose of McKenzie with one punch after having dropped him earlier with a body check behind the net, despite the colorful goaltender Gerry Cheevers recently proclaiming McKenzie "the greatest corner man in the league." That bout was the last of a series of three scraps that night, first with Jerry Korab of the Hawks taking on Carol Vadnais, then McKenzie going after Korab, and then Magnuson downing McKenzie. Just as McKenzie was sent sailing to the ice, however, Don Awrey came from behind and tried to pull Magnuson off of him, at which point Bobby Hull reached in to grab Awrey to keep it a fair fight. By late 1971, the escalation of such moblike brawls was something the NHL felt it needed to begin addressing.

Many national hockey writers considered this conduct typical of the Boston team. However, these brawls changed substantially in the 1971–72 season—even for teams known for regularly employing such tactics such as the Bruins and the Flyers—as it was the first year that the "Third Man In" rule was instituted in the NHL. The rule stated that a man interfering with a two-man fight was automatically ejected with a game misconduct penalty and slapped with a $100 fine. The effect on the Boston club had been obvious to Stan Fischler, one of those writers who did not care for the methodology of Harry Sinden's men.

"The Bruins are gang fighters, or at least they used to be," Fischler scoffed. "Guys like Sanderson aren't as eager to get into fights now." Overall, fights would indeed drop considerably over the winter of 1971–72; by March, Magnuson himself would have accumulated only nine fighting-major penalties—half the number he had posted at the same point in the previous season.

"At least with this rule, we know who the fighters are," Magnuson added in a positive tone about the change. "The linesmen don't break up fights as quickly as they used to, so a fellow has to be kind of careful who he gets involved with."

Magnuson also believed the new rule would help curb those players whom he liked to refer to as "homers"—and many of them resided in Boston.

"It's a term we use to describe those exhibitionists who are reluctant to play rough except in front of a home crowd," Magnuson explained, "where their teammates will have to back them up once anything gets started. That's why some players in this league are actually scared to play in Boston. It's like walking into gangland."

Mike Peluso, who in the 1990s would become an on-ice policeman for the Black Hawks for several seasons, readily admitted that there was an advantage to fighting on home ice.

"As a fighter it was way better fighting at home, because your home fans gave you even that much more adrenaline," he said. "A good crowd, like at the Chicago Stadium, was a huge advantage for you. The fear you had going into it [the fight] wasn't so much about getting hurt, but rather about losing and disappointing them."

Despite all the temper troubles between the Hawks and the Bruins, Cheevers, Orr, and a large majority of the other Boston players had a great deal of respect for Magnuson and his teammates.

"Let me tell you about Chicago," Cheevers said. "The Hawks are by far the most difficult test for any goaltender... They all shoot the puck so hard. You have to be alert every second against them because they can move the puck quickly to get someone in position to drill one... There's a mental tension for the whole 60 minutes against Chicago."

In addition to their dominance in the Stadium, the Hawks had been strong on the road through the fall, including a 4–1 win on December 22 over the struggling Seals in Oakland. The defense was completely suffocating opponents, and people around the league were beginning to take more notice of the continued improvement of Magnuson and Doug Jarrett as a defensive pair, along with Pat Stapleton and Bill White. In the game against Charlie Finley's team, Bobby Hull recorded his 28th hat trick against former Hawks goalie Gilles Meloche, extending his NHL record in this category. It was also an evening that held another bout for Magnuson; he took on future Chicago teammate Ivan Boldirev, who surprised Magnuson in felling the Hawks defenseman with one big right hand.

With the sourness of the 1971 Finals behind them and a robust start to the new schedule, it finally looked to be the Hawks' year. Evidence of this was shown by the nine Chicago players who were chosen to represent the Western Division squad in the 1972 NHL All-Star Game in Minneapolis, breaking their single-team record from the year before. No other team would come close to that total.

The New York Rangers led the East squad with six selections. The Hawks present were Tony Esposito, Bobby and Dennis Hull, Chico Maki, Pit Martin, Stan Mikita, Stapleton, White, and Magnuson.

Magnuson was grateful for the honor, but for a true competitor like Keith, seeing and speaking with his regular opponents in the lobby of the hotel where the players stayed during All-Star week was uncomfortable—especially Orr, McKenzie, Phil Esposito, and Dallas Smith, who were there representing Boston. Magnuson simply did not care to get too friendly with those with whom he would have to compete the following week—much in the same way that St. Louis Cardinals pitcher Bob Gibson approached his appearances in the Major League Baseball All-Star Game with begrudging tolerance.

"Back then, we never socialized off the ice," Magnuson would reflect years later, with a disdain in his voice for the way in which opposing athletes appear so comfortable in comingling in modern times. "So we were skating around before the game and Orr says to me, 'Hey, Magnuson, we don't fight in this game.' I just looked at him."

Dave Schultz, the man being groomed at the time as Earl Heiskala's replacement as the policeman for the Flyers, would cite another such circumstance a couple of years later, when Magnuson could not check his competitiveness at the social door.

"In 1974, after the season, I had to fly to Detroit to speak at a banquet," Schultz recounted. "Keith was there. He wouldn't even talk to me. He said to someone, 'Look, he and I are going to go at it again next year. I don't want to talk to him.' I certainly understood that."

Unfortunately, during their stay at the hotel, the players would have to deal with more than just the discomfort of close quarters with their usual adversaries. While relaxing in his room, Martin happened to wander out to his balcony window at the same time that Danny Meyer, a front office worker in the minor leagues of professional hockey, approached his own balcony ledge in the adjoining room. In the next instant, a distraught Martin watched as Meyer suddenly leapt to his death below.

Greatly shaken, Martin at first had no interest in playing in the game after witnessing the tragedy. "I was shocked by the whole thing," Martin said, "but I figured that if I played, I would get my mind off it." In between periods of the All-Star Game, Martin, Maki, Bobby Hull, and Toronto's Paul Henderson—the last of whom had been rooming with Martin—were interrogated by the city coroner about the incident. Hull and Maki had been staying in the room beneath Meyer's; Maki had woken up the sleeping Hull in a state of panic, exclaiming that a man had jumped off the building.

Back on the ice, Hull scored the game's first goal with three minutes remaining in the opening period, but ultimately the Hawks-laden West team fell to the East 3–2.

Despite the success the Hawks had enjoyed in the past two years—in addition to its dominance of the All-Star roster—they continued to be subjected to second-class coverage in much of the Chicago sports media, at least according to some within the organization (with the exception of Bob Verdi's work in the *Tribune*). Don Murphy, the team's publicist, made his feelings known in a February 1972 interview with *The Sporting News*. "The [local newspapers] treat hockey like a stepchild," he said. "While the Black Hawks are the only team in Chicago that has won anything since 1963, it is the team that gets the worst treatment in the Chicago press."

Perhaps the recent shuffling of the roster had been confusing to the media and fans alike; the trade of Foley was just the first of a number of changes the team experienced over the course of the 1971–72 season. On February 8—just two nights after his picture appeared on the cover of the game program sold at the Stadium—Danny O'Shea, nearly a hero the previous season after his goal in Game 7 against the

Canadiens, was traded to St. Louis after reputed disagreement with Tommy Ivan over his contract. Coming to the Hawks in return was a grateful Christian Bordeleau, fresh after missing a month with a broken foot, who called his new outfit "a sophisticated team." Bordeleau's brother Jean-Pierre—better known as J.P.—was currently playing in Chicago's farm system at the time and had been a former first-round draft pick of the Hawks in 1969.

After being selected by the Hawks in the draft, J.P.—much in the same method used on Magnuson by Ivan—was hastily handed a standard contract from the general manager that he was expected to sign immediately. For Bordeleau, the "negotiation" occurred while he was on his first team flight with the Hawks. Bordeleau had quickly come to trust Mikita in their short time together, so he went to the back of the plane where Stan was sitting and asked him if it was a fair deal. Mikita said it was, so Bordeleau agreed to put his name on it.

Along with Foley and O'Shea, also departed from Chicago was Gerry Pinder (following his confrontation with Billy Reay in the previous year during the playoffs) and Paul Shmyr. Both of them would cause trouble for Magnuson in the Hawks' next visit to Oakland on March 3, 1972. As they met in the corner for a loose puck, Pinder gave Magnuson a shot from behind that sent him flying into the boards. When Magnuson got up to respond, Shmyr jumped in between them and dropped the gloves with Keith. It was the first time Magnuson could recall fighting a former teammate, and it did not sit well with him. Shmyr later felt badly about it as well, and while dining in the same establishment later that night, he sent a contrite note to Magnuson at his table.

A week later, on March 12 in Detroit, another first for Magnuson and his fighting narrative occurred: it was the first (and last) time he could recall a fight in which he and his opponent were permitted by the linesman to punch themselves out until exhaustion. The scrap with the Red Wings' Nick Libett thus ended with each man grasping the shoulder of each other's jersey, struggling to stay upright from fatigue.

• • •

While the Hawks were marching easily toward another Western Division title in the spring of 1972, on the business side of hockey, storm clouds were starting to form on the horizon, the likes of which no one had ever witnessed before. That same April, Major League Baseball saw its first-ever wholesale players' strike, which cancelled the first two weeks of the schedule before the owners and the players' union could come to a new collective bargaining agreement. A different yet equally destructive issue was rearing its head for the National Hockey League, as the upstart World Hockey Association was getting ready to begin play in the fall—and was also readying to immediately raid the rosters of NHL teams to stock its own. No player was beyond the new league's reach, even those of esteemed owners such as Arthur Wirtz of the Hawks, recently inducted into the Hockey Hall of Fame in 1971 for his contributions to the sport.

And in the crosshairs of Ben Hatskin, the owner of the Winnipeg entry in the WHA and a former professional football player in that city, was Bobby Hull.

On March 25 in Boston, Hull scored his 600th NHL goal against Cheevers with 2:26 left in the game (Cheevers had permitted Hull's 400th goal, four years earlier, as well). After the game, there were congratulations all around for Hull for yet another milestone achieved. Even the crowd at the Garden—normally hostile to the men wearing the Chicago crest—gave him a 30-second standing ovation. "Did Chicago's management at least buy a beer for Bobby?" wondered Dan Stoneking of *The Sporting News*. It was even reported that Ivan walked right by Hull in the locker room and said nothing to him; perhaps it was because news had broken in the *Chicago Tribune* that very same day that Hull and others had been approached by the WHA with contract offers.

In response to the gossip about his alleged discussions with the other league, Hull was frank and direct. "If Winnipeg makes a sensational offer," Hull said, "I'd be a fool not to look it over. And I have a feeling the Chicago people might not match it."

Stoneking, however, believed that ultimately Hull would be back in a Black Hawks uniform for the 1972–73 season. "To be sure, Chicago owner Wirtz won't let Robert slip into the hands of the enemy," the writer assured. "So look for Hull to sign the largest contract ever by an NHLer."

An article released by Fischler had listed Magnuson as one of several other NHL stars contacted by WHA agents for the possibility of jumping leagues (a list that also included Mikita, Martin, Dennis Hull, Ken Dryden, New York Rangers defenseman Brad Park, legendary goalie Jacques Plante, and several other notable names). Back in February, the WHA had conducted its General Player Draft, in which they "selected" players already on NHL rosters. The event was mere symbolic saber-rattling, but it also suggested that the WHA meant business.

Magnuson, at the time, admitted that the money the WHA was throwing around "gives every decent player in the NHL a little extra bargaining power for salaries" in discussing contractual matters with his current team. Mikita recalled being offered a five-year, $1.5 million deal to join the new Chicago Cougars of the WHA, but made it clear—as did Magnuson—that his loyalty remained with the Hawks.

Shortly after Hatskin's pursuit of Bobby Hull went public, Jim Pappin, Martin, and Dennis Hull suddenly got new raises from Wirtz. Now 33 years old and looking for one big payday before he retired,

Bobby—as unbelievable as it may have been—was ready to consider playing for a team other than the Black Hawks.

"When Hull was setting scoring records and featured on the covers of *Sports Illustrated* in his midtwenties," wrote Gare Joyce, "he wanted to be the highest-paid player in the league. Arthur Wirtz and general manager Tommy Ivan assured him that he was, though they offered no proof of the fact."

In an interview with *Sport* magazine around that time, Hull revealed to scribe John Devaney that he was starting to lose his love of hockey—in part because of the financial aspects that were becoming more prevalent in the sport. "Ten or 15 years ago I just wanted to play hockey," Hull was quoted as saying. "I loved hockey…it's more of a business now, scoring goals to win games. Instead of my legs I use [what's] upstairs."

By mid-April, the amount Hull was offered by Winnipeg was finally revealed. With all the bonuses and incentives thrown in, the total came to $275,000 per season for 10 years for a dual role of player and coach. It was clear to all that Hull would be impossible to replace, both for the Hawks as well as for the NHL.

"He has been the most glamorous shiny ambassador over the past decade," Fischler wrote of the Golden Jet, "patiently delivering lengthy interviews with newsmen when a Bobby Orr will hide in the trainer's room and endlessly signing autographs when a Derek Sanderson will tell a lad to bugger-off."

Consequently, the Hawks countered by offering Hull $1 million over five years for him to stay in Chicago and the NHL, something for him to ponder for the coming months as the battle lines stabilized. What was exceedingly painful for Hull's teammates was knowing they were so close to achieving the Stanley Cup—if only they could keep him. "The players even said they'd give up a little bit of their salary so they could pay Bobby the extra amount," his brother Dennis revealed.

Thus, beginning in mid-March 1972, a pall hung over the Hawks for the rest of the season, as the players and fans wondered what would become of their superstar. The team continued to dominate the West, ending the season by tying the franchise record set in the previous season, 107 points. They had lost only three times in the Chicago Stadium all season, and permitted a mere 166 goals—25 fewer than the next-closest team in the league, as Esposito shared his second Vezina Trophy with his backup, Gary Smith.

In the opening playoff round, they made quick work of the Pittsburgh Penguins in a four-game sweep. In the series, Dennis Hull had one of his sticks confiscated by the officials because it was over the limit in terms of the permitted blade curve; the Hawks momentarily threatened to not play the remaining games in protest, but later relented as Hull agreed to paying a league fine.

A few years earlier, Mikita had gotten the blade of his stick caught in the swinging door by the bench one day at a practice session. Finally able to free it after several yanks, Mikita noticed that the blade had splintered slightly and had warped, with a curve on the end of it as a result of the tugging. Not wishing to scale down the 21 stairs to the locker room in the Stadium's basement for another stick and then having to climb 21 stairs back up (in the midst of a grueling workout at the hands of Reay), Mikita instead skated over to the steps and banged on the glass to get the attention of the equipment staff and requisition a new stick.

In the meantime, a frustrated Mikita grew bored and saw some pucks lying near the faceoff circle. He started slapping some shots toward the goal, attempting to pass the time until the new stick was delivered. On the first playful drive, he noticed a strange tailing action to the puck as it was launched from his curved blade. Thinking it was simply an errant strike on his part, Mikita took another shot, and then another, and then another; and soon, like many great inventors, he realized he may have just stumbled upon a tremendous revelation by accident.

Bobby Hull was watching from a distance, and noticed the pronounced dips, slices, hooks, and tails that the puck displayed off Mikita's curved blade. Soon, both men were either ordering their sticks with a curved blade built in, or did it themselves by softening the wood with a blowtorch and then forming it to their liking. They also liked the fact that the curved blade allowed for better handling of the puck, as well as helping to conceal it from defenders. But when goalies began complaining of the erratic, unpredictable movements of the puck from the "innovation," the NHL imposed a limit on the blade curve to no more than one inch.

In meeting the Penguins in the first round of the playoffs, it was expected that Magnuson and his 201 penalty minutes that year would lead him to Pittsburgh's Bryan Watson, who had topped the league with 212. But instead it was Eddie Shack whom Magnuson sought out, a 14-year veteran of the league but a player not widely known as a frequent fighter. By now, Magnuson felt he had proven and himself and gave no heed to an opponent's tenure, be it Shack nor any other elder player. So when Shack got his stick up on Magnuson—again, one of the methods that he hated the most—Keith felt the need to return a message. (Magnuson and Watson would not cross paths for another few seasons, at which point an ugly scene would alter the latter years of Magnuson's career.)

After walking over the Penguins, the Hawks suddenly made a disappointingly quick exit in the next round, the Rangers returning the favor from the previous year by downing Chicago in four games.

Many were worried the flat performance and rapid ousting from the postseason would hasten Hull's deliberation in signing with the WHA—a feeling shared by some in the locker room as well. Many had fully expected it to finally be the Hawks' time, but the

Cup instead went to the Bruins. In winning, Orr once again ran off with a bunch of hardware in capturing the Norris, Hart, and Conn Smythe Trophies.

As the lazy summer months came upon the lonely Stadium, the ice went away and Elvis Presley appeared to give two sold-out performances in the building on June 16 and 17 as part of his 15-city American tour.

Around the time of Presley's appearance, the announcement was made official regarding the local star. For the first time since 1957, Bobby Hull—the king of hockey—would not be in a Chicago uniform.

Magnuson—whom Hull had long favored and had nicknamed "Man O' War" in honor of the toughness that Keith had brought to the team—was understanding of the reasoning for Hull's departure to Winnipeg and the new league.

"For a true professional, the decision is as clear as black and white," Magnuson reflected. "We'd all have done the same thing in his lucky shoes. More power to him...but what I'll remember most about Bobby is his endless generosity to everyone."

Magnuson recalled many instances of Hull's good-heartedness, but pointed in particular to the time when trainer Skip Thayer joined the team. Thayer had gotten an apartment in Chicago for his wife and two children just as the Hawks were scheduled to immediately go on the road for a couple of weeks. Thayer's first paycheck would not be coming for a while, and with little money in the bank, he was worried that he might not have the deposit money ready for the apartment. The day before the team left for the road trip, Hull waited until everyone except Thayer was gone from the training room. He then handed Thayer an envelope with money inside—the exact amount needed for the deposit. It was the very kind of thing, Magnuson remembered, that Hull would do with no one watching, without any fanfare, done with "that irresistible wink and magnetic grin. Skip will never forget the moment," Keith recollected fondly. "Hope this helps a little," Hull said to Thayer while slipping him the envelope.

Another time during a brutal Chicago winter storm, Hull gave his only overcoat to Pinder when the team's travel plans had suddenly changed to an earlier flight and Pinder had already sent his own coat to the cleaners, thinking there would be plenty of time to get it back for the trip.

Just like with his own teammates, the fans always wanted to be around Hull as well. "Bobby is like that wherever we play," confirmed Maki. "People want to be near Bobby and he obliges. And we hold the bus for him." Added Tony Esposito, "I've never seen him turn his back on a kid."

As expected, the Hull signing unlocked a floodgate of others who followed in suit—players who were afraid to make the move to the WHA until Hull went first. Boston's Sanderson was one; after leading the NHL with seven shorthanded goals in 1971–72, he signed for $2.65 million over 10 years with the new Philadelphia Blazers. The image of Sanderson in any kind of Philly uniform was indeed hard to imagine, given the brewing rivalry between the two cities in hockey circles; nonetheless, as with Hull, few could blame him for accepting the offer.

"A year ago," Damata of the *Tribune* observed in October 1972, "Sanderson held out for $40,000 and settled for $37,500. Today the National [Hockey League's] $12,000 minimum is even a laughing matter in the minor leagues."

In what Blazers officials hoped would be a gala spectacle on their opening night the following autumn, they instead selected Sanderson to be the bearer of bad news. Sanderson proceeded out to the arena to inform the crowd that the team's very first game would have to be canceled, because the Zamboni had crashed through the ice at the old Philadelphia Civic Center—at which point Sanderson was pelted with souvenir pucks the team had distributed in commemoration of the inaugural. (As it turned out, Sanderson would play in only eight games for the Blazers before getting injured, and he came back to the Bruins in February 1973 with his hat in his hands.)

As the WHA defections continued through the summer of 1972, Damata mentioned a topic in his *Tribune* column that was haunting Major League Baseball business negotiations at the very same time. "The World Hockey Association is banking on the premise that the reserve clause is illegal." It was an idea to which NHL president Clarence Campbell replied, "The reserve clause is quite valid in National Hockey League contracts and it will be enforceable by injunction...we are not going to be [in partnership] with the World Hockey Association."

The WHA was equally and undauntedly pursuing prospects and established stars in its roster raids. For example, after three years with the Philadelphia Flyers and one season in 1971–72 with the Hawks, the gifted Lacroix became one of the new league's highest-paid players; he certainly earned his keep, winning two scoring titles in his time in the WHA. Joining Hull in Winnipeg would be Christian Bordeleau, after spending just half of one productive season in a Hawks uniform. Chicago also lost center Bryan Campbell to the Blazers as well as Gerry Desjardins, a valuable second-string goalie behind Esposito. The departure of Desjardins, however, could not be blamed on the WHA. He was picked up by the New York Islanders in the NHL expansion draft. The new team began play in Uniondale, New York, in the fall of 1972 in their sparkling new arena, the Nassau County Coliseum, adjacent to the campus of Hofstra University.

Despite lucrative WHA contract offers being thrown about like peanuts on an airplane, many stars chose to remain with the Hawks, including Magnuson, Pappin, Martin, and Dennis Hull. The latter three continued to comprise the "MPH" line, which Reay would purposefully undermine in the press for a strategic reason.

"Billy made sure that nobody thought the best line Chicago was Martin-Pappin-Hull," Dennis once revealed. "He always said the best players were Stan Mikita and Bobby Hull. 'If you stop those two guys, you stop the Black Hawks,' he said, time and time again."

It is hard to estimate how many scoring chances Reay's words opened up for the MPH line, but the statistics bear out the group's immense worth to the Hawks of the early 1970s. Similar to the way the scoring statistics of Scottie Pippen suddenly rose with the (temporary) retirement of Michael Jordan from the Chicago Bulls in 1993, the MPH line enjoyed its greatest season ever in 1972–73 with Bobby Hull removed from the Black Hawks lineup.

Bobby finished his NHL career with 604 goals, second only to Gordie Howe's 786 at the time. However, Stoneking also pointed out that Hull had averaged 40 goals per season in his 15 years in the league, while Howe averaged 31.2 in his own first 15 seasons. While many people reading the newspapers decided that Hull's decision to go to the WHA was purely because of money—something which Hull himself admitted was a large factor—it also had to do with being respected, at least in the player's mind. "In the NHL, they treat you like cattle; in the WHA, they treat you like a human being," Bobby would tell Verdi later that summer.

After Hull left the Chicago Stadium dressing room to remove his personal belongings for the final time, Maki moved into his locker—not because it was better real estate, but because he wanted to maintain the dignity of the space by keeping it orderly. Maki, who enjoyed smoking a pipe while strumming a guitar in the clubhouse, would miss playing the country tunes for Hull that Bobby loved so much.

"[Cliff] Koroll thinks that if we had won the Cup in 1971," Mikita once stated in a wishful tone, "we would have begun a run of several Cups and that Bobby would never have left."

• • •

If the 1972 off-season talk in hockey was not centered around the encroachment of the WHA on the NHL's turf, it instead focused upon the monumental upcoming "Summit Series" in September, an eight-game slate in which Canadian-born NHL stars would take on the best players of the Soviet Union for the first time, in a battleground of the Cold War.

Sinden of the Bruins was selected as the head coach of the NHL contingent, but when invitations went out from the league to select players with whom he would work, Bobby Hull was not among them. Bill Wirtz was in charge of the North American side of the contract negotiations for the series, and had inserted a stipulation that all participating players had to be under a signed NHL contract by the beginning of the tournament. Naturally, it was believed that Wirtz was using this angle as leverage in his contract negotiations with Hull, believing that Hull—who had a strong desire to play for his home country in the Series—would accept less money to stay with the Hawks as September drew closer. The alleged gamesmanship by Wirtz caused dissension, even among his fellow power brokers in hockey who believed the requirement would affect other players besides Hull.

"I don't care if he signed with a team in China," scoffed Toronto Maple Leafs owner Howard Ballard in response to the Hull-Wirtz feud. "He's a Canadian and should be on the Canadian team."

Even so, this response was seen by Joyce as posturing by Ballard, who was not really willing to risk losing the benefits of being part of the Series.

"His objections to [Clarence] Campbell's and Wirtz's end run weren't so deeply felt that he was going to decline having his arena [Maple Leaf Gardens] as Team Canada's training camp home and site of Game 2 of the Summit Series," Joyce pointed out. The first four games would be held at professional venues across Canada (the Montreal Forum, the Maple Leaf Gardens, the Winnipeg Arena, and the Pacific Coliseum in Vancouver), while the final four contests would take place at the Luzhniki Ice Palace in Moscow. In the end, Wirtz's rule would stand—it was definite that Hull would not play in the Summit Series.

"Sinden, who had privately wished to have Hull on the roster, would see his own Bruins Cheevers and Sanderson excluded for the same reason as well," Joyce continued. "Bobby Hull was out. It wouldn't be the last time the NHL left him twisting in the wind."

Magnuson was disappointed that he had to sit out the Summit Series himself—not because of a contract issue, but rather because he needed to further rehabilitate his knee during the summer of 1972. (He had been among those who received an invitational letter to try out for the team.) Maggie would have significant company in watching from the sideline. Orr had withstood much pain in his own knee in leading the Bruins to the Cup in May 1972, a prelude to his own surgery that summer which left the Canadian team without his services as well.

As the first game of the Summit Series commenced in Montreal, the normally reserved hockey crowd in that city was more raucous than usual; few in Canada could recall a time in that country when so much national pride was at stake. And when Phil Esposito scored less than a minute after the first puck was dropped, it appeared that the series would be the "laugher" that many NHL followers expected it would be.

But the Soviets were intent on applying a form of a "rope-a-dope" on the Canadians. As Magnuson had noted from his college days at Denver, the Soviets displayed superior physical conditioning as compared to the NHL players, appearing to be sprinting around the ice at full speed even late into the third period. As September was typically the time of year when the NHL players were just arriving at training camps for purpose of getting into shape (as opposed to today's players who train year-round), they noticed that their international counterparts were far ahead of them.

A flurry of Soviet shots on Dryden's home ice resulted in several going past him in a 7–3 win for the Russians in the opener. Tony Esposito responded well in the second contest, however, and led an NHL team awoken from its slumber to a 4–1 win in Toronto.

After a 4–4 tie in Winnipeg, the NHL team put on another unenthused showing in Game 4 at Vancouver in a 5–3 defeat, and then proceeded to blow a 4–1 lead in a 5–4 loss in Game 5 in Moscow which put the Canadians one defeat away from losing the Series altogether. Being booed off the ice at the end of the game in Vancouver, many of the NHL players—especially Phil Esposito—publicly voiced their disgust for the lack of support from the fans.

Perhaps sensing that something extraordinary was now needed to boost his team's energy, former Montreal intimidator John Ferguson—an assistant coach with the Canadian team—turned to one of the emerging personalities in hockey to jolt the squad. Center Bobby Clarke was 23 years old at the time, fresh off his claim to the Bill Masterton Trophy from the end of the 1972 season, which, named for the former University of Denver and NHL player, annually goes to the player who "best exemplifies the qualities of perseverance, sportsmanship, and dedication to ice hockey." Clarke had won the award for his ability to overcome the diabetic seizures he suffered at the start of his career. He was one of the rising stars of the league by the fall of 1972, part of an improving Philadelphia Flyers squad that was threatening to make a leap into the upper echelon of NHL teams in the coming season.

Clarke, however, had also already gained a sullied reputation around the league as a win-at-all-costs type of player and agitator, and Ferguson decided to use these traits to the Canadian team's advantage. In Game 6 in Moscow, he directed Clarke to go after Soviet star forward Valeri Kharlamov; and while not being specific as to the method, Ferguson instructed the player to render Kharlamov "ineffective" for the remainder of the contest.

At one point in the game, as Kharlamov raced into the Canadian zone with the puck, Clarke sensed his opportunity and soared in on him at an angle, and from behind. As Clarke approached him, television viewers could plainly see Clarke slide his left hand down the shaft of his stick in joining his right hand at the knob, as if he were a baseball player preparing to take a swing of the bat. With one vicious chop, he violently slashed the heel of the Soviet player. To all watching (games had been sent back to North America on national Canadian networks as well as selected American stations), the blow was as intentional and flagrant as it could be, with Clarke directly in the center of the television camera's lens. Kharlamov's ankle was broken instantly. And while he would finish the game at a severely limited capacity, Kharlamov naturally had been neutralized for the final two contests of the series as well.

Canada won the sixth game 3–2 as a worldwide hockey debate was launched. Some felt Clarke's attack was an intolerable, cowardly play, while others believed it was an understandable decision by him and Ferguson in order to shift the momentum (some Canadians even called the chop a "patriotic" blow). In any event, the game's result kept Canada alive in the Series.

After Paul Henderson scored late to clinch a 4–3 Canada win in Game 7, a heated, winner-take-all eighth match was set for Moscow on September 28. The game was marred by several strange off-the-ice eruptions, such as NHL player agent Alan Eagleson being restrained in the stands by Moscow police in his protest of the goal light not being illuminated after an obvious Canadian goal, and Sinden hurling a chair onto the playing surface in another moment of objection to a referee's call.

With anger still lingering from the Kharlamov incident, jeers were exchanged all evening long between the Soviet crowd and Canadian players, and the NHL team found itself trailing 5–3 heading into the final period. The players emerged from the locker room for the final 20 minutes with reckless abandon, however; Montreal forward Yvan Cournoyer and Phil Esposito knotted the score at 5–5 with their goals. Then, with 34 seconds remaining in regulation and a beehive of activity swirling around the Russian net, Henderson tapped in a rebound off an Esposito shot which instantly became known as "the goal all Canadians would remember." A delirious celebration was set off from Nova Scotia to British Columbia as the NHL took the series by a 6–5 final score in the last game, swelling the pride of all Canadian hearts with a feeling described by Todd Denault as "one of those rare shared moments in the history of a country, an unforgettable experience, a defining moment."

Oddly enough, the moment was so powerful it was difficult to remember there was a full schedule of games still to play back home. "After the excitement of the just-concluded Summit Series," Denault added, "the upcoming NHL season felt like an anticlimax."

For many years, the location of the actual puck that Henderson shot into the net was a mystery. Naturally, many museums as well as private collectors would have liked to have possessed it, but only recently did Bill White—who along with Mikita, Stapleton, and Dennis Hull was a key member of the Canadian team in the series—reveal its location.

"Pat and I were on the ice when Henderson scored and until the game ended [34 seconds later]," White said in a 2010 interview with Verdi. "Look at the tape. When it's over, Pat circles around and takes the puck. He's never really admitted it. In fact, he tells people I have it. I still get calls from reporters asking me why I don't donate the puck or sell it to the Hockey Hall of Fame. And I tell them, 'I don't have it. Pat Stapleton has it. Call him.'"

In 2010, the Canadian team sweater that Henderson was wearing when he scored the goal was auctioned off for nearly $1.7 million, reputed to be the highest amount ever paid for a single piece of hockey memorabilia.

• • •

While it was perhaps "anticlimactic," as Denault put it, the 1972–73 NHL season nonetheless began with renewed sense of dignity for the sport's founding nation. Canada's victory over the Soviets in the Summit Series tempered at least some of the tension that was sure to come from the splitting of major league hockey into two factions.

As expected, all did not proceed smoothly in the opening acts for the WHA. For example, Hull would be 15 games late in joining the Winnipeg Jets at the start of the year, as the legitimacy of his contract was still being contested by the Hawks well into October. Magnuson, determined to help fill the void of leadership left behind in Chicago, demonstrated as much in his first fight with the new Boston Bruins tough man, Terry O'Reilly, in an exhibition game at the Stadium on September 22 (the night after all of Canada was forlorn with the Game 5 loss during the Summit Series in Moscow).

"Magnuson flexed his muscles early," the *Tribune* proclaimed about the fracas that was launched only a minute into the contest, just as Magnuson was in the process of heading to the penalty box for hooking the Bruins' Chris Hayes. "Young Terry slammed Keith into the boards. The Hawk defenseman took umbrage and posed in the classic [Johnny] Coulon stance: left hand extended and right cocked."

O'Reilly got the best of him in their initial encounter, however, pinning Magnuson up against the boards and freeing himself for a few good shots. But, once again in the spirit of "cold-dish revenge" in the Howe and Mikita tradition, Magnuson made sure he would get other chances at O'Reilly down the road.

Six weeks after the regular season started, Magnuson had a first-time bout with another new pugilist entering the NHL. Dave Schultz was already a legend in the Juniors system, having racked up more than 350 penalty minutes in remote Canadian villages in the minor leagues in each of the past three seasons. And when the Hawks met the Flyers at the latter's wondrous five-year-old home, the Spectrum, on November 9, 1972, Magnuson and Schultz soon converged. They began throwing hands without much of a prelude or warning—in one of at least 20 fights that Schultz would have in his first NHL year—and the Flyers rookie proved himself a force with which to be reckoned, even at the top level of the sport. He landed right cross after right cross upon Magnuson, who flailed away in return, kept taking shots, and still kept coming back too Schultz for more.

"My first meeting with Magnuson was typical of the manner in which a hockey fight between two ice cops begins," Schultz remembered about that evening. The two players had collided behind the Chicago net, and Schultz launched a preemptive strike before Magnuson could get him first. "I drove him in the mouth with my right," the Philadelphia player said. "In a split second his lips were redder than his hair. Blood red."

Schultz's assault had been so quick that it was reported that Magnuson, when assisted in the training room, did not know who it was who hit him—despite being keenly aware of Schultz's reputation from his days in the Juniors, and readying for him as Magnuson prepared his pregame plans in the locker room.

"I felt I had to prove myself," Schultz continued. "Magnuson had already been in the league for three years and had earned a reputation as a good and very energetic fighter."

Magnuson returned later in the game and chided Schultz from the moment he returned to the ice. Midway through the third period, Schultz got his stick up on Magnuson again, and garnered another five-minute major penalty for drawing blood. Keith's lip was severed once again with a blow that required a few more stitches, but the resultant penalty also resulted in a power-play goal by Dennis Hull. It was becoming commonplace for Philadelphia to regularly try to intimidate opponents who came into the Spectrum, but Keith remained unfazed. "Magnuson is just so busy all the time," former Flyers coach Vic Stasiuk had said back in 1970. "He gets the hell beat out of him, but he keeps coming back for more. You have to like a kid like that."

While the nucleus of the strong Black Hawks teams of years past was still in place—even without his famous linemate in Hull, Mikita enjoyed his best start ever to a season in posting eight points in his first three games—there were still growing pains to be endured as the club proceeded without the Golden Jet. The St. Louis Blues beating the Hawks 3–1 on October 15—which was the first time the Blues had beaten Chicago on Stadium ice in five years. (St. Louis had been 0–11–3 in their previous 14 visits to the Stadium; the Blues would take the next game on Madison Street as well, on December 27.) The loss also ended a 16-game unbeaten streak for the Hawks in regular season play, dating back to the previous year. And by midseason, it was evident that the other expansion teams with which the Hawks had been placed in the Western Division were showing marked improvement. In February 1973, the surging Flyers—with the irrepressible Clarke leading the way and the rookie Schultz now hammering away at everyone in sight—won in the Stadium for the first time ever. It was the same week that the precocious Clarke was named their captain, believed to be the youngest in league history, and the Philadelphia club was suddenly becoming a major player in the standings. Schultz would wind up leading the NHL in penalty minutes with 259 in his rookie season, a warning to the rest of the league that a surly collection of renegades was forming in Philadelphia.

So Reay continued to make adjustments, which included the occasional pairing of Magnuson with physical rookie Phil Russell on the defensive line, to give the aging Jarrett more rest. Russell, the Hawks' first-round pick from the previous year's draft, brought not only scoring abilities to the back line but relieved some of the fighting load off Magnuson with his own tough, aggressive spirit. So did another rookie brought to the roster, University of North Dakota product and 1968's ninth-overall pick John Marks, who possessed approximately the same size as Russell (6'2", 205) and who displayed a penchant for left wing as well as defenseman. Marks, a collegiate opponent of Magnuson's, was paired on the blue line with White; Reay then moved Stapleton to center to free up his skating ability, a position he last played in the Western Hockey League in 1964–65 at Portland, where he scored 29 goals during the season.

Just a few months after he left town, Chicago hockey fans would have chance to see Hull skate on local ice once again as the Winnipeg Jets arrived on December 22 to take on the Cougars. The Cougars' home ice was the International Amphitheatre, a quaint, small arena on the city's south side and adjacent to the infamous old Chicago Stockyards, which had just closed in the previous year after more than a century of operation. The Amphitheatre had been made famous worldwide four years earlier in hosting the meetings of the raucous 1968 Democratic National Convention, in which Chicago mayor Richard J. Daley hollered from the crowd against speakers at the podium who were denouncing the violence occurring in the city streets as the convention proceeded.

While the Amphitheatre had its charm and coziness, the Chicago Stadium still commanded the top local indoor events of the era as the "Amp" was relegated to hosting little more than Cougars games and the circus. (The majority of the Amphitheatre's business had revolved around livestock shows, a trend which naturally diminished in the wake of the Stockyards closing in 1971.) The Bulls moved from the Amphitheatre to the Stadium after their first season of play (1967), and in January 1973, the Stadium hosted its first NBA All-Star Game. Popular music acts continued to fill the Stadium as well; in addition to Elvis Presley's two-day stop there the previous summer, January 3, 1973, saw 1960s icon Bob Dylan appear in the Stadium for the initial show on his first tour in eight years.

As he emerged from the visitors' locker room at the Amphitheatre, Hull, still donning the same old shoulder pads he had worn when he broke into the NHL 15 years earlier, was greeted with a mixed reception. Even by the time he was finished in the WHA, he would still be wearing them, as he found the pair to be comfortable and lightweight, even though they offered almost no protection. "I have no doubt that Bobby Hull took more physical punishment on the ice than anyone who has ever played the game," Pappin once said. The Golden Jet did not want anything to slow him down, and like a fighter plane being stripped of unnecessary encumbrance for maximum speed, he went with the bare minimum.

There was no doubt that a fire raged in Hull's eyes in returning to Chicago. The hometown Cougars carried a 3–2 win out of the Amphitheatre, but Bobby had skated with a fury, which included viciously beating on former Hawks teammate Reggie Fleming in a fight.

"Hull threw Fleming around like a bale of hay," wrote Joyce in reference to Hull's farming roots in Ontario, "twisting him down to the ice until he was on his knees. Hull rained blows down on the back of Fleming's head, the nape of his neck and unhelmeted temples."

Despite the severe punishment, after the game the two combatants acted as if nothing had happened, speaking pleasantly while standing near each other by the seating area and signing autographs for children. "Hull and Fleming reprised the roles of the sheepdog and Wile E. Coyote," Joyce continued in a humorous reference to a famous cartoon, "the Looney Tunes characters who fought almost to the death and then came to a dead halt, punching the clock at the end of their shift."

Even with the amicable ending, the brutal bout had likely hastened the twilight of the career of the former Magnuson family favorite. (Fleming had been the recipient of thousands of blows in his fight-filled professional career and passed away in 2009 at the age of 73. His family later authorized a further examination of his brain, and it was determined that Fleming had experienced prolonged, massive head trauma that contributed to him suffering a neurological deterioration that resembled Alzheimer's disease.)

Meanwhile, on NHL ice just a couple of miles to the north of the Amphitheatre, the Hawks continued to roll through the winter at the Stadium. By January 17, after winning 6–4 that night, they were unbeaten in their last 14 games against the Detroit Red Wings.

Of course, respecting superstitions was paramount during such a winning streak, and Magnuson and Koroll were not taking any chances in this regard. As the roommates left their apartment in Park Ridge and headed down the Kennedy Expressway to the Stadium, they would look for the same electronic billboard to flash each trip, which read, LISTEN TO THE BLACK HAWKS—8:15 ON WMAQ. Magnuson would say that they "simply have to" see the sign if the two were going to have a good game that night. "A few times I've had to slow down to a crawl in the emergency lane until this comes on," he claimed.

Their driving antics did not stop once they got off the Kennedy, however. Magnuson and Koroll, in pursuit of another serving of good luck, would then attempt to drive all the way to the Stadium along certain local streets without ever applying the brakes—and that meant *ever*.

"We'd be creeping along, trying to hit it [the light] when it would turn green," Magnuson was quoted as saying by writer Andrew Podnieks. "We'd have cars honking at us, but we thought that if we could get through all those lights that we'd definitely win that night."

Upon arriving at the Stadium, the other Hawks players made it a point to regularly visit Keith's vehicle to see the aftermath of what they called "Maggie's Latest." Once, he backed into the wall of the Stadium itself when intending to pull forward from his parking space. Magnuson recalled one incident with his vehicle in his second year with the Hawks. "I hit another car on a freeway," he said. "The guy stopped and jumped out, ready to kill me. Then he saw who I was, shook my hand, and told me if I had any trouble about insurance, he'd testify for me in court. Now that's a hockey fan for you."

Just getting the car started, however, often was a challenge for Magnuson, according to Koroll. "One day, he walked into the apartment about 4:00 in the afternoon," Cliff said, "and said he left his car running in the lot so he could charge the battery. Well, we have dinner and whatever, and it's about 11:00 that night when we're watching TV and a car commercial comes on. Maggie jumps from the couch in his bathrobe and runs outside in the snow. He forgot to turn the car off."

Their attempts to acquire good luck were perhaps not as strange, however, as the ritual of goaltender Gary Smith at the Stadium on nights when he played. Although called upon rather infrequently since Esposito was primarily in the nets for Chicago, Smith, when given a starting assignment by Reay, would strip down to the nude between periods. He then put all his equipment back on shortly before the next period began, Dennis Hull remembered.

Back at Magnuson and Koroll's apartment, the two bachelors had decorated the place in the most stunning of 1970s motifs, a design which would have made the Brady Bunch's home look like it was crafted by modernist David Bromstad on HGTV.

"When they moved in last year, an interior designer offered to furnish and decorate it for them for a cut rate $5,000. They agreed," reported Paul King for *Canadian* magazine on the living arrangements. "'But when we saw all the stuff coming in,' Keith said, 'we *really* flipped. We're guys from Saskatoon. We're not what you'd call super mod.'"

King himself hardly found the words to describe the place. "It was easy to see why they flipped…a living room filled with plastic see-through chairs and three bare white tree branches stuck in huge white flower pots, a dining room papered in black-and-white stripes like a referee's shirt, and a burnt-orange bedroom with a fake leopard's bedspread. There was also one black-and-white and three color TV sets and three stereo sets in the apartment. On Magnuson's bedroom wall was the mounted bill of a 150-pound marlin he caught last year in Jamaica."

But domestic pursuits would not allay Magnuson's ferocity on the ice. On March 15, he broke the jaw of New York Ranger Gene Carr in a bout at the Stadium. Pappin had just scored the game's final goal at the 7:37 mark of the third period to make the score 4–2 in favor of the Hawks when the fireworks erupted. "A minute later, in the center of a stadium where many great ones have fought," Verdi wrote, "Magnuson dropped gloves with Gene Carr, a young Ranger with the prettiest locks this side of [St. Louis'] Garry Unger." Magnuson finished things with a tremendous right hand that shattered Carr's chin, as New York's Brad Park tried to jump in to aid his teammate—for which Park got the newly requisite game misconduct penalty as per the third-man-in rule.

"It was just a lucky punch," Maggie said later in the locker room regarding the coup de grace, a statement at which Doug Jarrett snickered in agreement from across the way. Magnuson nodded to concur.

"I haven't won that many, have I?" he said back to Jarrett.

In just a month's time, however, Park would avenge his teammate's injury, albeit unintentionally.

The pistons of Reay's machine continued to fire through the spring. By season's end, Magnuson and the Black Hawks were able to get the same result without Bobby Hull as they had the past three years with him: a division title. The MPH line of Martin, Pappin, and Dennis Hull would indeed have its best year in Bobby's first in absentia, as the trio totaled 272 points—a Black Hawks record for a line at the time, with Pappin netting 41 goals, Hull 39, and Martin 29.

• • •

The 1973 postseason began with the famous goalie of the Montreal Canadiens issuing a warning.

"The Rangers, Bruins, and Black Hawks had better win the Cup this year," Ken Dryden had said before the start of the playoffs, "because with the talent we have coming up, I'm afraid the Cup will be in Montreal for many years after."

The young crop of new talent the Canadiens had cultivated in the past couple of seasons was indeed ready to blossom, as a fresh roster of hopefuls prepared to take the place of Beliveau, Richard, and the other aging superstars who had carried the team for more than a decade.

In their quest for the elusive title, the first step for Magnuson and the Hawks involved getting past the St. Louis Blues. The series would be the first of many more postseason clashes to come in subsequent years with their neighbors to the south.

"The rivalry ensured the series would be hotly contested," said Mark Magnuson, Keith's nephew, who at the age of nine attended the first game of the 1973 series in the Stadium, a 7–1 blowout for the Hawks on April 4. Mikita posted a team-playoff-record five assists in the victory. Joe and Birdie had flown to Chicago to watch their son play, and brought Mark along as a special treat for the youngster. "What a thrill!" Mark continued. "For a small boy on the prairie, to be flying to Chicago to watch the NHL playoffs! I think I told half of Saskatoon. As a proud nephew, I let everyone know he [Keith] was my uncle."

The evening was about to become even more exciting for him, as Mark described:

> *Keith left hours early for the Stadium that day. Grandpa and Grandma and I were given a ride from a friend of Keith's who took us to our seats about 30 minutes before game time, about five rows above the penalty box and directly opposite the home and visitor player boxes. The game became very chippy and penalty-filled. At one point, Phil Roberto of St. Louis was called for a penalty and headed to the box to serve his two minutes. The fans behind the penalty box began to jeer Roberto and, frustrated by the game and the certain outcome, he began to jaw back until, finally, he exploded and turned around and started swinging his stick at the fans behind the glass. One fan managed to grab his stick and pull it away; Roberto then scaled the glass and threatened to jump into the crowd. Some of his teammates had seen the initial verbal confrontation, and the Plager brothers [Barclay and Bob], known as belligerent players, hopped onto the dasher board and held onto the top of the glass with their hands, also threatening to enter the stands. Meanwhile, the well-known Andy Frain security guards*

were trying to make their way to the fans directly behind the box and locate Roberto's stick.

Whenever a melee of any sort breaks out in hockey, the fans rise in unison to watch the event unfold. As a nine year old, I quickly lost my view of Roberto and the Blues' reaction to the fans in front of me. Then, suddenly, I felt myself lifted up high into the air and gently placed onto my grandfather's shoulders. I now had the best view in the Stadium, not two rows from the fans exchanging pleasantries with Roberto and the Blues hanging on the glass. I was in the old Chicago Stadium, watching my one hero, Uncle Keith, fight while his team dominated their opponent, while my other hero, Grandpa Joe, had ensured I wouldn't miss an event I have remembered my entire life.

It was a wild start to a wild week of hockey, as Chicago won the series in five games while posting a team-record 22 goals, the most ever by the Hawks in a five-game postseason round. Meanwhile, Magnuson and the rest of the defensive crew helped Esposito keep St. Louis to only nine goals of their own.

A short time after being eliminated by Chicago, the Blues head coaching position would be taken over by one of the Hawks players from the series in Lou Angotti. Angotti left for St. Louis in June 1973 for what was known as the "intraleague draft," which was designed to make the former expansion more competitive in a quicker amount of time. (During the 1973–74 schedule, Angotti, who in 1967 had become the first captain of the Philadelphia Flyers, spent the final 23 games of that season as player-coach of the Blues.)

Fortunes were flying high for the Hawks after their easy opening-round triumph; however, they would soon turn quickly for Magnuson in the other direction.

In the semifinals against New York, the Hawks regrouped after losing Game 1 at the Stadium and took a 5–4 win in Game 2. It was the first of four straight they would grab from the Rangers, sending themselves to the Stanley Cup Finals against the Canadiens for the second time in three years. Reay had the club rolling once again, and the multitalented youngster Marks was moved from the defensive line and placed on left wing with Mikita and Koroll.

But in the second game of the series, on April 15, Magnuson's jaw was shattered on a slap shot by Park in the second period—the result of Magnuson selflessly falling in front of the shot in an attempt to block it during a Rangers power play.

Esposito had always told Magnuson (as well as the rest of the Chicago defensemen) that if they try to block a shot, they had better get a piece of it—otherwise he would not be able to see the puck. Get a piece Magnuson did, and he dropped to the ice as a stunned audience sat in silence. Mikita later vividly remembered the impact of the vulcanized rubber striking Magnuson's face. "You could hear it reverberate throughout the old stadium," he said.

A stretcher was summoned, but Magnuson waved it off and willed himself up to his knees. He then pushed upward onto his skates and finally insisted on skating off the ice, with slight assistance from Marks and Maki, receiving a thunderous ovation from the crowd that snapped itself from its frightened silence in an instant. Skip Thayer was of course on the scene immediately to aid Magnuson, but Magnuson would dismiss Thayer as well, only permitting the trainer to give him a towel, nothing more. When Thayer later thought about that scene, he just shook his head in disbelief; Thayer could not conceive Magnuson's high threshold of pain. "You couldn't hurt that kid's head with an axe," the trainer marveled.

In addition to having his jaw set and secured, Magnuson also received 75 stitches for the wide cut that resulted from the blow.

Even so, he simply wanted to know from Thayer if he would be able to return for the next period of play that same evening. "It was a five-on-three [shorthanded situation] and it saved a goal," Magnuson remembered proudly in 2000 in replaying the crucial moment in the game. He also recalled how, during the healing period for the broken jaw, he had to carry around a pair of scissors every place he went, just in case the myriad rubber bands that held his top and lower plates together started to gag him.

Despite Magnuson's bravery, he was in no condition to play in the Stanley Cup rematch with the Canadiens, and the Black Hawks were forced to go without their leader on the blue line. Wearing a protective mask while he skated in practice, Magnuson was withheld from game situations by Reay. "I thought I could be playing a week and a half ago, but no soap," a disappointed Keith would tell a writer by the middle of the final series. "The coach keeps saying no. He's thinking about my health, and about my future. But how many Stanley Cup games does a guy get to play in?"

Montreal, meanwhile, certainly looked as if it was heading into another dynasty, just as Dryden had predicted. Under second-year coach Scotty Bowman, they had rolled off a league-leading 120 points during the regular season, which included only 10 losses—an NHL record they would break again in 1976–77 with only eight that season. Their roster boasted an amazing total of 11 future Hall of Famers, including Cournoyer, a diminutive winger who, along with Lemaire, had taken over as one of the team's top scoring threats. Cournoyer, nicknamed "the Roadrunner" for his incredible acceleration with the puck when attacking in the opponent's zone, had been playing half the season with a lingering stomach issue after being speared in the abdomen by Minnesota's Ted Harris back on January 8.

The absence of Magnuson from the Chicago defense was obvious, and Montreal assailed Esposito with eight goals in Game 1 at the Forum. After dropping the second contest by a 4–1 score, the Hawks were able to manage a split of two games at the Stadium and then another shootout in Game 5 at Montreal, prolonging the series by surviving an 8–7 squeaker. Stapleton finished the game with a plus-minus rating of +1—he was on the ice for all 15 goals—and he kept the Hawks alive for another night as Game 6 shifted back to Madison Street.

Esposito, despite all the pucks flying past him in the previous week and missing Magnuson in front of him, was nonetheless his usual calm self before another decisive game. "He reminded me a lot of Glenn Hall," Mikita would say of his longtime goaltender, "except that Tony didn't throw up before games. Tony got prepared by just sitting in front of his locker without saying a word, staring off into space. You didn't dare talk to Tony before a game…He would just look through you like you were invisible."

Just as in the infamous Game 7 of two seasons ago in the same building, the Hawks jumped out to a quick 2–0 lead in this sixth game of the 1973 series. And just as in that 1971 classic, Lemaire would play a major part in a Canadiens comeback.

With Montreal engaging the Hawks in a 4–4 tie near the halfway point of the final period, Lemaire fired a puck into the Chicago zone from center ice that eerily resembled his disastrous dump-in from two years prior. But unlike his shot that helped doom the Hawks in 1971, this long attempt sailed well wide of an unconcerned Esposito, who briefly glanced at the passing missile. Unfortunately, it took an unusual hop off the boards behind him. Waiting in front of the goal was the Roadrunner, and Cournoyer instantly knocked it into the net with one flash of his stick for his 15th goal of the 1973 postseason, a new league mark that topped Frank Mahovlich's total from the 1971 playoffs. It would ultimately be a 6–4 final for Montreal, giving Bowman his first

Stanley Cup. (Almost 20 years later, Bowman defeated the Hawks in the Finals yet again as the coach of the Pittsburgh Penguins.)

It was also the first title for three young Canadiens named Guy Lafleur, Steve Shutt, and Larry Robinson—three of those 11 future Hall of Famers on the 1973 roster, who would lead the Montreal franchise into an unmatched stretch of dominance during the latter part of the decade. The most heralded among them was Lafleur, an even bigger star in the juniors than Rejean Houle. Lafleur had amassed an unfathomable 233 goals in his 118 games for two years' work in the Quebec Major Junior League before coming to the Canadiens.

Dryden, who was stellar once again between the pipes, would actually sit out the 1973–74 season in a contract dispute with the team before returning.

Heading into the off-season, Chicago desperately needed Magnuson's leadership more than ever—it was clear the roster was evolving, with several of the team's longtime workhorses going by the wayside.

Among the outgoing was Pat Stapleton. No one would realize that Game 6 of the 1973 Stanley Cup Finals would be his last played in a Black Hawks uniform.

6

New Bullies

"In the NHL jungle, an enforcer learns that winning a battle does not necessarily mean winning the war, if only because the loser of one fight—if he has any gumption at all—is likely to come back the next time with all guns blazing. So it was with Magnuson on another night at Chicago Stadium."

—Dave Schultz

A week after the Hawks fell to the Canadiens in the 1973 Stanley Cup Finals, Chicago drafted talented left wing Darcy Rota in the first round. Rota had posted remarkable scoring numbers with the Edmonton Oil Kings in the Juniors, and as a 20-year-old rookie he jumped right into NHL play in the following autumn. Keith Magnuson allowed Rota to stay with him at his condominium, since Maggie and Cliff Koroll had gone their separate ways after Cliff's wedding.

Meanwhile, Billy Reay and Tommy Ivan fully expected Magnuson to not only return from having broken his jaw, but once again assume the undisputed role of the enforcer on the team. For four days after the conclusion of the 1973 Finals, the two men worked to trade Jerry Korab and Gary Smith to Vancouver for Dale Tallon, who like John Marks was a versatile young player in showing an ability to play either defenseman or forward. But in dealing the potential fighter in Korab, the Hawks left Magnuson (except for the continuingly developing Phil Russell) as the lone established policeman on the team.

The other void on the blue line would be the impending absence of Pat Stapleton, along with Doug Jarrett and Bill White the senior Hawks defenseman, who announced on July 24, 1973, that he was heading across town to the Amphitheatre and the Cougars of the WHA for $1 million over five years—nearly the same money Bobby Hull had gotten with Winnipeg. As with Hull, part of Stapleton's responsibilities with the Cougars would be administrative, as he was to serve as player-coach for the first three seasons of his contract and then as coach alone for the final two.

Stapleton, a former captain of the Black Hawks, was reported to have never been given a reason from the front office for being stripped of that title after the 1969–70 season. The team would have no captain until 1975. At the same time Stapleton decided to sign with the Cougars, Brad Park—Magnuson's most recent nemesis after his powerful slap shot to the jaw, but also another of the league's top defensemen—had been given $200,000 by the Rangers for the upcoming season, making him the highest-paid player in the league.

In one of his national columns, addressing Park's contract alongside the Stapleton situation in Chicago, Stan Fischler claimed that Stapleton was worth at least three-quarters of that figure to the Hawks, but had been denied such a salary by the ownership. Both the agents for Hull and Stapleton would later claim that their salary requests were never even acknowledged by the Chicago executives, let alone heard and/or denied. "There's no excuse for one of the sport's richest franchises to treat two of its most distinguished athletes as shabbily as the Black Hawks have treated Hull and Stapleton," Fischler concluded. Therefore, Stapleton—like Hull—saw not only larger dollar signs in the WHA, but perhaps also believed those dollar signs could be a proverbial slap in the face to the Hawks' perceived stinginess.

But Stapleton's gripe was not with the entire administrative wing of the Hawks. In joining the upstart Cougars (who had just finished with a league-worst record of 26–50–2 in their first WHA season, under coach Marcel Pronovost), one of the most difficult aspects of Stapleton's decision to leave the Hawks—perhaps in addition to no longer being able to pull pranks on willing victim Magnuson—was that he would be parted with Reay, his longtime coach, whom he loved and respected. "He was a gentleman," Stapleton said, "and I really can't say anything bad about the man. I played eight years for him in Chicago, and if there's a regret in leaving the Black Hawks, it's leaving him."

Upon taking the coaching reins of the Cougars, Stapleton made it a priority to court Magnuson across town to join him. In fact, he also had his eye on several former teammates toward the same purpose—and the biggest names on the Hawks roster were among them.

"The No. 1 order of business is getting Stan Mikita [for the Cougars]," Stapleton would boldly announce on August 10. "We'll have a good team, and by 1974, we'll have a new rink." Stapleton was referring to the in-progress Horizon being constructed in the northwest Chicago suburb of Rosemont, designed to be the permanent home of the Cougars and replace the aging Amphitheatre.

In addition to Mikita and Magnuson, Stapleton also set his sights on Koroll, veteran Ralph Backstrom, and young Hawks prospect Dan Maloney—all of whom, as Bob Verdi pointed out, were "able bodies who like Chicago, like security, and like Stapleton." Of these, only

Backstrom made the move, but it proved that Stapleton would not be standing pat with the roster he inherited from Pronovost. (Lou Angotti would be yet another ex-Hawk who Stapleton was able to recruit to the Cougars, leaving his newfound role in St. Louis to play one abbreviated season for Stapleton in the WHA in 1975, at the age of 37.)

Not to be upstaged by the Cougars' clamoring for a new arena, Arthur Wirtz—with backing from Mayor Daley—also announced that same month that he wished to expand Chicago Stadium to 30,000 seats by selling $15 million worth of municipal bonds. Despite Wirtz's outright ownership of the building, however, the project encountered an insurmountable number of hurdles in getting off the ground.

• • •

Magnuson arrived at training camp in September 1973 with his broken jaw healed, yet he once again encountered misfortune. In a collision with a teammate during a practice session, he cracked an elbow which forced him to be shelved for the first portion of the regular season schedule. Taking his place on the roster would be another University of Denver Pioneer, 21-year-old rookie center Rob Palmer, who had made the squad. Palmer would play in only one game that season (and a total of only 16 in his three-year NHL career), but he was further testimony to the quality of players that Murray Armstrong was continuing to produce.

Returning to the ice in mid-autumn, Magnuson was surprised to discover a new cast of "tough guys" had entered the league. As had Dave Schultz, these individuals appeared to go out of their way in an attempt to make their marks. Among them was Garry Howatt of the fledgling New York Islanders, who would challenge Magnuson to fisticuffs with just under four minutes left in a game on Long Island on December 15, 1973. Former Hawks player Al Arbour—one of the few bespectacled skaters in league history—had taken over as head coach of the second-year expansion team in New York, and was searching for an identity for his inexperienced club. The undersized rookie Howatt was, like Schultz, seeking to take on seasoned fighters like Magnuson in order to more quickly establish a reputation in the league—even if that meant resulting to unconventional tactics.

"Howatt is small," Schultz said of the 5'9" winger, "but the first thing he would do is go for the hair. He was ultimately responsible for what would fittingly be known as the hair-pulling rule. The NHL voted a game misconduct penalty for anyone who pulled hair during a fight."

The melee started when Magnuson planted Howatt with a hard check as he entered the Chicago zone, battling to keep the puck away from the Hawks net to maintain a 3–3 tie. Howatt grabbed hold of Keith's jersey, showing impressive strength for one of his stature, and threw Magnuson down to the ice as the diminutive Howatt unleashed a flurry of wild punches. Finally freeing himself, Magnuson matched the voracious Islander blow-for-blow, ultimately knocking Howatt's helmet off his head as a hearty cheer from the novice Uniondale hockey crowd followed the two men to the penalty box.

"Magnuson said afterward that the brawl didn't do his ailing right elbow any good," Verdi reported in reference to Keith's training camp injury. "'But I owed it to him,'" Maggie said.

Just one week later, it would be Schultz's turn, again with Magnuson, as the legend of both men had been growing further around the NHL.

Schultz was from Rosetown, Saskatchewan, on the other side of the province from Magnuson's hometown of Wadena. He claimed to have never had a street fight, even as a kid, but yet came from the same tough western Canadian turf as Keith. "I grew up on the thin edge of poverty, moving from town to town across the Saskatchewan prairie," Schultz recalled from his youth. In contrast to how some sports historians have painted him—as a lifetime goon—Schultz was actually quite the opposite type of player in amateur hockey before coming into the professional ranks—and was extremely frank in admitting so.

"I wanted no part of that rough stuff," Schultz said of avoiding physical play early in his career and into his first year of Juniors. "[I] let other guys fight my battles. I was a coward and I proved it when a fight broke out on the ice in Flin Flon. I hid in the bench area. If I could have crawled under the bench I would have."

Soon, however, Schultz would shed this initial self-image and become one of the most feared players in the game. In three years of play in the minors from 1969 to 1972, Schultz accumulated season totals in penalty minutes of 369, 382, and 392, respectively. By the start of his rookie season in Philadelphia in the fall of 1972, he was a perfect fit for the Flyers, who intimidated opponents who entered the Spectrum with their unrelenting brutish play. The team had acquired such nicknames as "the Mad Squad" and "Freddy's Philistines" (after head coach Fred Shero) as they solidified into a unit. But their most famous moniker was that of the "Broad Street Bullies," a name surmised by *Philadelphia Bulletin* reporter Jack Chevalier and headline writer Pete Cafone which first appeared in that paper on January 4, 1973. Cafone's banner that morning read BROAD STREET BULLIES MUSCLE ATLANTA after the Flyers had savagely beaten upon the Flames the prior evening.

Word quickly spread around the league about the terror that teams were starting to feel in visiting the City of Brotherly Love.

"I used to hear stories from opposing players about when they would have to come into Philly to play us at the Spectrum," Schultz said. "They would all be laughing and joking on the bus from the airport until they came to the Walt Whitman Bridge, then the entire bus would go silent." According to Schultz, some visiting players would even feign an injury to avoid playing in a game in Philadelphia. "We were proud of guys coming down with 'Philly Flu,' because that meant they were intimidated before they even stepped foot in our building.

"Intimidation went both ways, though. Going into Boston to play the Big Bad Bruins was tough. I will never forget sitting in the penalty box and having Bobby Orr and Phil Esposito skate by and say, 'Hey asshole, the boys are going to get you tonight.' There were times I had the 'Boston Flu' too, trust me."

But his coach generally disagreed, saying that Schultz himself made the Flyers a formidable opponent, even as a visiting team. "So many clubs are tough only in their own rinks," Shero would say. "But Schultz gave us courage on the road. You can't measure the value of a man like that."

Nonetheless, having a team-wide reputation of thuggery had its downside, and Schultz believed there was prejudice on the part of NHL officials when dealing with him and the other Flyers. "I believe referees get up for certain games, just like players," he added. "And when they're assigned to the Flyers, they're automatically watching me closer than anyone else."

According to several NHL experts, what made a 1970s Philadelphia Flyers player different from the basic, traditionally tough hockey man was that, in fighting and other matters of physical play, they generally did not obey the Code. In opposition to the Code's protocol, the Flyers would attack the opponents' skill or "finesse" players—who, while able with the puck, were generally weaker fighters, or not even fighters at all—just as frequently as they did the opponents' enforcers. And in an era when bench-clearing brawls could still occur (despite the implementation of the third man in rule), the inevitable "pairing up" that followed was typically very bad news for another team's finesse player—as even the Flyers' skill players were dangerous customers. "So, if you were a goal scorer," advised 1990s NHL fighter Marty McSorley, "you might have to square up with Bobby Clarke, who was tough as hell. A lot of teams were simply afraid of them."

McSorley echoed a sentiment that Magnuson had professed over and over throughout his career.

"And once your opponents are afraid in this business," he added, "the game is over before it even begins."

Borje Salming, a talented player for the Toronto Maple Leafs during the 1970s who later became a chef and author, was one of the many Flyers opponents who did not look forward to a game on Philadelphia ice.

"It wasn't just two or three guys you had to worry about," Salming said of Shero's men. "It was 20 guys. You would see their sticks come flying at you. If they hit you, you'd be dead... They really tried to kill you. They really tried to force you out of the game. If they did some of those things today, they would be suspended for life."

Salming, while one of the league's best defensemen, was also Swedish—one of the very few Europeans in the NHL at the time—and the Europeans were accustomed to their style of play from across the pond that involved much less contact.

But while they indeed had a considerable amount of actual hockey skills, the Flyers were hardly concerned with spending any great deal of time honing them. On this topic, Shero was as unapologetic as any of his players.

"If it's pretty skating the people want," he said of local fans, "let them go to the Ice Capades."

Shero had been an amateur boxer, and was well aware of the psychological edge that the simple willingness to fight—or "showing up," as Magnuson called it—which Schultz and his other players outwardly possessed, could give a player or an entire team.

"We lose as many fights as we win," the coach pointed out, "but that's not important. We use our bodies to get the puck in the corners and along the boards and, when we can, to open things in front of the net."

And the numbers supported Shero's claim, as the team's tactics were indeed opening up scoring opportunities—not only for Clarke, Bill Barber, and other top-line forwards on the Flyers, but even for third- and fourth-line checking forwards such as Don Saleski, Bob Kelly, and Schultz himself. In fact, in an eight-day stretch in January 1974, and a few weeks after the Flyers hosted the Hawks in the vaunted Spectrum, Schultz posted two hat tricks, and his 18-of-75 shooting to start the season, to the surprise of many, led the league in scoring percentage.

Clarke, the Philadelphia captain and Canada's motivational hero/villain of the Summit Series (with his stick chop at Valeri Kharlamov), was as unrepentant as Shero, Schultz, or anyone else on the Flyers about what he saw as the necessary, brutal side of hockey.

"If I hadn't learned to lay on a two-hander once in a while," Clarke uttered, "I'd never have left Flin Flon."

His statement was in reference to the rugged community from which many of the game's roughest personalities had come, a blue-collar mining town on the Manitoba-Saskatchewan border comprised of old houses built on stone and with many sewer pipes running above ground.

By the end of the 1973–74 season, Clarke was named by a panel of retired players (including John Ferguson, the man who allegedly green-lighted him to go after Kharlamov) as the "league's toughest player;" he had also been nicknamed "Captain Courageous" by some, for his leadership of the Flyers. Many around the league, however, would highly dispute the legitimacy of these titles—including Schultz. Schultz's reaction to such praise of Clarke seemed not to be out of jealousy, but rather for the way in which Clarke conducted his business on the ice.

"If ever a player led by inspiration, Clarke was the man," Schultz admitted. "But there was a darker side to him, one that many Philadelphians and Flyers personnel chose to ignore or, at the very least, dismiss as irrelevant. I am referring to the manner in which Bobby played the game. Dirty. Very dirty."

In particular, Schultz over time became resentful that he had to clean up the messes when Clarke chose to be underhanded with an opponent.

"The unwritten rule was that he could dish out the rough stuff but that nobody on the opposition was allowed to retaliate," Schultz explained.

Specifically, Schultz felt that Clarke—along with Wayne Cashman and Bobby Schmautz of the Bruins and Dennis Hextall of the North Stars (and later, the Red Wings), among others—was extremely dangerous in the way he wielded his stick, "at times employing it in a manner of an infantryman handling a bayonet," Schultz claimed. And while Schultz, like Magnuson, firmly believed in the requisite role that honorable fighting played in professional hockey, he felt that attacks with the stick were not only dangerous but cowardly. Schultz asserted that Clarke's run at Kharlamov would not have been considered so "heroic" if it had been an NHL player on the receiving end—particularly a noteworthy player—rather than a Cold War opponent.

"Any penalty involving the illegal use of the stick should be increased to a five-minute major penalty rather than a two-minute minor as is the case today," the slugger would state near the end of his career, in the late 1970s.

Schultz also made it clear that he held his team's captain among the most culpable for hit-and-run attacks. "It is an indisputable fact that Clarke rarely backed up his stickwork with his fists," he added

Keith's parents, Joe and Birdie Magnuson.

The Magnuson children, circa 1950: Meridel, Dale, Wayne, and Keith.

"I wanted to be a hockey player," Magnuson said. "And there's no better place than Denver for that." (University of Denver)

Magnuson celebrates winning the 1969 NCAA national championship with boyhood friend Tim Gould (right) and Tom Miller. (University of Denver)

Keith, coach Murray Armstrong, and teammates celebrate winning the NCAA title. (University of Denver)

Magnuson and goalie Tony Esposito work to stop Detroit's Alex Delvecchio. The two Chicago teammates would compete for the Calder Trophy as the NHL's top rookie in 1970. (AP Images)

An inconsolable Magnuson laments what might have been after his team's loss to the Canadiens in the 1971 Finals.

Over the years, Magnuson often engaged his heated rivals from Philadelphia and Montreal, including Bob Kelly (above) and Pete Mahovlich (below). (AP Images)

Keith, his wife, Cindy, and children, Kevin and Molly, in 1981.

The Magnusons celebrate Kevin's senior day at the University of Michigan in 2000.

Cliff Koroll and Magnuson were lifelong friends who met in Saskatoon when they were 10 years old. The two were teammates at the University of Denver and on the Black Hawks, and coached together in Chicago for parts of two seasons. (The Koroll family)

Kevin Magnuson (front, left) leads the pallbearers carrying his father's casket after Keith's funeral service on December 20, 2003. (AP Images)

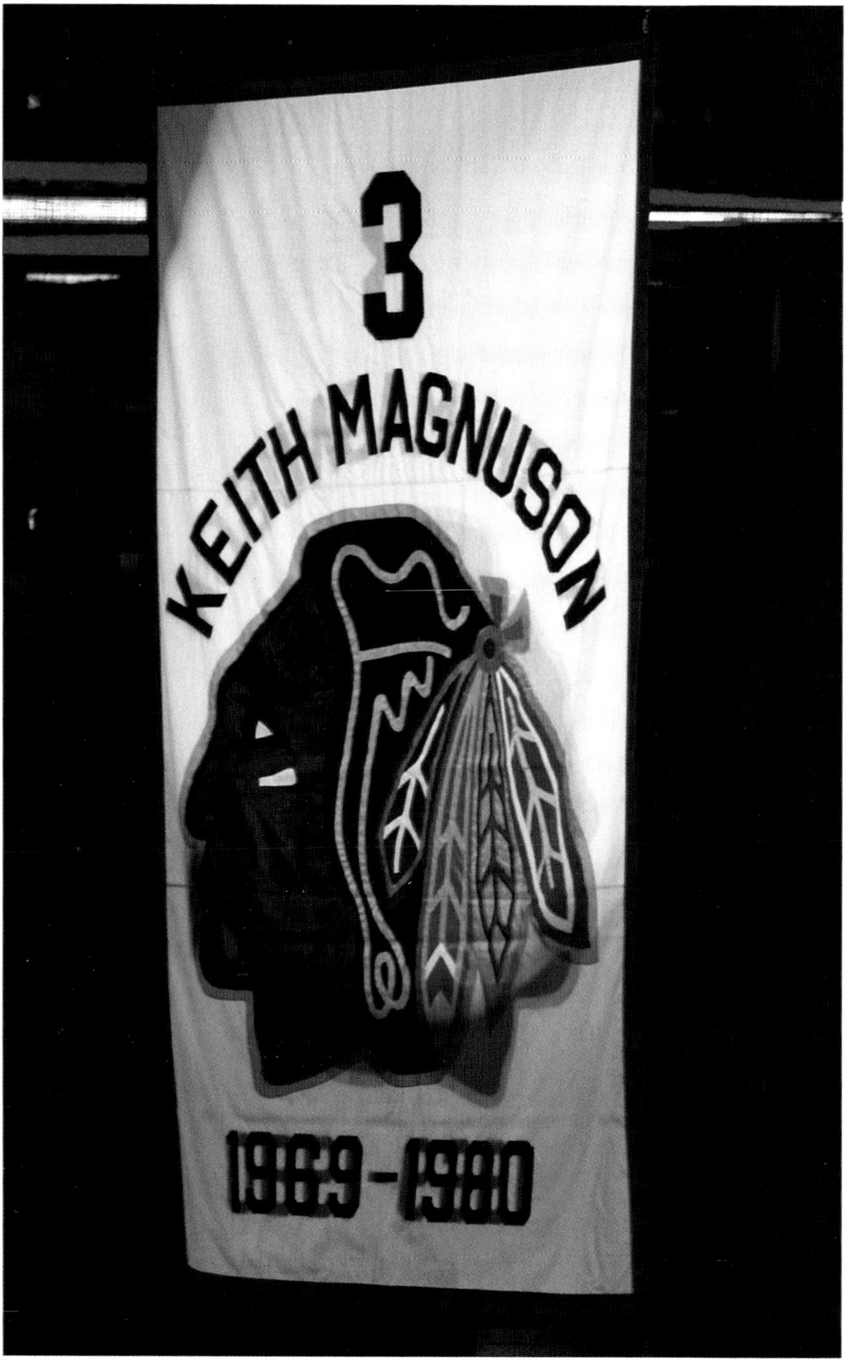

On November 12, 2008, the Blackhawks retired Keith Magnuson's No. 3 and raised a banner to the United Center rafters. (AP Images)

plainly. "Too often, I was called upon to do the fighting for him... I felt that if he was going to start something he should have been able to finish it; when he didn't, I lost respect for him."

Writing in the midst of the Flyers' rise to NHL prominence in the mid-1970s, *New York Post* reporter Mike Shalin felt much the same way. "Bobby Clarke is a very dirty hockey player, perhaps the dirtiest hockey player ever to lace on a pair of skates," he wrote. "The victims of his vicious attacks are too many to name... Why has nobody taken it upon himself (or themselves) to beat the living stuffings out of this counterfeit angel?"

The answer to that question was that the opposition would then have to go toe-to-toe with Schultz, Saleski, Kelly, Andre Dupont, Mel Bridgman, and other willing fighters on the Philadelphia roster, Schultz explained.

So despite countless tussles in front of Tony Esposito and the Hawks net, Magnuson never threw fists with Clarke in an NHL game—but he went the distance with Schultz four times.

And on December 22, 1973, the Black Hawks were the visitors at the Philadelphia Spectrum, as the Flyers sought to wrestle control of the NHL's Western Division from Chicago—in any manner they needed. The two teams had played 10 days earlier in the Stadium to a 2–2 tie without a major extracurricular incident, but a simmering powder keg was about to go off.

By now, Magnuson was as seasoned as anyone in the league at all forms of physical tactics, and was not about to let anyone intimidate him, even in the hostile Philly environment. Before a faceoff in the Chicago zone, he and Schultz circled around each other with angry glares, as if they were a couple of stray dogs with a piece of meat sitting between them. Magnuson then took the initiative, readying himself with his patented "shoulder shrug" in loosening his arms before battle, and sprung upon Schultz, striking him with several right hands before the Flyer returned multiple strong blows himself. The Chicago defenseman stood his ground and gave some damage right back to him. In the end, Magnuson generally took a larger share of the beating as people reviewing the fight gave Schultz the edge in the "decision." Later in the game, heavyweights Phil Russell and Don Saleski exchanged blows as well.

"My double triumph [this particular fight and the one with Magnuson from the previous season] over so significant a foe as Magnuson was a substantial boost for both my ego and the Flyers'," Schultz reflected years later. "And within a month, our club's image had done an about-face. Kelly and Saleski and I had the NHL on the run."

It was the most evenly matched of all the Schultz-Magnuson scraps over the years, and also played a major role in Schultz soon acquiring his nickname, "the Hammer."

After the *Sports Illustrated* cover was printed in his rookie season with his tooth-missing grin, as well as the subsequent article in *Time* magazine about his role as a hockey policeman, it took a while for people following the sport to understand the other side of Magnuson. It was a side far removed from the blood-splattering, tenacious defenseman seen on the ice, and the one of great humanitarianism with empathy, as raised with Dale, Wayne, and Meridel by Joe and Birdie back in Saskatchewan. Only six days after the bloody Schultz fight on December 28, Magnuson had displayed his good nature by helping out the Pittsburgh Penguins' promotional staff the night before the Hawks were scheduled to play in the city. Magnuson was in attendance as the Penguins played the Blues, and Keith was asked came down to the ice and take part in a between-periods contest. While more arrogant professional athletes might have considered such a request beneath them, Magnuson did so happily, and greeted the fans with his infectious smile and pleasant disposition.

"He showed me something by going down and helping out," one Penguins public relations person said afterward. "Too many athletes are too stuck up and think they are too good for something like this."

Schultz and the Flyers would return to Chicago in late February 1974, a month after the Stadium had hosted its first NHL All-Star Game since 1961. While another free-for-all was expected from Shero's men, the Flyers instead displayed a lighter side, and the Hawks won 3–1, their seventh victory in a row.

Before the game, Clarke and Philadelphia defenseman Ed Van Impe got into a playful punching match in the visitor's locker room—while both happened to be naked. Clarke let fly with an open-handed slap that was harder than intended, and just as what happens in the schoolyard in such circumstances, the recipient became incensed and a real fight ensued. Van Impe then chased Clarke through the tunnels of the Stadium and out into the seating area—both still naked. As Van Impe scrambled over row after row of seats to get at Clarke (all while both tried not to damage critical body parts), Billy Reay happened to pass by.

"How in the hell do you sons of bitches ever win a hockey game?" the Chicago coached yelled to them from a distance.

But by the end of the year, the Hawks could not stop the rampaging Flyers, nor could anyone else. Chicago would actually set a club record during 1973–74 for the fewest losses in a season with 14 (as well as a team-record 23 ties), but Philadelphia ended the Hawks' string of divisional titles with their own impressive totals of 50 wins and 112 points.

After getting past coach Bob Pulford's Los Angeles Kings in the first round of the playoffs in five games, Chicago succumbed to the Bruins in the semifinals in six—yet another hard-fought series. The third game against the Bruins was played on Esposito's 31st birthday; and with four minutes left in the game, Magnuson once again encountered the new Boston bruiser Terry O'Reilly. Magnuson endured several punches from the eager youngster, but his aggressiveness nonetheless buoyed his mates to rally for a 4–3 overtime win for Chicago, and a 2–1 lead in the series at the time.

"I didn't do that to get things going necessarily," Magnuson would say later in front of his locker at the Stadium. "I lost it [the fight], for sure. My record is good—three wins and a hundred losses. But if it helped, it helped."

Ultimately, the Bruins—while still putting up video-game-type scoring numbers behind Orr and Phil Esposito—were the final victim of the Flyers, as Philadelphia became the first expansion team to win the Stanley Cup. Orr continued his personal mastery of a certain piece of hardware among his other league awards.

"A lot of people ask me if I'm bothered that Orr wins the Norris Trophy every year," Bill White had said in a gracious tone, one also echoed by Magnuson. "But I'm not. He's the best and he deserves it. I get my recognition in other ways."

As expected, Schultz and O'Reilly ultimately converged in an epic bout in the second game of the championship round, a game in which Schultz would set up Clarke's winning goal in overtime as well, rebounding the Flyers from a loss in the series opener. "The fight and the goal not only gave us a win," Schultz pointed out, "but also a psychological lift in the series. No longer were we afraid of the Bruins, as we proved by winning the next two games and taking a 3–1 lead in the Finals."

Among postseason laurels, Tony Esposito once again had a share in the Vezina Trophy as the league's top goalie, this time splitting it with Flyers netminder Bernie Parent. The two men had been the unwavering workhorses between the pipes for their teams, playing in an astounding 70 and 73 games, respectively, while posting 10 and 12 shutouts as well. Behind Magnuson and his blue-line cohorts, the

Hawks continued their grinding, defensive style that permitted scant scoring chances—a fact noticed by Angotti, who now had an opponent's perspective in St. Louis.

"You just can't get behind that team," Lou said of his former teammates. "They don't make any mistakes on their own, so you don't get any chances to catch up. If you try to open up, their defensemen handle the puck so well that they'll trap you and pretty soon you're even farther behind. But that's the benefit of having some defensemen who've played together for two or three years. They know what they're doing."

One of those defensemen who had been a Black Hawk for so long, however, was now over in the WHA. Pat Stapleton's stellar play continued, and he was named the top defenseman in his first year in the new league.

Schultz, meanwhile, proceeded to obliterate Magnuson's three-year-old regular season NHL record for penalty minutes of 291 with 348 of his own. The Flyers showed no fear of placing themselves in shorthanded situations, even during the playoffs; if anything, Schultz and his teammates had actually upped their aggression during the 1974 postseason. Schultz, including his fight in the Finals with O'Reilly, added a playoff-record 139 penalty minutes throughout Philadelphia's 17 postseason games in '74, while the imposing defenseman Dupont logged 67 of his own. (By comparison, Magnuson's 63 penalty minutes in the 1971 playoffs was a Hawks team record at the time.)

With the exceptions of Eric Nesterenko and third-pair defenseman Darryl Maggs, Stapleton would not be able to raid the Hawks roster of any more significant players. Bill Wirtz re-signed Magnuson and Koroll, both established pillars of the team, to multiyear contracts in the off-season of 1974 while drafting Alain Daigle, a forward who posted remarkable scoring figures in the Juniors and who would become one of the team's first French Canadian players in the modern era.

Still, the aging of other veterans necessitated the further development of other younger players such as Marks (moved permanently to left wing), other first-round draft picks Rota and Grant Mulvey at forward, as well as Russell and Dick Redmond on defense. It remained to be seen if the evolving roster would produce the same high-caliber teams as in past years, but Billy Reay, for one, was confident.

"Overall, this is the most solid team we've had here in the last eight seasons," he would say in September 1974. "I don't believe we've ever been this deep in good defensemen."

Going into the 1974–75 season, Reay needed only 37 wins to catch Toe Blake (at 500) for second place on the all-time coaching list behind Dick Irvin's 692.

The O'Reilly fight in the 1974 playoffs was yet another in which Magnuson stood his ground bravely, took on the other team's toughest opponent, and absorbed tremendous punishment. The cumulative effect of Magnuson's bouts were admittedly starting to wear on him, as such blows, as well as lingering knee problems and new injuries, had limited him to only 57 games in 1973–74. Even so, he took the aches and pains in stride—and always with a sense of humor.

"Long ago I gave up counting the stitches above my own neck when I reached 250," he had noted a year earlier.

As with many hockey players, Keith also had the misfortune of losing some of his teeth—particularly before the advent of modern protective and corrective devices. As a result, Magnuson wore a plate in his mouth and occasionally asked equipment manager Lou Varga for a pair of pliers so that he could straighten them himself. When the plate would crack, Magnuson would attempt a temporary repair with household cement—a solution, he said, that would last only a month or two, and which of course came with a nasty taste.

"Almost all hockey players have missing teeth and wear plates off the ice," Magnuson explained. "Occasionally the teeth will loosen and start to flop around. Dentists can handle this, of course, but they cost money. Besides, just getting to a dentist in the middle of a season is a task all its own."

Once, Magnuson recalled being the featured guest at a dinner banquet in Chicago, where he was to give a short speech. At the meal before his talk, Keith had bitten into a dinner roll and suddenly, one of his loose teeth popped out and started bouncing across the floor. Scrambling with his hands for a moment under the table, he was able to retrieve it without anyone noticing and placed it in his pocket. Later, at the microphone, he revealed to the audience and restaurant staff what had happened, saying good-naturedly to the servers that he remembered having "tangled with a lot of noted pugilists, but never having been really nailed until meeting one of their buns."

Varga, like most everyone, had become very fond of Magnuson and was happy to indulge whatever he needed—be it pliers for his dentures or some other requirement. As another example of Magnuson's unique equipment needs, he asked Varga to acquire specially made skates for him in order to ensure a proper feel on the ice. Keith wore a size 11 shoe, but his left foot was larger than his right. Magnuson also admitted that he was the only Hawks player not to wear socks while playing, as he preferred the natural feel of the boot against his bare feet. Keith was also very particular about the hour-by-hour condition of his skates, asking Varga to sharpen them multiple times a day and usually in between periods of games as well. It was certainly a long way from Magnuson's boyhood days in Wadena and Saskatoon when, because of the expense, his father would permit him to have his skates sharpened only once a year.

Hockey gloves were yet another example of Magnuson carefully crafting the gear to his liking. Varga would cringe whenever Magnuson would take a knife or scissors and cut out the palms of a brand-new pair that the manager had just taken out of the box. Just as with his sockless skates, he believed it gave him a more natural feel for the stick—and it also did not hurt in helping him to grab the jersey of an opponent.

• • •

Such obsessions with fine-tuning his hockey gear and his game drove Magnuson's life, as looking for advantages on the ice was his single-minded objective each day. He had not seriously considered any long-term personal relationships to this point. Jarrett, his partner on defense, had gotten married at age 18 and already had five kids when he came to play for the Hawks. Thus, Magnuson would turn to Jarrett for "life advice," such as knowing the right time to win over the right gal. "Don't worry—you'll find her," Jarrett would always tell him. "You'll know when the time comes."

When Magnuson first started with the Black Hawks, he was immediately proactive and organized about whom he permitted into his personal life. "If you're a pro athlete," he said in a magazine interview in 1971, "you've got to find a really great girl if you're going to get married. She's got to understand that you're always away from home. It isn't easy."

Keith would indeed find one.

Magnuson, like Koroll, Mikita, and many other players, spent a good deal of his free time in the summer playing golf. One of his favorite courses was the Park Ridge Country Club in suburban Chicago. Part of his preference for the location was the lovely lady working in the course's pro shop, Cynthia White. For her daily reliability, she simply became known around the club as "Pro Shop Cindy," and even answered the phone as such.

It was at a celebrity tournament at Park Ridge in 1974 where Keith first saw Cindy. He was stunned by her beauty, and asked her out on a date, right there on the spot. While flattered, Cindy—at the time unaware of Magnuson's celebrity—politely mentioned that she already had a boyfriend but was appreciative of the gesture. Later that day, Cindy mentioned to her twin brother, John, what had transpired earlier in the afternoon, and he in turn gave Cindy a little more background on her red-headed suitor. Cindy was still relatively unimpressed, however, and finished her summer at the pro shop before heading back to her studies at the University of Missouri that autumn.

For his part, Magnuson—displaying the same dogged persistence that constituted his play on the ice—was undaunted.

"I remember Maggie phoned me," Koroll said of their very next conversation after Keith had encountered Cindy, "and told me he met this beautiful lady and he was going to marry her. The second sentence he said: 'But she won't go out with me.'"

With Cindy in Columbia, Missouri, Magnuson took it upon himself to get to know her mother, Marjorie, back in Chicago, by phone. By the time Cindy had come home for Christmas break, Magnuson had made such an impression on Mrs. White that she convinced her daughter to give him a one-date tryout.

"That shows you the character and perseverance Maggie had," Koroll said. "He was bound and determined to marry Cindy, and he did."

The wedding took place less than seven months later, and a year later, they welcomed their son, Kevin, to the world, followed by their daughter, Molly, in 1979.

"I've been lucky," Keith would say often. "Cindy is a great girl."

• • •

Just as 1974–75 looked to be a rebuilding year for the Hawks, the season would have a new look for the league as well, as it split itself into two new conferences of two divisions each. Chicago was placed in the Smythe Division of the Clarence Campbell Conference (which also included the Patrick Division with Philadelphia, Atlanta, and the New York teams), and just as with their move to the old Western Division in 1970, many felt it would be one which the Hawks would easily dominate. Joining the Hawks in the Smythe would be St. Louis, Minnesota, and Vancouver—all mediocre teams, at best, at the time—as well as another expansion team, the Kansas City Scouts. Another first-year team, the Washington Capitals, would compete in the Norris Division of the Prince of Wales Conference, which also included the Adams Division.

Magnuson began the year with his usual determination, starting in the exhibition season. In a game against Toronto on September 29 at the Stadium, he followed Esposito in leading the team out onto the ice as usual, sprinting laps around the Hawks' half of the rink before all of his teammates had even joined him. Shortly after the first drop of the puck, he was challenged by a 20-year-old Toronto rookie named Dave Williams, who had acquired the nickname of "Tiger" back in his boyhood home of Saskatchewan, when he was five years old. Williams—in his very first week of NHL action—had gone after Larry Carriere of the Sabres in Buffalo the night before and had gained a reputation as a fighter in Juniors before coming into the league.

But there were lessons to be learned about the top level of play, and Magnuson rang the school bell quickly. As the two squared off, Keith knocked Williams' helmet off, clutched his jersey with his palmless gloves, and slammed him down to the ice. The blitzkrieg strike of bombs that followed was "by far the best start of Magnuson's six-year fistic career," Verdi said. While Williams later complained to have been caught off guard. "I was still talking when they started punching," Williams said, in making it sound as if Magnuson was receiving help from other Hawks players. He then referred to himself in the third person, as if his status was already legendary. "The Tiger is bruised but untamed," Williams happily continued. "There will be other nights and other fights. Tonight, I talked when I should have socked." Later that evening, Russell also picked apart Toronto's main scoring threat, Darryl Sittler, in another fight that also lasted only mere seconds.

Indeed, there would be other nights and other fights for Williams. He would go on to an NHL career that would last nearly 15 years, through 1988, during which he would amass 3,966 minutes in penalties —the most in league history.

Unfortunately, any early momentum for the Hawks would not last. After a solid start to the season in which Chicago won six of its first nine games, the team fell into a pattern of lethargy and losing streaks, having to battle with other less-established teams in the new Smythe Division simply to attain a playoff berth. As part of their early-season inconsistency, the Hawks also had the ignominious distinction of being the first team to ever lose to the expansion Capitals, on October 17. The Washington team was on its way to completing the single-worst season in league history, finishing the 1974–75 schedule by managing only eight wins and five ties against 67 losses.

The demoralizing defeat was a prime example of the erratic performance of the Black Hawks that season, and further changes to the club appeared imminent. On December 15, the Hawks' new divisional adversary, the Vancouver Canucks, came calling at the Stadium. Four minutes into the game, a fight erupted between Magnuson and Canucks defenseman Harold Snepsts. Immediately after Magnuson got out of the penalty box, he took on Vancouver forward Chris Oddleifson with even more fury, breaking Oddleifson's jaw with a tremendous right hand. Noticing that the fist with which Magnuson was punching was taped (which was illegal), referee Bruce Hood gave Keith a game misconduct penalty—something that was somehow overlooked during the earlier bout with Snepsts. Oddleifson, meanwhile, would miss the Canucks' next 18 games with his injury while the Vancouver team already began contemplating its revenge.

"It's a long season, and we'll get Magnuson," vowed coach Phil Maloney.

Reay immediately came to Magnuson's defense, saying that his player knew the rule but had forgotten to keep his gloves on.

Shortly thereafter, Canucks officials would appeal to the league for Magnuson to be suspended for as long as Oddleifson was out; instead, Keith was off the ice for only three games. And while waiting to serve his punishment, he was permitted to play and had other battles to wage.

Two weeks later, on December 28, he fought Schultz for the third time, with the champion Flyers visiting Chicago and their confidence at an all-time high. Yet despite his earlier victories, Schultz knew better than to take any confrontation with Magnuson lightly.

"In the NHL jungle, an enforcer learns that winning a battle does not necessarily mean winning the war, if only because the loser of one fight—if he has any gumption at all—is likely to come back the next time with all guns blazing," Schultz said. "So it was with Magnuson on another night at Chicago Stadium."

Less than two minutes into the game. Magnuson had given Philadelphia center Rick MacLeish a crushing hit at the whistle, to which Schultz took exception. Schultz jumped in between them as he knocked into Maggie while holding both gloves up by his chest, using them like a bumper before the fists started flying.

"Magnuson scored early but Schultz scored heavily and late," said Verdi, summarizing the bout.

Video of the incident shows Magnuson's head recoiling violently and multiple times from the pulverizing shots, though he was remarkably able to stay on his skates. Schultz, known for getting in one last punch as officials pulled him off his opponent, uncorked a final right hand on Magnuson that shook the defenseman once again. Schultz laughed in being separated from Maggie. The Stadium crowd was delirious with rage at the Philadelphia player, hurling insults in his direction.

After the two had been finally escorted off the ice by the linesmen, Schultz never sat down in the penalty box—instead he chose to stand on top of the seat and beckon angrily across the ice to the Chicago bench, challenging anyone who wished to go at it again.

"There were no takers," Verdi disappointedly noticed.

Later in the game, Phil Russell would have some words for Schultz during a stoppage in play, but nothing came of it. Dennis Hull was able to notch his 250th career goal, which permitted Chicago to sneak out with a 2–1 victory.

Despite the win, several writers—including Verdi—were beginning to believe that a majority of the Hawks (save for Magnuson, Russell, and a few others) were clearly displaying a lack of heart when it came to the ever-increasing physical tone of play dominating the NHL at the time. Fred Shero had noticed it as well.

"The players don't back each other up," the Philadelphia coach would tell *The Sporting News* a month later in his assessment of the Hawks. "For years, the fans in Chicago Stadium have been booing Jim Pappin," Shero gave as an example. "He's one of their best players, and yet not one of the players has stood up and defended Pappin."

Shero pointed out how the same thing had happened the previous year in Philadelphia with one of his defensemen, Tom Bladon, and that the other Flyers players put an end to it by telling the Philly fans the criticism was unwarranted. "That might not be a very good thing to tell your own fans, but the team comes first... There are things I would do for my players that I wouldn't do for my own family," he said.

So it was up to Magnuson, despite all his pain, to provide inspiration to a lethargic team once again. And the pain continued to worsen; by late spring of 1975 it was a lingering high ankle sprain. It was part of the reason Magnuson would not score his first goal of the season until March 26 at 2:10 in the first period of a home game against Buffalo, a feed off a smooth behind-the-net pass from Mikita in a 5–1 Hawks win.

Magnuson would be on the other side of a "taped fist" situation on January 29, just a month after the Oddleifson incident. With the Hawks in Pittsburgh to face the Penguins, Magnuson ran into another Bob Kelly—not the one who fought alongside Schultz with the Flyers, but another with the first name of "J. Bob," or as he was known around the league, "Battleship." A few seasons later, Kelly would become a teammate of Magnuson's in Chicago, but on this night they squared off on the ice of the Civic Arena in the Steel City.

Kelly had been picked up by Pittsburgh in the middle of the previous season from St. Louis, along with defenseman Steve Durbano. Both young players had piled up immense penalty minutes in the Juniors. Durbano, in fact—a former first-round draft pick of the Rangers in 1971—would surpass the 400-minute mark in 1972 with Omaha of the Central League. And after just one year of NHL play, Kelly had established his own reputation as one of hockey's tougher fighters.

"On the ice in the National Hockey League, nobody messes around with Pittsburgh Penguin Bob 'Battleship' Kelly," asserted John Clayton a couple weeks after Kelly's encounter with the Hawks. (Clayton was then a college student at Duquesne University, covering the Penguins and football's Pittsburgh Steelers for the Beaver County *Times*.)

Kelly thought of himself as a scorer, and was in fact proving himself as one—he was on the way to posting 27 goals during the season, a level he would not reach again. Still, he publicly wondered why he was not getting the puck more often from his center, 19-year-old rookie Pierre Larouche. "You can't score if you don't get the puck," he complained to Clayton.

When referee Wally Harris saw Kelly with the taped fist in his fight with Magnuson, he was suspended two games and fined $250. Kelly did not mind.

"I don't care how much the league tries to suspend the players for fighting," the unconcerned player said after the news of his banishment. "It is still part of the game. When I played in the American Hockey League, there were only a few players that fought and the refs could watch certain players. In the NHL, everybody can potentially explode into a fight, so they can't watch certain players."

"Referees are all bad," Kelly then concluded. "Some are just worse."

Joining Kelly on the Penguins' scratched list over the next couple of games was Durbano himself, out with an injury. But in one year's time, by the spring of 1976, Durbano would take the league penalty-minutes title away from Schultz with 370 as he split the year between Pittsburgh and Kansas City. Durbano's career would fade in the WHA, while Kelly would land in Chicago in the fall of 1977.

To the surprise of many, the moribund Hawks—now with lots of unexpected competition in the Smythe Division, thanks to their own inconsistent play—had missed their own chance to retool by letting the NHL trading deadline pass without making a deal. Left leading the team were veterans Magnuson, Koroll, Mikita, Martin, White, and Dennis Hull, several of whom were recently injured. Along with Magnuson's ankle, Hull and White were both suffering significant back problems. The Hawks front office had indicated some measure of interest in finding a replacement or two, but claimed there was nothing available to be had.

"This league isn't like it used to be in pre-expansion days," Reay explained of the general reluctance most clubs were having of parting with anyone. "Not many teams have great depth."

Meanwhile, Vancouver had recently won in the Stadium for the first time in 14 tries, snapping their 0–11–2 stretch in Chicago and Snepsts, Oddleifson, and Magnuson engaged each other this time without incident. The two teams played on three more occasions in close succession at the end of the regular season schedule, with first place up for grabs in each contest (and a first-round bye in the playoffs at stake).

In the midst of the stressful and turbulent year, the Hawks turned to humor, pranks, and preying upon the idiosyncrasies of each other even more often—even in the absence of Stapleton, perhaps the biggest jester the team had seen. That role now fell to Pappin, in what would be his last year in a Chicago jersey, and who with White's assistance still enjoyed pulling one of the team's more famous jokes on the rookies.

At the end of a team practice session at the Stadium, White would tell an unsuspecting first-year player that Pappin was an accomplished organist, a prospect at which the rookie would be skeptical. "Hey, Jim," White would then holler over to Pappin, "would you go up and play us a few tunes?" So Pappin would make the steep climb up the stairs to the box of Al Melgard—who in 1974 at the age of 85 was in his 41st and final year of playing the famous Stadium organ—and took a seat. Slowly and reverently stretching his fingers in an arm-circle above his head, Pappin then lowered his hands, raised them again dramatically with his palms down, and proceeded to slam them down onto the keyboard as he simultaneously pressed "Play" on a stereo that sent a recording of one of Melgard's performances blaring through the Stadium's speakers. Pappin then continued to run his fingers smoothly along the keyboard during his air-organ routine while gazing upon the stunned face of the rookie down on the ice.

Pappin, an integral part of Chicago's talented teams in the past decade, took his goal scoring and practical jokes to the California Golden Seals at the end of the season. Tommy Ivan then informed Dennis Hull that he would be next to go, as the Hawks had received a young forward named Joey Johnston from the Seals for Pappin. However, in the time when Hull was waiting for the call from a new team, Johnston was involved in an auto accident that prevented him from passing a physical and temporarily put the deal on hold. So Hull, though nearing the end of his career himself, was still a Black Hawk for the time being, although Ivan continued to shop him around while J.P. Bordeleau received more ice time in Pappin's spot on the old MPH Line.

Mikita, like Magnuson, was another veteran on whom Reay was counting for leadership. At age of 34, Stan continued to amaze hockey followers with his strong play at the center position. He led the Hawks in scoring once again in 1974–75 with 86 points, reaching 50 or more assists for the eighth time in his career.

"There's no way a wing can keep from scoring and playing well when Mikita is really going," Koroll said. "All you really have to do is give him the puck and get into position."

Mikita was legendary for taking great care of his body with his in- and off-season diet and exercise regimen, and even worked to improve his eyesight in the same manner as Boston Red Sox slugger Ted Williams had—Mikita would look at the license plate numbers of approaching cars while driving, attempting to see which ones added up to 21 (his jersey number). Mikita and Martin (the two whom Magnuson claimed to be the sharpest dressers on the team) were named cocaptains of the Hawks in 1975, the first time the club had named any captains in the five years since the title was taken away from Stapleton.

With his team in desperate need of all available and experienced bodies for the 1975 playoffs, Magnuson returned from his ankle injury earlier than anticipated. On April 10, with the Hawks already down 1–0 in their opening-round series with the Bruins, he exchanged punches with Terry O'Reilly once again, the third time in which the two men had squared off in the NHL. The fight, at 8:24 of the second period, inspired the Chicago team in a 4–3 overtime win at the Stadium. The next night, in Boston, Magnuson—still in tremendous pain from his ankle, in addition to his scrap with O'Reilly—scored on the Hawks' first shot of the game, part of a 6–4 win, as Esposito turned away 52 shots from the formidable Boston offense to help give Chicago an upset in the best-of-three series. Esposito had shown remarkable resilience after being pulled in Game 1 by Reay in favor of Michel Dumas, when Tony surrendered seven Boston goals in a game in which Phil Esposito noticed that his brother looked overly fatigued.

No one would realize at the time that the series was the last hurrah for Bobby Orr, who in the regular season had smashed his own record of goals by a defenseman with 46. The loss to Chicago signaled the end of his final, dominant year, as more knee problems and a schism with Boston management would unravel a sequence of stunning events with the player in the final years of his career, which lay just ahead.

The Hawks' season, meanwhile, ended in a five-game loss to Buffalo in the following round of the postseason. Nonetheless, with Magnuson fighting through his pain, a renewed sense of spirit was seen in the club and on the new faces of Mulvey, Rota, and others. (That past fall, Mulvey had become the youngest player—at age 18 years and 32 days—to score a goal in the post-expansion era of the NHL.)

It was the Sabres—led by their high-scoring "French Connection" line of Gilbert Perreault, Richard Martin, and Rene Robert, with each man nearly totaling 100 points—that met the Flyers in the Finals as Philadelphia was looking for its second-straight Stanley Cup. Fred Shero's team would not be denied, as Schultz and company slugged its way to a six-game victory. Bernie Parent permitted only 12 goals, taking home another Conn Smythe Trophy as playoff MVP as well as the Vezina, and Bobby Clarke claimed his second Hart Trophy as the league MVP.

The unadorned Schultz, meanwhile, had shattered his own NHL single-season penalty minutes record from the previous year with a whopping 472, still a league record to this day (comprising nearly eight full games' worth of playing time, and nearly twice the impressive second-place figure that his teammate Dupont had logged with 276). In third place on the league's penalty list was Phil Russell of the Hawks with 260; it was apparent that Magnuson was finally getting some assistance in the carrying the fighting load for the team.

"Billy Reay would instruct me and Maggie to find someone to hit right after the opening whistle, and have us nail him as hard as possible," Russell said. "That way, the other team knows it's in for a fight the entire night."

Magnuson, dogged by his ailments the entire year, played in a total of only 48 games, which had limited his own ledger to 117 minutes in the penalty box. Russell had established himself as another force on the blue line, and while he had offensive skills, Russell's first preference was the physical aspect of the sport.

"I remember Stan Mikita asking [former Detroit and Chicago player] Ted Lindsay one time, 'How do you stay in the league so long?'" Russell recalled. "His answer was three words: 'You hit first.'"

But with fighting in the NHL at an all-time high, the topic became the elephant in the room that the league was forced to confront. Some individuals, who felt fighting unnecessarily debased the sport, wished to see it gone altogether. In November 1975, *Sports Illustrated* ran an article lamenting the amount of fighting in professional hockey (as well as its general brutality, as perceived by the writer of the article), and would call upon its immediate cessation—a possibility, the magazine granted, that was unlikely.

"The NHL will continue to be plagued by a split personality that threatens a ruinous alienation of affections," wrote Ray Kennedy in his piece entitled "Wanted: An End to Mayhem." Bobby Hull, interviewed for the article, concurred with Kennedy's premise.

"[Fighting] will ruin the game for all of us," Hull was quoted as saying. "I've never seen such vicious stuff going on. Instead of making hockey a better game, we're tolerating people and things that are forcing a deterioration of the game."

Soon, officials in Canada including the attorney general, members of Parliament, and prominent Toronto lawyer Bill McMurtry, were calling for criminal penalties for players who wantonly and senselessly attacked opponents on the ice. But on the other side, some hockey legends were not so sure that the problem was out of control.

"I don't think we need any of his [McMurtry's] legislation," Gordie Howe said when interviewed by the *Toronto Star* about the lawyer's plan.

Thus, the sport appeared to be at a crossroads heading into the 1975–76 season. With fighting contributing to hockey's growing popularity, would the NHL be prepared, or even willing, to curb it?

7

Transitions

"One thing you've got to have to be a success in this league can't be taught... The ingredient is guts—and this means not being afraid of anyone."

—Keith Magnuson

Times were changing at the old Chicago Stadium. While still a respected elder among indoor arenas, by the mid-1970s the Stadium had been falling behind other venues in the NHL, particularly those of recent expansion teams which received brand-new buildings, such as in Washington, D.C., and Kansas City.

While the Black Hawks still did not have player names on the backs of their jerseys as of yet, a more pressing modernization need was about to be addressed. By 1976, a new scoreboard that included a modern digital clock would be hung above center ice at the Stadium, replacing the old analog clock that players, coaches, officials, spectators, and the media had tried to decipher for decades. The analog clock, in use at the Stadium since 1943, had faced in all four directions, with the "big hands" keeping the game time and the "little hands" keeping the time for penalties. The new scoreboard, however, was still of the most basic variety compared to others seen around the league; a more advanced board would not be placed in the Stadium until 1984.

Changes were also occurring within the Hawks broadcast booth. The 1975–76 season would mark the final one for Lloyd Pettit at the radio microphone, as the popular announcer decided to retire to Wisconsin—whereupon he would purchase the Milwaukee Admirals of the American Hockey League with the hopes of one day landing an expansion NHL franchise in the city. Over the following four years, a parade of different play-by-play announcers would pass through the Stadium, all primarily paired with Lou Angotti as the color man, and the team moved its broadcasts from WMAQ back to WCFL, the station that had previously carried the team's games before WGN assumed the role. WCFL, whose call letters stood for "Chicago Federation of Labor," had been one of two major pop music stations on the AM dial in the city (along with WLS) until its switch to an adult-contemporary format in the same year it added the Black Hawks. Billing itself as "the Voice of Labor" since going on the air in 1926, WCFL had formerly published a newsletter for Chicago union workers.

With the departure of Pettit, stability in the Hawks play-by-play radio chair would not arrive until the appearance of 26-year-old Pat Foley in 1980. The Chicago-area native would come back home after attending Michigan State University and subsequently broadcasting the games for the Grand Rapids Owls of the International Hockey League.

Back in 1975, Pettit began his final season in the Stadium by witnessing a poor showing on Madison Street with a 5–3 defeat at the hands of the Los Angeles Kings. Reay said such losses were being caused by inattentiveness on the defensive end, with some players putting too much focus on trying to score goals. (Another reason may have been the departure of Doug Jarrett, Magnuson's longtime partner on defense, who was dealt to the New York Rangers shortly after the season had started. Jarrett had finally made his first All-Star Game the season before, an honor which Magnuson felt was long overdue.)

"Come contract time and all they talk about is the goals they scored," Reay complained of some of the team's forwards. "We should bring up the goals that were scored against us when those guys were on the ice."

Reay was speaking indirectly to the "plus-minus" statistic, in which individual players receive a "+1" each time he is on the ice when his team scores, and a "-1" each time he is on the ice when the opponent scores. The aggregate sum is then meant to judge a player's relative worth to his team. Magnuson, despite his modest yearly goal and assist totals, had piled impressive numbers in this department since his rookie year:

SEASON	+/-	TEAM RANKING
1969–70	+38	1
1970–71	+32	4
1971–72	+52	2 (second-best in team history, behind Bobby Hull's +54 from the same season)
1972–73	+24	7
1973–74	+16	10
1974–75	+10	5

The loss to the Kings served as a wake-up call, however, as the Hawks rebounded in their next game three nights later, beating the Canadiens 2–1 at the Stadium in what developed into yet another great battle between Tony Esposito and Ken Dryden. It was the second of only two losses that Montreal would suffer in the first month of the season, and one of only 11 times they would be defeated the entire year (a standard they would actually surpass in the following season).

"It just proves that against supposedly easier teams, you have to go all out, all game," said Cliff Koroll afterward. "You can't just show up in your uniform and expect to win."

Magnuson was playing with a renewed sense of vigor, finally healthy and now being paired more often on defense with Dale Tallon, something with which Reay had experimented two years previous.

"He was my first partner when I came to Chicago," Tallon recalled. "I would always tell him make sure nobody touches me."

Tallon, with three excellent years in Vancouver before coming to the Hawks in 1973, joined Phil Russell and Dick Redmond as another true force on the Chicago blue line after a great career in the Juniors.

Nonetheless, momentum for Chicago proved to be difficult to grasp. The team fell into a deep early-season tailspin once again; the Hawks won just once from November 19 to December 19. Soon, the first widespread grumblings about Reay's job began to be heard around Chicago. There appeared to be somewhat of a generation gap forming between Reay's old-school philosophies and some of the younger players who were joining the team.

"Though the old guys were all Billy's players," Dennis Hull pointed out, "the new ones didn't fit in with Billy's thoughts on the game. It caused some friction. Some of the new guys would be off the ice as soon as practice was done. But that wasn't Billy's way. Most of us veterans would be on the ice for an hour after practice was officially over. It was a new breed of player."

Additionally, the Wirtz family was trying to modernize the team in its training procedures.

"Fitness was all the rage," Hull continued in his recollection of the Hawks from the mid-1970s. "There were all these machines in our dressing room. I think we used them one day and then hung our coats on them. It just wasn't the way Billy ran his team. Billy Wirtz told him we had to work on fitness. We'd do sit-ups and push-ups on the ice. It was bizarre."

Meanwhile, the WHA was already showing signs of financial decline after just four years of operation. The fledgling league continued to hang its hopes on the retention of a handful of ex-NHL superstars. "Had the Black Hawks somehow persuaded Hull to remain in the NHL," Stan Fischler wrote in early 1976, "there wouldn't be a WHA today, or in 1975, 1974, or 1973. But they didn't, and Hull kept the league and the Winnipeg Jets in business."

Fischler went on to say that certain average or above-average NHL players, such as the former Boston goalie Gerry Cheevers, "were deluded into thinking they really were stars and that lots and lots of people would come and see them [in WHA games]...instead, what Cheevers learned in Cleveland [with the Crusaders, the city's WHA entry] was that he had the personal drawing power of a dead battery on a zero-cold night."

Pat Stapleton, meanwhile, had left Chicago and the Cougars after being claimed by the Indianapolis Racers in the WHA's "dispersal draft." Fischler unapologetically not only saw him as a deserter of the Black Hawks and the NHL, but one who accelerated the demise of the Cougars and the entire WHA as well. "Stapleton not only didn't save the Cougars," Fischler claimed, "he marched with them toward extinction, then jumped off the bandwagon and re-leaped again at Indianapolis."

Stapleton would play two seasons in Indianapolis and then one with Cincinnati's entry in the WHA, the Stingers, before returning to Indy to coach the team in the league's final year, 1978–79. For the first eight games in that concluding season, one of Stapleton's charges was a 17-year-old center from Brantford, Ontario, named

Wayne Gretzky, who would be traded to the Edmonton Oilers on November 2.

• • •

In the wake of the excitement that had been generated by the Summit Series in 1972, the event had been repeated in 1974. Bobby Hull was permitted to play this time, and would lead the series in scoring with nine points despite the Soviets getting their revenge with four wins against one victory for the Canadians (and three ties). Then, the NHL would announce on May 28, 1975, that a select number teams would play exhibition games against the two top teams from the Soviet Union—the Soviet Wings and the Central Red Army—over the upcoming holiday season.

The plan was the culmination of the vision of legendary Soviet hockey godfather Anatoli Tarasov, who long dreamed of sending his country's best players up against the premier teams in North America. The new set of games would be called the "Super Series," as promoted by NHL president Clarence Campbell. "At the time being," Campbell said, "I believe it is the only way to develop the game of hockey."

Eight contests would be scheduled, with the Central Red Army (which was considered the elite Soviet team) taking on Montreal, Boston, Philadelphia, and the New York Rangers (with all those contests televised on the Canadian Broadcasting System) while the Black Hawks would join Buffalo, Pittsburgh, and the New York Islanders in games against the Wings (with only the Buffalo contest televised). As part of the agreement between the two parties, NHL rules would be used in the games to coincide with a Soviet referee. Additionally, the Soviet teams were allowed to add players to the Wings and Red Army rosters from other clubs around Russia.

Like the famed Summit Series tilt of 1972, the political importance of the games was in no way being underestimated by the media, as exemplified by Al Strachan of the *Montreal Gazette*. "In approximately seven weeks," Strachan pronounced solemnly that autumn, "the National Hockey League will begin the most crucial two-week period of its 50-year history."

When it was announced that the Wings would play a game in Chicago Stadium, Magnuson once again was reminded of his battle against the Russians as an amateur at the University of Denver back in December 1967 at the Colorado Springs tournament, and how the Soviet players displayed unparalleled physical conditioning. "If I were to rate the best hockey teams in the world today," Keith had noted back in 1973, "I'd have to put the Russians right up beside Boston, New York, Chicago, and Montreal."

So in the midst of the Hawks struggling to find their new identity, a standing-room-only crowd of at least 18,500—well beyond the fire code–permitted 16,666 that was usually listed officially for sellouts—entered the Stadium on January 7 to see the Soviets take on the hometown Black Hawks. Just a few days earlier, the Buffalo Sabres had rattled the Wings by a 12–6 final score. The Wings had watched Buffalo's 9–6 loss to the Los Angeles Kings on New Year's Day and consequently had pegged the Sabres as a weak team.

For most of the contest, the fans in Chicago would lambast the Russian referee, Yuri Karandin, for a perceived inequitable amount of calls against the Hawks (although both of the linesmen, Matt Pavelich and Neil Armstrong, were from the NHL).

The game was broadcast back to Russia on radio, with an actor from the Moscow Arts Theatre named Nikolai Ozerov conducting the descriptions. Ozerov told his audience to "watch Phil Russell—he is a good and experienced defenseman" And as the game progressed, even Ozerov criticized Karandin when Russian player Sergei

Kapustin slashed Bill White and opened a gash on the leg of the Hawks defenseman. "They gave him two minutes when they could easily have given him five," he told his listeners back in the U.S.S.R. of the referee, while praising Armstrong and Pavelich during the evening as "exact and just."

Over the course of the game, the Hawks would be called for twice as many minor penalties as the Soviets (12 to six), but Bob Verdi still believed the team was playing soft—as he had been noting quite regularly over the past couple of years.

"The Black Hawks sometimes play as if they covet the Nobel Peace Prize," Verdi wrote after watching the international contest. "[They are] one of the National Hockey League's most polite squads, who [tonight] suddenly turned chippy. They couldn't have picked a more untimely occasion."

Young John Marks, quickly assuming a leadership role on the team, concurred with Verdi's assessment. "What are we, last in the league in penalty minutes?" he asked anyone who could respond with an answer.

Due to an intestinal blockage that was now hampering him, Magnuson—whom Reay and other observers believed was off to the best start to a season in his career—did not appear in the game. Redmond filled his role well, aggressively going after the Russian players at every opportunity and scoring the first Hawks goal, which left the game tied at 1–1 at the end of the first period.

Chicago fell behind, and then a long Dennis Hull slap shot that got past Wings goaltender Alexander Sidelnikov pulled the Hawks to within a two-goal deficit in the third period, but that was as close as they would come. Ozerov was impressed with Stan Mikita and called him "a good and experienced one," but decided that the Black Hawks "just cannot restrain our young players." The final score was 4–2 in favor of the Soviets, with the Hawks managing only 18 total shots on the Russian net.

Other Chicago players claimed that there was overt bias displayed during the evening on the part of Karandin, as the Russians scored three of their four goals on the numerous power-play chances they enjoyed, which proved to be the difference in the game.

"When you get the kind of refereeing we saw tonight," added Pit Martin, "after a while, you just say to yourself, 'What the hell's the use?' It's a shame that the game had to turn into that, but it did."

In postgame comments by both Ozerov and Wings coach Boris Kulagin, the point was repeatedly stressed that the Russian players were merely "amateurs" playing against professionals in the NHL, apparently to make the effort all the more impressive.

Eight days earlier, on New Year's Eve 1974, the Soviets' Red Army squad had played to an epic tie with the Canadiens in the Forum in Montreal. In retrospect, it would be considered one of the most competitive matches in hockey history. Additionally, the Red Army had also beaten the powerful Bruins in the Boston Garden despite the Russian players' almost mystical reverence of Bobby Orr, who did not play in the game, instead continuing the rehabilitation of his knee. According to Todd Denault, the Russians stood numb, with mouths agape, when noticing Orr's No. 4 jersey hanging in his locker when receiving a tour of the Bruins dressing room at the Garden. They reached out respectfully to place their fingers on it, as well as the array of equipment he had left on the floor in front of the locker, as if the items were holy relics through which some supernatural power would be transmitted.

"They just kept touching everything that was his, stroking his sweater," recalled NHL chief of security Frank Torpey, who was watching the scene. "It was really strange."

Later, when a Russian player found his hockey sticks broken before the game with the Bruins, he had to borrow one from the Boston club. The Bruins equipment man brought him one that happened to have the name "Orr" stamped on the top of the shaft. Immediately, the other Soviet players began grabbing at it, each wanting to claim it as his own.

On January 11, the Red Army would play the final game of the Super Series against the bullying Flyers at the Spectrum, with tension already building days before the match.

"For Fred Shero and his Flyers," wrote Denault, "this game was nothing less than the unofficial World Championship of hockey."

Shero had long admired the Soviet style of play, even to the point of once traveling to Russia to study their methods with 100 other North American hockey coaches; Shero, in leading the pilgrimage, was the only NHL-level coach.

The atmosphere in the stands at the Spectrum was as turbulent as it was down on the ice, with Philadelphia fans displaying as much fervor as the Flyers themselves. Faces were torn open with rage toward the communist visitors, as disparaging signs hung from the railings, some even in the Russian Cyrillic alphabet, many of which read FREE RUSSIAN JEWS.

Once again, the high-scoring Soviet forward Valeri Kharlamov was the prime target, just as he was more than four years earlier in the attack from Bobby Clarke—who was also on the ice again this evening. In addition to that infamous Summit Series assault from 1972, the 5'9", 165-pound Kharlamov had also been beaten badly in a postgame fight with the New England Whalers' Rick Ley during one of the games from the 1974 version of the Summit Series.

Halfway through the first period, Ed Van Impe—a Saskatoon native who previously had wrestled with Clarke in the Chicago Stadium seats and who been a Black Hawk defenseman 10 years earlier as a rookie—knocked Kharlamov to the ice with a tremendous hit. Kharlamov was in the process of receiving the puck in front of the Philadelphia net, so the timing on the check was legal, but the blow also came mostly from behind, and with Van Impe's forearms thrust into the back of Kharlamov's head.

When Van Impe's act went unpenalized, Red Army coach Konstantin Lotkev became enraged and took his team off the ice, at which point Lotkev himself was whistled for a delay-of-game penalty by the referee when he called them over to the bench. The Russians then retreated to the dressing room, none of whom wanted to return—as confirmed by their star goalie Vladislav Tretiak.

"No Red Army player wanted to play against the Philadelphia Flyers," Tretiak said. "Each of us could have been hit from behind, cross-checked, kicked—what kind of sport was this? It had nothing at all in common with the sport of hockey... The Stanley Cup winners demonstrated their highly unfriendly, if not hostile, attitude. Nobody came over to welcome us [before the game]."

In a short time, however, the Soviets returned to the game when informed they would not be paid if they did not finish the evening's play. Some writers felt that Van Impe's check was nothing beyond a strong hit commonly seen in a typical NHL game, and that Kharlamov's subsequent sprawl to the ice was planned acting—directed by his superiors—in an effort to illustrate to the world what they viewed as the "barbaric" North American version of hockey. (Van Impe himself later claimed that he had dealt many other harder hits in his professional career.)

Clearly shaken, the Central Red Army lost that evening for the only time on their North American tour, by a 4–1 score. Tretiak was pounded with 49 shots as the physical Flyers dominated the play in the Soviets' zone, while Philadelphia goalie Wayne Stephenson (subbing for the injured Bernie Parent) handled a mere 13 tries during the entire contest.

Thus, once again it was the unfortunate Kharlamov who was placed at the center of a geopolitical sports battle. One of the greatest players the game has ever known, Kharlamov would be struck again by violence both on and off the ice. A few months later, injuries from his involvement in an automobile accident would prevent his playing in the Canada Cup tournament. He had helped lead the Soviets to the gold medal in the Winter Olympics in February, just after the Soviets' tour of North America. Five years later, another auto collision would take Kharlamov's life at the age of 33. In 2005 he was posthumously inducted into the Hockey Hall of Fame, while the Kharlamov Trophy was established to recognize the top Russian player in the NHL each season, as voted upon by the Russians in the league at the time.

• • •

Just a week after their victory over the Soviets, the Flyers would face an opponent which would prove to be even tougher—the resurgent Chicago Black Hawks, and the return of their passionate director of the blue line, Keith Magnuson.

By the time the two-time defending Stanley Cup–champion Philadelphia team took the ice at the Stadium on January 18, the Hawks had lost only once in their last 11 games. Reay's club met the Flyers with a vengeance. "The Black Hawks not only took the usual punishment meted out by the Philadelphia Flyers," decided a newly impressed Verdi about the team's aggressiveness that evening, "but kept their team on the ice for 60 minutes to down the Stanley Cup champions 2–0 in a brilliant Stadium checkoff."

Magnuson had led the charge in the shutout for Esposito, once again throwing fists with Dave Schultz to the delight of the Chicago crowd. Magnuson emerged the bloodier combatant once again after yet another beating from the Philadelphia enforcer, but he got such a roar from the crowd that Verdi claimed "he could have bumped Dick

Daley in a mayoral election if a vote had been taken on the scene." Despite Schultz's reputation growing with each season, Magnuson showed no signs of backing down—from him nor anyone else. "One thing you've got to have to be a success in this league can't be taught," Keith would say. "The ingredient is guts—and this means not being afraid of anyone."

As Verdi continued with his column, he illustrated how Magnuson, as usual, also deflected any laurels. "But Magnuson, Chicago's spiritual leader, accepted no praises afterward," he wrote. "Instead, he pointed his swollen hand to the cubicle of Tony Esposito… 'Don't talk about the fight,' said Maggie. 'There's a guy who's more important to talk about… He is the big reason we are where we are.'"

As he had been in previous seasons of overuse, Esposito was noticeably fatigued, having started his 19th straight game that night in posting the 56th shutout of his career, as well as his fourth of the season. And while the approaching All-Star break would be a welcome rest for him, Hawks players Marks and Russell wondered why Esposito was not invited to the All-Star Game as they had been. After the win against Philly in the Stadium, the Hawks won three of their next four as well to lift their record to 21–11–16.

Schultz was amazed that Magnuson kept coming after him season after season—a factor which can even wear on the aggressor, as pointed out by Jim Wiste. "If I was a tough guy on another team," Wiste offered, "I wouldn't want to fight Maggie. You could beat him five times, and he'd get you on the sixth." But to Keith, it was simply a job that needed to be done.

"He once said to me that I was nuts to keep coming back," Magnuson said of Schultz. "But I look at it like if you go down to block a shot and you catch it in the face. The next day in practice you work on doing it so the next time it doesn't hurt. It's the same way with an altercation."

It was the final timc that the two seasoned fighters would square off.

After their playing days were over, Schultz and Magnuson became good friends, as the respect was mutual. "He wasn't dirty," Schultz said in admiration of Chicago defenseman in reflecting upon the countless times they collided on the ice. Magnuson, his longtime nemesis claimed, was different from many other players around the league; the red-haired kid from Saskatchewan invariably performed his duties with honor. "He could have hit me [many times] from the side," Schultz would remember, "but there was no way."

Upon his return to the lineup, the cheers Magnuson heard once again from the Stadium crowd were not just the result of his scrapping. He was getting recognized around Chicago and beyond as a gentleman and a philanthropist off the ice, performing charitable functions above and beyond what was typically done by athletes. As an example, he had recently received a call from a man he did not know, named Robert DeAngeles, whose 12-year-old son was undergoing surgery for a malignant tumor at Gottlieb Hospital in Maywood, a nearby suburb. Magnuson drove through an intense Chicago snowstorm to reach the hospital, and then gladly spent an hour with the boy. "We'll never forget what a good guy [Magnuson] was," the boy's brother, Steven DeAngeles, would say years later.

The charge the Hawks mustered in the middle of the season ultimately enabled them to finish in first place in the Smythe Division—by the narrowest of margins—in 1976, edging out the Canucks by a single point by virtue of a 7–2 dismantling of the St. Louis Blues on the final day of the season. Along the way, Tallon set a Chicago record for a defenseman during the season with 62 points on 15 goals and 47 assists.

The Hawks were paired up in the first round of the playoffs against their old postseason adversary the Canadiens, who were on the brink of beginning a stretch of complete league domination. Magnuson still maintained his tradition of being the first one charging out the door to hit the ice after the goaltender as the Hawks came out of the locker room, now with Russell and Grant Mulvey usually right behind him. "Going a hundred miles an hour," Montreal center Doug Risebrough had noticed of Maggie doing his ritual in the previous season, Risebrough's first in the NHL. "I remember my rookie year I thought he was going to come right at me and hit me [during warm-ups]."

The Hawks, completely overwhelmed by the mass of talent that the Canadiens had assembled, wound up scoring only three total goals in a four-game sweep by Montreal. And in the fourth game on April 18, White would suffer an eventual career-ending neck injury.

The Hawks still appeared to be in a holding pattern, stuck between relishing past glories with their veterans and the incorporation of talented new youngsters. Thus, looking to bolster the team's star power after the departure of Bobby Hull, the Wirtz family saw an opportunity to claim a damaged luminary from another team—one of the game's greats with, hopefully, some of his magic still remaining.

For all intents and purposes, the Boston hockey club had been prepared to make Bobby Orr a Bruin for life. In the fall of 1975, terms were announced that set forth a new 10-year contract extension for Orr that would pay him more than $4 million. However, after the extraordinary player made his delayed season debut on November 8 (the day after Phil Esposito had been traded to the Rangers), Orr learned he would need to have another surgery on his shattered knee just three weeks later. At that point, the club wished to renegotiate the previous offer, exchanging a large chunk of his player's salary with nearly 19 percent ownership of the team coming to Orr by 1980. He was talked out of the deal by his agent, Alan Eagleson, who claimed it was in Orr's best interest to stay out of the management side of the game.

Orr was ultimately granted free agency; and thus Bill Wirtz saw an opportunity for what he viewed as a surefire boost for the sagging attendance at Hawks games at the Stadium. He moved in on Orr and offered a five-year contract worth $3 million; it was accepted and finalized on June 8, 1976. The once-indivisible marriage between Orr and Boston was now over, and the Bruins would receive no form of compensation from the Hawks in signing him. With their two top stars now playing elsewhere, the irate Boston fans threatened to boycott games at the Garden.

While perhaps a better long-term strategy for lengthening his NHL career would have been to use the summer and early fall of 1976 to heal his knee, Orr felt compelled to follow a greater short-term purpose. Like Magnuson, he had missed the entire Summit Series in 1972 and 1974 because of earlier problems with the knee, and Orr knew that time was running out to represent his home country in international play. Thus, after signing the contract, he sought and received permission from Wirtz to participate in the 1976 Canada Cup, which offered NHL stars another high-profile shot at the Soviets.

The tournament would be much broader than the Summit Series, involving teams from multiple nations—including an American contingent. Team Canada and the Soviets were naturally considered the favorites, and the two met in the last round-robin contest on September 11 to see which would proceed to the finals against Czechoslovakia. In front of a packed house at Maple Leaf Gardens in Toronto, Orr—who could barely walk into the arena from the parking lot because of the soreness in his knee—powered the Canadians to a 3–1 win over the Russians, as well a two-game sweep of the Czechs in the best-of-three final round. The wounded Orr put forth a heroic effort and was named the tournament MVP, tying for the overall lead with nine points on two goals and seven assists. As his Canadian teammate

Sittler concluded about the games, "Bobby Orr was better on one leg than anyone else was on two."

The gutsy display furthered Magnuson's respect for Orr's toughness; despite their several run-ins over the years in the great rivalry between the Bruins and the Hawks, the two men, now teammates, admired one another's gritty play.

As training camp for the 1976–77 season opened for the Black Hawks and exhibition games began soon after, Orr would need to inform Reay—rumored to be retiring after the conclusion of the season—shortly before each game if his knee was ready for action on the particular night. It therefore became a mystery to Black Hawks fans heading to the Stadium each evening as to whether or not they would get to view the living legend in action—which, while no fault of Orr's, somewhat defeated the purpose Wirtz had in signing him in the first place.

Attendance had recently been down all around hockey, and the presence of Orr on the Hawks' roster, to the surprise of many, did not help much in Chicago either. In the first two Sunday night home games for the season, less than two-thirds of the Stadium was full. More than 13,000 had seen the Hawks play an exhibition game in Denver with Orr in uniform (against the new Colorado Rockies, formerly the Scouts, which had played just two seasons in Kansas City), but only 7,000 attendees returned just two weeks later for a regular season rematch between the two teams (the high attendance for the exhibition contest was perhaps due to the "2-for-1" ticket giveaway night that evening).

Denver, while long a bastion of collegiate hockey, was looking to reestablish itself at the professional level in opening a sparkling new rink, McNichols Arena. Magnuson was happy to return to the scene of his undergraduate glory. "The record for pro hockey in Denver is not good," Keith admitted, "but once the people who followed college hockey come out, they should get caught up in the excitement of the NHL."

By the following spring of 1977, few teams around the NHL would see improvement at the gate. At that time, Hawks publicity director Don Murphy even had to expel a film crew from the Stadium when it compiled footage of the many empty seats at the games; an independent filmmaker was trying to use the images to contrast the scene with pictures of the building being filled during seasons past. In mid-October 1976, Elvis Presley had returned to the Stadium to gave two of his last live performances—two of the few times over the coming months when the building would be full.

Scoring also became less and less frequent, which did not help in attendance matters. Tommy Ivan and Reay decided that until the young forwards came further along, it was best for the team to continue emphasizing a defensive strategy. But a horrific injury would derail Magnuson's season once again, in an attack many would term as "cowardly" on the part of an opponent.

On October 30, 1976, in a game at the Olympia in Detroit, Magnuson was harassing the Red Wings' Mike Bloom near the boards midway through the final period. In doing so, Magnuson got his stick up on Bloom by accident, an anomaly for him, and something which he later admitted doing in this particular case. Watching from across the ice was Bryan Watson, the policeman of the Red Wings, who charged the width of the rink to come to Bloom's aid. With Magnuson mostly facing the opposite direction, Watson cross-checked the Chicago defenseman to the side of the face, and Keith's jaw was broken once again. With Magnuson sprawled on the ice, the other Hawks players angrily surrounded Watson with their sticks pointed in his direction. The Code had been breached.

"It's the worst thing I've ever seen in hockey," Reay said simply after the game.

Before making that statement to the press, the coach had chased referee John McAuley down the corridor of the arena to give him another earful and telephoned Campbell at the NHL's head office as well.

"And for however long Keith is out, that's how long Watson should be out," Reay claimed, citing Magnuson's incident with Oddleifson from a couple years back after which the Vancouver club made the same appeal. "There's no place for what Watson did, and no place for Watson in this league."

Added Tallon, "It's the cheapest shot I've ever seen." Marks warned, "Watson better keep his head up the next time we play." Mulvey, sitting on the Chicago bench at the time of the incident, filed it away, ready to confront Watson at the right time.

While sitting on an examination table at a Detroit hospital and spitting out words sporadically with a jaw that would have to be wired shut, Magnuson tried to reconstruct the event and, despite repeated deliberations, could not comprehend Watson's action.

"If I'd been going around the league doing things like that myself, I could understand it. But I've never taken any cheap shots at anybody. I always try to drop my stick and I never get a guy from behind. I've never even had any real run-ins with Watson."

After having the jaw set, Keith was able to immediately return to the team's hotel and join them on the flight home.

Watson ultimately received a 10-game suspension for the hit—after which he would be traded to the Washington Capitals—while Magnuson would only miss four games; he was able to play with a football-like face mask to protect the jaw, like ones previously donned by Bobby Hull and Kenny Wharram when sustaining similar injuries.

Interestingly, Watson would later claim that he was being unfairly targeted by Campbell, whom Watson insisted was being pressured by

Ontario attorney general Roy McMurtry. McMurtry was currently pursuing assault charges against Dave "Tiger" Williams, and, along with his brother, Bill, was still on a personal crusade to stamp out unnecessary violence in hockey. As for Watson's theory, Campbell replied, "Bryan Watson isn't the most reliable guy I know. I wouldn't take his word for anything."

During Magnuson's brief absence, Orr had gotten off to a strong start in posting 23 points in 20 games, and the Hawks stood with an even 9–9–2 record by mid-November. But both men were two wounded grizzlies, fending off surrounding hunters in the NHL's black forest as their bodies creaked with pain. Orr's knee finally gave out for good in the late fall (even though Reay stated in early November that Orr "will be back with us in less than two weeks"); he would miss the rest of the season, all of the 1977–78 campaign, and would play in only six contests early in the autumn of 1978 before calling it quits for good.

The person upon whom both Orr and Magnuson had come to regularly rely—Hawks trainer Skip Thayer—had been nicknamed "Superman" by the players for his resemblance to Clark Kent. But even the caped superhero could not have gotten the team through a rash of key injuries that would impact the 1976–77 season—injuries which would help bring about a monumental change in the organization.

• • •

Christmastime in Chicago, 1976. The air becomes more biting as the shoppers finish their searching and scrambling along Michigan Avenue and State Street, pausing only to gaze at the marvelous seasonal displays in the windows of Marshall Field & Co.

But amidst the holiday rush, the city was rocked by startling news on December 20. While in to see his physician for a routine checkup,

Mayor Richard J. Daley suffered a heart attack. The medical staff on the scene was unable to revive him, and Chicago's leader of 21 years was dead at the age of 74.

The Black Hawks had been in Minnesota at the time for a one-game road trip. The team scratched out a 3–3 tie with the North Stars on the night of December 21, which nonetheless kept them winless in their last 11 games; their overall record stood at a dismal 10–19–5 after being at the .500 mark before Orr went down.

The team arrived late back in Chicago after the game to find the somber city streets respectfully quiet after a soft snowfall. Heading into his office at the Stadium the next morning, Reay noticed that the flags around the city had been lowered to half-staff. Reay wanted to get an early start on his work, looking for some angle that would snap his team out of its doldrums.

Unbeknownst to him, a meeting had taken place among several of the franchise's power brokers while the team was in Minnesota. Bill Wirtz and Ivan had instructed Mikita, Orr, and White (all injured and not in uniform) to meet them at the Bismarck Hotel before the rest of the team got back to town.

"I looked at Bobby [Orr] and asked him, in pantomime, what was going on," Mikita recounted of the odd scene. "He pointed to White. He was the new coach. Bobby and I were going to be his assistants."

Reay, the Hawks coach for 14 seasons, had been fired.

"It was all very strange, and it got even weirder when we were in the meeting and heard that Mayor Richard Daley had just died," Mikita continued.

Verdi would write in his column a couple of days later that the Hawks informed the media of the move "in a 10-paragraph press release which not once mentioned Reay's name."

The *Tribune* writer also noted that, only a month earlier, Wirtz had publicly labeled Reay as "the best coach in the business" and that there had been plans for Reay to soon take over for Ivan as general manager. This, too, was now out of the question. Reportedly, Reay declined the offer of the general manager's position when told by Wirtz that he would not be allowed to name his own head coach. (According to Dennis Hull, Wirtz had wanted Bobby Kromm installed—who had been coaching the Winnipeg Jets in the WHA after Bobby Hull had completed his stint in that role as coach in Reay's place. Kromm would not take the job, but would surface as the head man of the Detroit Red Wings the following season.)

"It's against everything we stand for—firing people in the middle of the season, firing people during the holidays," explained Wirtz of Reay's expulsion. "But it had to be done… We need to get this thing straightened out right away."

Soon after, however, it was discovered that the team's administration had not informed Reay of his dismissal in person, but instead by slipping a note under his office door.

"That's a rotten way to treat a guy who been in your organization for 17 years," said one player under the condition of anonymity. Then, the player rethought the words he wished to use.

"I'll take that back. It's a disgrace."

On the contrary, it was also reported that some on the Chicago roster felt Reay's time had come.

"Three years ago, almost no Hawk players would have dared questioned Reay's modus operandi," wrote Verdi. "But lately, there have been whispers here and whispers there that other teams were passing the Hawks by because of better systems."

White, at the age of 37, assumed the title of interim head coach for the rest of the season. Reay ended his NHL career with 542 wins, second in league history at the time.

Mikita did not have any plans to coach, but for the good of the team he reluctantly agreed to be an assistant while continuing to play as well. Before the team had a morning workout on Wednesday, December 22, Mikita had a brief, closed-door meeting with Reay from which, according to Verdi, Stan emerged wet in the eyes.

"Deep down, I really believed that if this group of players was not going to produce for Billy Reay, they weren't going to play for anybody," he wrote. "When White was asked what his first move would be as head coach, he responded, 'I'm going to take all my doors off their hinges [to prevent any further notes under the coach's office door].'"

White's next move was to name the universally respected Keith Magnuson as his captain (Mikita had started the year as Reay's captain, but had to surrender the role in becoming a player-coach). But even this serious shift in the organization's structure did not come without White pulling one more of his famous pranks, with poor Maggie on the receiving end one last time.

"I called him [Magnuson] and asked to have dinner with Keith and his wife, Cindy," White remembered. "We had a nice meal, then I told Keith I wanted him to be our captain. He deserved it. He was very happy about it, I think. Then I got up and left him with the check. Why shouldn't he pay for dinner? He's our captain, right?"

Reay, meanwhile, quickly adjusted to his new reality. "I sort of had a feeling that, the way things were, there might be a change," he told the Chicago papers two days after his dismissal. "I'll never have any bad words to say about Billy Wirtz. Never. Did the players let me down by not putting out? Oh, I could never say that. I don't think that."

Then, motioning with his hand toward the other side of the hall from his office in the Stadium, he added, "I only wish the guys in that locker room the best of luck."

For several veterans on the Hawks roster, including Magnuson and Dennis Hull, Reay was the only NHL coach they had ever known. Hull himself admitted an immediate desire to quit the game he loved after Reay was fired, especially for the way in which the change had transpired.

The new coaching plan met with skepticism in the Chicago press. "This year [the Hawks] gambled heavily on Bobby Orr's knees and the gamble appears to be lost," Robert Markus of the *Tribune* summarized. "The crowds have fallen off alarmingly and perhaps that panicked Bill Wirtz into making a move. The move seems pointless. It had already been announced that Reay would retire at the end of the season."

When a friend reminded Reay that now he could at least celebrate New Year's Eve in the coming week without any work obligations, Reay responded, "Yeah, but like Tony Esposito says, 'I'd rather play. It costs less.'"

Shortly after the holidays, more rumors started to swirl. The new gossip was that Bob Pulford of the Los Angeles Kings was Wirtz's choice to take over the team on a permanent basis, perhaps as the general manager in addition to being the head coach.

Temporarily unavailable to the team while his jaw continued to heal, Magnuson began watching the Hawks games from the press box at the Stadium. On February 9, 1977, Watson and the Washington Capitals came to Chicago, and as Maggie looked on from high above, one of his teammates would once again illustrate that there was no statute of limitations in handing out hockey justice.

With four minutes left in the second period, Mulvey finally got his first shift of the night. Immediately after hopping over the boards, he dashed all the way across the ice from his right wing position to Watson's spot on right defense for the Capitals. Mulvey then proceeded to bombard Watson with a wave of punches, taking the Washington player down to the surface of the Stadium. Mulvey was promptly ejected for launching the attack, but to him, the price was well worth it. The location of the fight was only a few strides away from the gate that led down the stairs to the Chicago locker room, and hearty cheers from the partisan crowd carried him off.

Upon seeing what Mulvey had done, Magnuson sprang up from his seat and was seen bolting out of the press box. And even before Mulvey had made the short trip out the gate and down the 21 stairs to the Hawks clubhouse, Maggie was already there waiting for him, "teeth clenched and wired shut," according to Mulvey. Grateful for what "Granny" had done, Keith gave him "the biggest hug and welcomed me into his inner circle. That was our bonding moment," Mulvey would say years later.

Watson, meanwhile, did not think that Mulvey's assault was in retaliation for what he had done to Magnuson. "Naw, I don't think that," Watson was quoted by the *Tribune* after the game. "Mulvey is a pretty straight shooter and it was his first shift on the ice, so he probably was just letting out his frustration."

The captaincy that White had granted to Magnuson—and which was fully endorsed by the players—actually would be short-lived. Magnuson was forced to give up the title for the remainder of the year when he encountered yet one more devastating injury, a ruptured Achilles' tendon later in February which would cause him to miss the last three months of the schedule. Martin donned the *C* on his sweater in his place.

• • •

If ever a lame-duck finish to a season was visited upon the Chicago Black Hawks, it came about in the spring of 1977. They nudged their way into the playoffs, but once again suffered a quick exit.

As part of the bizarre chain of events witnessed over the past few months, one of the Hawks' home playoffs games against the New York Islanders actually had to be played on the road. On April 7, the

Chicago Stadium had been previously booked for a Led Zeppelin rock concert, which the management of the band and the building were unwilling to cancel or reschedule.

It had been alleged that Chicago's front office had the option of buying out the concert and moving it to another date, but instead decided to allow the Hawks to play the entire series on the road—which infuriated the players.

"It's almost as though the people upstairs decided to write us off completely," second-year defenseman Bob Murray bluntly said, in doing so "summing up the sentiments of 17 other players," according to Neil Milbert. Much of the players' anger stemmed largely from the fact that the Islanders had been in nearly the same predicament, but that the New York ownership had found negotiating room. The Bugs Bunny Easter Show was set for the Nassau County Coliseum during the playoff series dates; and while it was perhaps not the same task as rearranging a Led Zeppelin tour, the Islanders nonetheless worked out an agreement with the show's organizers to postpone the famous rabbit's performance for another time.

So, while Robert Plant, Jimmy Page, and the rest of the band played on in Chicago, the Islanders won the transported playoff game on their own ice and then swept the opening-round, best-of-three series.

It was the end of a nightmarish few months that Magnuson, like most of the Hawks, was happy to have behind him.

"One afternoon, following a typically dull Hawk effort," Verdi had noted, "the ailing Magnuson, complete with crutches, drove from his suburban domicile and talked to his teammates. His message, delivered behind closed doors, was a call to arms, and appeal to pride." It was a task Maggie felt compelled to do. "It was my role as captain to say something," he stated, even though the on-ice duties of the captaincy had been transferred to Martin. "I know not everybody appreciated it. Everything was said for one reason—to get people thinking about winning."

In addition to recovering from his latest round of injuries, Magnuson had lumbered through his only "negative" season to date in terms of the plus-minus statistic, logging a -11. And while Orr, Mikita, and White had top-shelf hockey acumen, the "tri-coaches" system (as Mikita mockingly called it) essentially failed, as some compared it to the infamous "College of Coaches" experiment of the Chicago Cubs from the early 1960s, in which Cubs owner Phil Wrigley decided to use a collection of men who took turns managing the team.

A true fresh start was needed. The Wirtz family looked to the outside, and found the man they wanted.

• • •

Considered a rising star behind the bench, Bob Pulford—a former player for Reay in Toronto—was indeed the organization's choice, as had been rumored. He would fill both titles of head coach and general manager once the 1977 playoffs had reached its conclusion, with Ivan moving into a new role as a team vice president.

A fervent disciple of the defensive aspects of hockey, Pulford was a rarity in the modern era of professional sports, having leapt straight from his last season as a player (1971–72) directly into a head coaching job (1972–73). After hovering around the .500 mark in his first two seasons in Los Angeles, Pulford's Kings exploded in 1975 with 105 points—still the highest total in franchise history, even with the modern advent of the "overtime loss" point in today's standings. Pulford directed a balanced offensive attack (11 players with double-digit goal totals) and enjoyed stellar goaltender play from Rogatien "Rogie" Vachon as Pulford was named the NHL Coach of the Year. Vachon, a former starter in the nets for Montreal, would also be an impregnable wall in 1976 for Team Canada in the Canada Cup, posting two shutouts and a 1.39 goals-against average in challenging Orr for the MVP honors for the tournament. Interestingly, it was also a young Vachon whom Pulford, while the latter was playing for the Maple Leafs, had beaten with an overtime goal in Game 3 of the 1967 Stanley Cup Finals.

The hiring of Pulford in Chicago raised few impressed eyebrows across the sport and drew little praise, despite the coach's relatively quick success in elevating the Kings. "Pulford's defensive style should be as big a bore as Billy Reay's used to be," wrote Stan Fischler, "which figures to keep fans away from Chicago Stadium once more."

However, with the Stadium rink still smaller (188' x 85') than other NHL arenas, some thought that the hiring of a defensive-minded coach was the correct path to take until the Stadium was replaced with a new, standard-sized facility.

"I'm really excited about our new coach," Magnuson said in support of Pulford. "I think some of our pride is returning, and that's what we've lacked more than anything in the last few years. He has a great mind for detail. Very organized."

Mikita, like Orr, would thus relinquish his short-lived role as a player-coach and return to being a player only. (By December 1977, the 29-year-old Orr was a front office man for Hawks without any official title; after his sixth knee operation in the preceding summer, doctors advised him to take a full year of rest before seeing if he could play again.) Mikita admitted that an animosity had existed between him and Pulford during their playing days, and he wondered if he would be next to follow Reay out of Chicago.

"One night in the [Los Angeles/Inglewood] Forum," Mikita recalled about a particular encounter with Pulford, "we got into it in the penalty box. We were both thrown out of the game, so we went toward our dressing rooms. Before we reached our destinations, we crossed paths and had a stick fight in the hallway... I didn't think our rivalry would continue, but it did. At least it did from his point of view."

Once Pulford's hiring was made public, Mikita figured that his days as a member of the Hawks were numbered, and he was, at least in part, correct. For Mikita soon got his own note under the door: a contract renewal offer from Pulford—one of his first actions while wearing the general manager's hat—with a 75 percent pay cut, which, not unlike Reay's firing, did not arrive to Mikita in person but through a secondary party.

"I learned of that through my agent," Mikita revealed, "whom I didn't talk to for three weeks because he said he was too embarrassed to call."

In the end, however, Mikita struck a deal that maintained his 1976–77 salary after getting Bill Wirtz involved in the discussion with Pulford about the contract.

It appeared that Pulford was seeking to immediately reshape the roster in his own image. No one on the team was safe—not even Esposito, one of the game's all-time great goaltenders. Pulford, not sold on backup Mike Veisor as a long-term solution, looked to install the team's future goalie—whomever it may be—between the pipes. Pulford was perhaps focused on Esposito's downturn in play during the 1976–77 season, in which his goals-against average skyrocketed to 3.45, the likes of which he had never reached before. His teammates, however—especially those who had been around him the longest—had not had their faith shaken in their netminder.

"I was never worried," Magnuson reflected on Esposito's struggles during that period. "Tony didn't sulk when things were going bad. He just worked harder. A real man, I tell you. Tony is a winner."

Veisor, serving as Esposito's understudy for the previous three years, had learned many things from his mentor. Included among these lessons was one that came at a team practice session in November 1977, when Veisor witnessed Esposito being struck in the eye with a slap shot that shattered the old-fashioned, form-fitting mask that Esposito and most goalies of the era still wore. In seeing the limited protection those masks actually offered, Veisor chose to become one of the first North American goaltenders to wear a cage-style mask, which would become popular in the NHL in the 1980s and which had been already donned by many European goalies. "You'd never get me to wear one of them, with all that weight and padding around the head," a defiant, old-school Esposito said of the new style that Veisor soon was wearing. Esposito did agree to compromise, however, as the serious injury prompted him to install small bars near the eyeholes of his old mask for more protection in the final years of his career.

One of Pulford's first targets to acquire from the outside was J. Bob Kelly, an effort to add more toughness to the forward lines along with the feisty existing collection of Mulvey, Darcy Rota, Koroll, Ivan Boldirev, and Ted Bulley. Kelly was the man who was involved in the "taped hand" controversy in his fight with Magnuson three years earlier, and did help the team start the fall of '77 with more spirit; unfortunately, the end result was much of the same. With Magnuson again missing time early in the season by reinjuring the bad elbow in training camp, the Hawks once more limped to first place in a weak Smythe Division with a record barely over .500 (32–29–19), and were also once again whipped in the first round of the playoffs—this time at the hands of the Bruins in a four-game sweep.

The Hawks had perhaps been psychologically damaged by the Bruins after a 7–0 thrashing at the Boston Garden in late March, a game which Magnuson and Russell both missed with knee problems and in which talented rookie defenseman Doug Wilson would be limited to the first period only with a badly sprained ankle. In the team's previous meeting at the Stadium in February, Magnuson was injured four minutes into the game when Boston's John Wensink nearly knocked him out cold with a blindsiding hit. When the playoffs were over in late April, Magnuson would have a second surgery on his battered right knee.

The Hawks carried over their listless performance into the fall of 1978. Orr had to hang up his skates for good, with his final point coming on October 28 on a goal against the Red Wings in Detroit. Four days later, on November 1, the Vancouver Canucks—after many years of struggling in games in the Stadium—walked into town and left with their fifth victory in their last seven games in Chicago. Boos were heard all evening long from the small crowd that gathered.

Magnuson and Mikita, two of the veteran leaders left on the club, did their best to provide instances of inspiration. One such moment came on December 9 in St. Louis (in the Checkerdome, the newly named facility that for decades had been known as the St. Louis Arena before its purchase by the Ralston-Purina Company) when Magnuson notched his first goal of the season on a beautifully won faceoff from Mikita, the latter's 900th assist in his glorious career.

Magnuson was finding the daily physical pain to be less and less bearable, and he was still going down to the ice to block shots, still shoving players out from in front of Esposito, and still going after the other team's toughest players in the corners. But at the behest of his wife, Cindy, Magnuson had starting wearing a helmet to protect himself against more blows to the head in fights that were sure to come—and as always, Keith honored her wishes. Her fears were well founded; after playing in every game on the schedule his rookie season of 1969–70, Magnuson would never play an entire Hawks schedule again.

"He would still take a puck to the face," Verdi had written the past autumn, "even if it meant another fracture of the jaw. And he would still drop his gloves to fight for another mate, even if it meant a fat lip, a roamin' nose, or a trip to the dentist. Literally, he bleeds for his team."

Exactly two weeks after Magnuson recorded the goal in St. Louis, the Flyers came to the Stadium once again, two days before Christmas, in what promised to be another physical, holiday-season battle between the two platoons. Magnuson, with all his aches and pains, knew he would be called upon to do the policing yet again. But in this matchup, many of the familiar faces wearing the Philadelphia logo would not be present.

The Flyers were, like the Hawks, another club in renewal as the 1970s came to a close, attempting to climb back to prominence after their two Stanley Cup championships in 1974 and 1975. Schultz was long gone from the team, having spent the past three years in Los Angeles and Pittsburgh, with dwindling ice time in suiting up for those organizations. Instead, Philadelphia went in the same direction that the Hawks had gone in 1969—by turning to a rookie defenseman as their new enforcer. His name was Behn Wilson; and like Schultz, Garry Howatt, Tiger Williams, and other similar players early in their NHL careers, Wilson sought out Magnuson when playing the Hawks in an attempt to more quickly establish a league-wide reputation as a fighter.

The fireworks began when the Flyers' talented 21-year-old goalie, Pete Peeters, slashed Rota in front of the Philadelphia net. Wilson shoved Rota as a follow-up message, and then Mulvey came over and took a shot at Wilson—for which Mulvey was ejected, deemed as the third man in on a fight that had not really begun. Mulvey, a big, strong player with scoring ability, was taking a leadership role in providing the kind of player Pulford had wanted to integrate into the forward lines.

"[Referee Bryan] Lewis told me later he made a bad call," Magnuson revealed after the game about the Mulvey ejection, getting word from the official as he was once again the captain. "The original thing was between the goalie and Rota. If anything, Wilson was [the] third man in. Mulvey just came in after Wilson got Rota, and Wilson didn't even get a penalty for that."

After Clarke and Marks tussled with each other after a whistle at 10:21 of the second period, Magnuson finally caught up with Wilson (as Wilson felt he now had to come to Clarke's assistance, as Schultz had done for many years). The Chicago veteran grabbed a hold of Wilson's jersey and "danced" with him for over a minute, giving Wilson an earful—likely an oral lesson for the rookie in learning about the NHL world. Lewis, shouting over the shoulders of his linesmen who were trying to separate Magnuson and Wilson, warned both players that each would get a 10-minute misconduct penalty if the dancing and jawing continued. Magnuson then let fly with a couple of rights that staggered the first-year player momentarily, but Wilson then capitalized on his larger size and downed Maggie with several hard shots.

J. Bob Kelly—once a hated foe of Magnuson but now an ally—then got ejected in the same manner as Mulvey for being a third man in while trying to help Keith. "I was just sitting on the bench when Bob Murray next to me said, 'Hey, we're a man short out there,'" Kelly said. "I just hopped out in case we needed help."

It was yet another of the countless confrontations that Magnuson had endured to inspire his team. He may not have won the fight, but his mere courage in "showing up" for it goaded the Hawks on to victory once again. An appreciative crowd of 14,197 at the Stadium—one of the larger seen there in recent months—was on hand for the 5–2 Chicago triumph that snapped a seven-game winless streak. The fans left no doubt that Magnuson's efforts had spurred them on, as the contest had lasted over three hours, the spectators' loyalty and rage so often escalated that a carpet of trash littered the Stadium ice in protest of officials' calls on three different occasions. The Hawks typically moribund offense, meanwhile, had jumped on Peeters early. The young goalie would become one of the NHL's best in the 1980s, but nonetheless appeared lackadaisical in the opening stages of this contest according to reports from the *Tribune*, giving up two quick goals that put the Flyers in an early hole.

Just as he had been in his jovial rookie season 10 years earlier, Magnuson was all smiles in the locker room, knowing that his enthusiasm had carried his team on the evening.

But he did not know that it would be his last fight in an NHL regular season game.

In the very next contest—on December 27, 1978, in the Stadium against the Blues—Magnuson and the Hawks were scrambling to protect a 4–3 lead in the last minute. As players for both sides jockeyed for position in front of the Chicago net, Magnuson collided with Harvey Bennett of St. Louis, and Bennett fell on top of him. The awkward toppling collapsed Magnuson's right knee yet again, and he lay immobile on the ice as the rest of the Hawks proceeded to hold on in the remaining seconds for the win.

After the horn sounded, cheers for the victory from the Stadium crowd waned as attention shifted to the player sprawled in the Hawks' zone. As spectators were leaving the Stadium over the next few minutes, Magnuson would be carted off the surface and then to the hospital where, that very same night, he underwent his third operation on the knee and his second in the past eight months. Rookie defenseman Mike O'Connell would be promoted from New Brunswick of the American Hockey League to take his place on the roster, making him the first Chicago-born player ever to play for the Hawks (despite spending much of his childhood in the Boston area).

With the latest blow to his knee, Magnuson seriously wrestled with the idea of retirement for the first time. The knee had been causing him further problems, even before the Bennett collision.

"It bothered me this season that I couldn't do some of the things I used to do, that I couldn't play as physically tough as I want to," he said. "And it bothered me that I felt I wasn't contributing like I should. When we had back-to-back games, or four games in five nights, the knee got sore—even when we were playing with six defensemen. "I wouldn't want to go through that again… I have some serious thinking to do."

The rest of the team was greatly troubled with the possibility of their leader being permanently sidelined.

"There isn't a player on this team who doesn't completely respect him. Or in the league," said Phil Russell. "The thought of him retiring…I don't even want to think of it."

As for Pulford, he stated that Magnuson "was just starting to play as well as he ever had when he got hurt."

Without Magnuson for the rest of the season, the Hawks' play continued to tail off as Mikita worked with Koroll (both in their final full seasons) to provide some sense of stability to the team. Pulford attempted to jump-start things by acquiring 34-year-old center Mike Walton in January—the same man who had squared off against Magnuson in the latter's first NHL fight in Keith's first exhibition game in Toronto in September 1969. Walton was able to help Chicago secure another lame-duck Smythe Division title—but this time it was even accomplished with a losing record (29–36–15)—and was followed by yet another sweep in the first round of the playoffs, an elimination again being served by Islanders (who, a year later, would end the Canadiens' run of Stanley Cup championships and begin a string of their own).

A gallant effort was turned in by Esposito in that series, who showed flashes of his old brilliant self. He would shut out the dangerous Islanders offense for three straight periods in Game 2 in New York—something that had not happened to the New York team in two and a half years—but yet Chicago fell to Al Arbour's club in overtime. The Hawks had now lost an amazing 16 straight playoff games dating back to the spring of 1975, and Pulford now found himself just as befuddled for answers as Reay had been in his own final seasons.

Magnuson knew he had some difficult decisions to make in the off-season—should he give the knee one more chance, or is the pain too much to endure? Does he call it quits on the game he loves and throw himself full-time into a new line of work?

Pondering these things while driving through the city, Magnuson looked down from the steering wheel for a moment to write one of his famous personal "to-do" notes, reminding himself to send a birthday card to a friend. In doing so, he rear-ended another car and jolted his bad knee—itself a reminder of the painful road to recovery still ahead of him if he wished to play again.

8

Coach Maggie

"There have been many finer athletes in Chicago, but not one finer person."

—Bob Verdi on Keith Magnuson in the *Chicago Tribune*, November 1, 1979

The new career offer outside of hockey Keith Magnuson had received was indeed tantalizing. It was lucrative, stable, and far removed from the nightly bone-crushing hits of the NHL ice.

For the past several off-seasons, he had been a spokesman and Chicago-area salesman for the 7-Up soft drink brand, a position obtained with the help of company vice president Bill O'Rourke and always held for him by the local Joyce Beverage distributorship when the summer months arrived. Always thinking ahead and a great planner, Maggie was happy put his degree in business administration he had earned from the University of Denver to use.

"At first, it was just making appearances at food stores," Magnuson explained. "Then, I took a sales training program and became an account executive."

"When a company such as ours takes on an athlete as an employee," O'Rourke explained, "the first thing people think is that we're doing it to showcase him, that we want him just as window dressing." But it was clear from the start that Magnuson was different. "He handles some of our biggest accounts," O'Rourke continued. "But he does the little things, too. He's ridden the delivery trucks, and he's made a point of getting to know the names of the men who drive the trucks, and the names of their kids. He cares, and the people whom he deals with like him and respect him for it."

In his very first year with the company, Magnuson was given the Chicago-area sales contracts for 7-Up for the chains of Walgreens and the old White Hen convenience stores.

"Maggie has been challenged, and he has responded," O'Rourke concluded. "He's not only intelligent but dedicated. He has a future here for the rest of his life."

With growing knee pain from hockey and his simultaneously growing success with Joyce Beverages, Magnuson had much to ponder over the summer of 1979 regarding his future. "It bothers me that I seem to be getting brittle," he had commented in the fall of 1977, reflecting upon the injuries that were lessening his time on the ice.

More changes were coming to the Black Hawks, and the NHL as a whole, which made Magnuson's future even cloudier.

As the NBA had done with the American Basketball Association a few years earlier, the NHL agreed to absorb some of the teams from the WHA in the fall of 1979 as the latter circuit finally folded. This made many of the players currently on NHL teams vulnerable to the "expansion draft," in which the rosters of the old WHA teams would be stocked, to a certain degree, with existing NHL talent.

To ensure he remained a Hawk, Chicago placed Magnuson on the "protected" list, making him among those ineligible for the draft. The Wirtz family wanted to make certain he stayed with the team, regardless of Magnuson's capacity to return from his knee problems. The Edmonton Oilers, located near Keith's home area in western Canada, had expressed a strong interest in selecting him. But after Magnuson was placed on the protected list, the Oilers instead chose Hawks defenseman Doug Hicks, who had shown promise briefly in Chicago in coming from the Minnesota North Stars, where he had played in every game except one during his first three years in the league.

In the final WHA season, 1978–79, the Oilers had been toppled for the league's last championship by the Winnipeg Jets. The 40-year-old Bobby Hull appeared in only four games for the Jets that season (posting five points in those four games) before announcing his retirement. (Hull would return to hockey, however, once it was announced the team was joining the NHL.) A consolation prize for Edmonton was that one of its players had claimed the WHA's final Rookie of the Year award—the gangly 18-year-old Wayne Gretzky, just acquired from Pat Stapleton's Indianapolis club. Finishing close behind Gretzky in the voting was a 20-year-old defenseman for the Birmingham club named Rob Ramage, who joined Gretzky as the lone rookies named to the WHA's final all-league team at season's end, along with former Hawks defenseman Paul Shmyr.

Edmonton owner Peter Pocklington planned to give the precocious Gretzky a 21-year contract through 1999—and thus have him don the jersey number "99." The teenager's influence was so profound, in fact, that Gretzky could have single-handedly held up the NHL/WHA merger. Pocklington had refused to allow Gretzky to be entered into the expansion (or "merger") draft, which was typically required for all first-year players; not wanting any snags in completing the merger, the NHL relented and permitted the steadfast Pocklington to keep him.

"He's one of those rare individuals who seems to improve with every game," Jets coach Tom McVie said after seeing Gretzky in his first pro season. "You wonder when he's going to stop."

Oilers coach Glen Sather also knew he had something special on his hands. "One of the biggest things about him is his intense desire to be one of the greats," Sather marveled. "Nothing seems to bother him. At 18, he's already exceeded our wildest expectations."

Gretzky continued to take nothing for granted in the future. As his first NHL season approached in the fall of 1979, he would actually be competing for his fifth straight rookie-of-the-year award in five different leagues, including the WHA and the Juniors.

"Each year I've had to prove myself," Gretzky said in the summer of 1979. "Each year they've told me the checking would be tighter, I'd get hit more and wouldn't score. Every year I've been told that I'm going to be run out of the rink. Next year, I'll have to prove myself all over again."

Citing a desire to focus on his general manager duties, Bob Pulford made an exit from the position of head coach of the Black Hawks after a brief two-year tenure. Elevated into his place was Eddie Johnston, who had enjoyed a successful year with the New Brunswick team in attaining 41 wins and a second-place finish in the AHL.

Magnuson felt positive about the change and decided to commit to training camp, going through the initial workouts to gauge the reaction of his knee to the stress. The joint ached with every movement, but Magnuson was able to labor his way through camp, helping a young defenseman named Keith Brown. The Hawks traveled to Montreal to take on the Canadiens in a preseason game on September 22. "I was mentored by him as a roommate, teammate, and a coach," Brown would say of Maggie in 2012. "I was one of the fortunate few."

In Montreal, Magnuson encountered Gilles Lupien, a man whom he had fought the previous March at the Stadium and who at 6'6" was a half foot taller than Keith. In what would be Magnuson's final bout on the ice, Lupien stunned him with several quick rights. By the time Magnuson regained his bearings the fight was already over, leaving him so angry at his failure to record a single punch that he shoved linesman Bob Luther in trying to get back at Lupien after the two were separated, thus receiving a game-misconduct penalty.

Magnuson now knew he was not the same player he had been, but nonetheless went to work each day and gave the best he could.

After the regular season began, the Bruins came to town a month later at the Stadium, on October 28. With Bobby Orr, Phil Esposito, and others from the talented Boston teams of the recent past then departed, new names were beginning to replace the old familiar ones on their roster. Among the fresh faces was a scrappy, 5'8" left wing named Stan Jonathan. The 24-year-old was a willing fighter, and had already proven himself to be a skilled craftsman with his stick as well, having led the NHL in shooting percentage (24 percent) in his rookie season three years earlier.

Shortly into the game, Jonathan set out to test Magnuson, as many others had done in the past 10 years. Bracing himself for yet another round of NHL combat, Magnuson set himself upon the heels of his skates and gave his patented shoulder shrug, readying his body for a bout as he had done hundreds of time before. But then, suddenly and instinctively, he backed away from Jonathan; his body was telling him at that very moment the he had endured enough. Much to the surprise of the crowd, the fight never happened as Magnuson retreated.

Forcing himself through the rest of the game in physical and mental anguish, Magnuson went straight to Pulford's office afterward. And on November 1, 1979, the news of Magnuson's retirement was made public.

The damage to his knee had finally been enough, and the team—for the first time in a decade—would be without its most spirited leader on skates. Though Magnuson was immediately named an assistant coach for Johnston, an era of Chicago hockey was coming to a close.

"From the first night he came bursting through the Stadium runway back in 1969, he never stopped trying. In the end, what more can a fan ask?" questioned Bob Verdi upon hearing what had transpired.

Twenty-five-year old center Terry Ruskowski, in his first season with Chicago but a veteran of five strong WHA seasons (after originally being drafted by the Hawks in 1974), was named the new captain in Magnuson's place. Joining Ruskowski on a formidable new forward line were Grant Mulvey and Rich Preston—the latter having been Ruskowski's teammate in Winnipeg and Houston in the WHA, and like Magnuson, yet another product from the University of Denver program. Soon, the three would become known as the "RPM Line," scoring at a rate not seen from a regular Hawks trio since the glory days of the early 1970s.

But Ruskowski wanted more than just goals. Crowds had continued to fall off at the Stadium, and the new captain wanted them back.

"This is no good," he said in pointing to the empty seats. "This is too good a hockey town, and hockey is too good a sport. I want to see this place full again. I'd like to see hockey back on the front pages of the newspapers and on the TV sports every night."

While the change in philosophy associated with Johnston's style rubbed some of the players the wrong way (including young defenseman Dave Logan, who was traded to Vancouver after he and Johnston get into an argument in the locker room after a game in Edmonton), the team as a whole—with the help of Ruskowski's and Magnuson's new leadership roles—blossomed. The Hawks finished with a much-improved 87 points, their best total in six years. They would also finally break their 16-game playoff losing streak, an unfortunate NHL record, by sweeping the Blues in the first round. They were then knocked out by the Buffalo Sabres, as the RPM Line finished the regular season with 39, 31, and 15 goals respectively for Mulvey, Preston, and Ruskowski (in addition to 26 from gifted newcomer Tom Lysiak, who had come from Atlanta). The energized Ruskowski also finished fifth in the league in penalty minutes with 252, while feeding his linemates often, totaling 55 assists.

As the season concluded, the spring of 1980 also brought the end for the playing days of Cliff Koroll, Magnuson's longtime friend, roommate, and confidant. Koroll joined the Hawks coaching staff as well. In fact, when their playing careers ended, Koroll and Magnuson had donned the Chicago sweater for the exact same span of years (1969 to 1980).

While Magnuson appreciated the opportunity to remain around the ice as a coach, he was torn between professional loyalties; he felt he could no longer split his attention between his two employers. Therefore, as the playoffs came to an end for the team in May, he announced that he was leaving hockey completely behind and resigned from his coaching position.

"I felt my work with Joyce Beverages was suffering because of the time I was putting in with the team, and vice versa," Magnuson said of the decision. "Being a coach takes a lot more time than being a player, and I got more involved than I thought I would. I felt I owed it to everyone to make a commitment either to Joyce Beverages or the Hawks."

The decision was not only career-based; there was a more important factor at stake. "My family life was another consideration," he added. "If I stayed in hockey as an assistant coach, I'd be missing a lot of family activities at night and on the weekend. My wife, Cindy, and our two children [Kevin, now age three and Molly, an infant] are the most important people in my life."

With the announcement of his departure from the Hawks, the Chicago members of the Professional Hockey Writers' Association immediately forwarded Magnuson's name as their nomination for the Bill Masterton Trophy in recognition of his dedication to the sport.

What Magnuson could not foresee, however, was the stunning chain of events that would occur during the next few weeks involving Johnston, Pulford, and the Wirtz family.

Rumors were circulating in the Chicago press that Pulford and Johnston could not come to an agreement on the coach's contract, with the general manager refusing to raise the compensation by an extra $5,000. Then Johnston, after one successful year, suddenly announced he had been fired by the Black Hawks, and he pulled no punches in referring to Pulford upon his departure.

"He's incompetent, has no business being a general manager, and the rest of the general managers in the league just laugh at him," Johnston assessed plainly. He added that he was never told directly by Pulford, Wirtz, or anyone else in the front office that he had been removed—instead receiving the information secondhand (which, if true, appeared to be a continuing pattern in the organization). "I have no respect for that man. It was my conflict with Pulford, not any money disagreements, that led to my dismissal. When it happened to Billy Reay, at least they slipped a Christmas card under his door to let him know," he continued.

When the paperwork for the dismissal was finalized, Johnston let loose even further in summarizing the past year, claiming that Pulford never listened to him on personnel matters, nor did he once promote a player from the minors whom Johnston suggested. Believing such actions were typical of the administrative side of the team, Verdi wrote in the wake of the move that "the Black Hawks have all the class of a ham sandwich. Public relations to them is not a lost art only because they have never had it."

The firing, however, must not have been a complete surprise to Johnston; for just three weeks earlier, on May 22, he had been given permission by Wirtz and Pulford to negotiate with other clubs that had openings for a head coach—specifically, the Quebec Nordiques,

Pittsburgh Penguins, and Boston Bruins—the last being the club with which Johnston had spent the majority of his playing career.

Johnston also tried to assert that there had been some conflict between him and Magnuson behind the bench, claiming this as another reason he was dismissed, and even suggested that Magnuson went for the assistant coaching position as a way to ultimately lobby for the head coaching spot.

"That's not true," Bill Wirtz refuted. "The only reason Eddie is no longer the coach is because he wouldn't accept our offer [for a new contract]."

As for his own relationship with Johnston, Magnuson was straightforward in his description. "I can look Eddie in the eye," he said. "The Black Hawks came to me. I didn't come to them soliciting the [assistant's] job."

In fact, Magnuson had been away from the team for several weeks when contacted by Pulford about the position of assistant coach. Furthermore, Johnston's agent, Bill Watters, confirmed that they had rejected Pulford's most recent contract offer. Pulford also pointed out that if Johnston had accepted the deal, only three other coaches in the league would have been making more money—Al Arbour with the Islanders (which had just won its first Stanley Cup), Al MacNeil with the Atlanta Flames (a team that was on its way to Calgary), and Roger Neilson with the Buffalo Sabres (Neilson had taken over for Scotty Bowman, who also had been general manager of the Sabres after departing from Montreal with four straight Cups; Fred Shero also had the dual role of head coach and general manager with the New York Rangers. Both Bowman and Shero would have had higher salaries than Johnston as well).

The bottom line was that Johnston was out, and Pulford and the Wirtz family knew that the position needed stability. They decided that the man for the job was Keith Magnuson, and the phone rang at his house at 3:00 in the morning.

"You won't believe this," Magnuson said to Cindy as he hung up the phone and rolled over in bed.

"What?" she responded.

"They'd like to know if I want to be coach."

And as Cindy later described the moment, "We both woke up real quick."

Just a month after leaving the team as an assistant to work full-time for Joyce Beverages, Magnuson—at age 33—was introduced on June 13, 1980, as the Black Hawks head coach, the team's fifth in five years. He would be the second-youngest head coach in the league, next to Gary Green of Washington.

"I never thought I'd be a [head] coach in the NHL," Magnuson told the writers in his first press conference as the top man. "A year ago, or even a month ago, if you told me it would happen, I'd have said 'Impossible.' When the job was offered, I talked the decision over with my wife, but we never really considered not taking it. It's an opportunity that if you passed it up, you'd regret it for the rest of your life."

In his *Tribune* column two days after the announcement, Neil Milbert resounded the feeling among the media that Magnuson deserved the opportunity. "The changing of the guard behind the Hawks' bench was accomplished with very little grace and a great deal of gall," Milbert decided about the tumultuous turn of events over the past few seasons in Chicago's leadership. "But Magnuson doesn't deserve to be made into a scapegoat. For more than a decade, he gave it all he had as a player. Anybody who knows him knows he's going to be the same kind of coach… [He] is an upstanding individual with immense loyalty and a ravenous appetite for hard work."

Koroll, standing by his side, joined Magnuson behind the bench as his assistant. Reactions among the coast-to-coast media—both in the United States and Canada—were favorable to the hiring as well.

"Magnuson, whose 10-year career as a Chicago player was characterized by reckless abandon, has given every indication that his coaching style will be rational and relatively relaxed," reported *The Hockey News* after Maggie's first few weeks on the job the following fall. "The stereo still blares after practice. The suds still flow after games. There are many new motivational slogans but no new rules."

Established NHL coaches were equally impressed with the choice. "Keith is going to be successful," said Arbour. "He's very intense, he's a hard worker, and he applies himself completely to whatever he does."

Magnuson knew, however, that the position would not come without pitfalls. "It was a tough transition for both Maggie and me," Koroll admitted. "One year you are playing and partying with your teammates and the next year you are the disciplinarian."

One such difficulty was his relationship with Tony Esposito, a rapport which appeared to have recently become strained—and one which Johnston, on his way out the door, predicted would worsen. According to Johnston, word had gotten to Esposito that Magnuson, Pulford, and Jack Davison (the Black Hawks director of player personnel) had berated the goaltender in the early morning hours following a 1980 playoff loss in Buffalo—which Johnston claimed, if true, was a prime example of Magnuson being too "pro-Pulford" in most disagreements the men would have with each other. Verdi, in his June 15 column which attempted to sort out the situation, suggested that the best move for Johnston would have been to sign the contract renewal for 1981 and hire a different assistant coach—pointing to a previous story reporting that Johnston had originally asked Lou Angotti to be his top assistant, but Pulford encouraged him to choose Magnuson instead.

The allegations that Magnuson was anti-Esposito proved to be unfounded. Just days after Magnuson was introduced as head coach, goalie Murray Bannerman was summoned from the minors as the new backup to Esposito and Mike Veisor was traded to Hartford—affirming that Maggie had every intention of Esposito remaining as his full-time man in the nets for at least one more season. Indeed, Esposito would lead the league in games played among goalies in Magnuson's first year as head coach in 1980–81, with 66, as well as 52 more in his second year.

"Magnuson had said he would break his neck for the Wirtzes, and several times he came close," Verdi had written back in November 1979 about Keith's unrelenting style when his retirement from playing was announced. "But that's the moral of the story. He kept coming. The greatest talent of all, after all, is the talent to work."

Johnston, meanwhile, was quickly scooped up by Pittsburgh, filling the Penguins' vacancy at the head coaching position.

• • •

As everyone expected, Magnuson attacked his new role with the same vigor and dedication with which he pursued everything else in his life. "I think we're going into this season well prepared," Lysiak, in his second full year with the Hawks, said during training camp. Lysiak had arrived in a blockbuster trade with Atlanta in March 1979 that saw Ivan Boldirev, Phil Russell, and Darcy Rota depart. "Maggie has brought us along gradually—a little harder, a little harder, a little harder. Everything is very organized. Maggie and Cliff go over what we have to work on and then at practice we apply what we've learned. Everybody knows what's expected. The atmosphere is good. I know I'm happy."

In addition to Koroll, Magnuson knew there were others to whom he could turn in the early stages of his tenure, including his captain Ruskowski and the quickly improving Mulvey. "Whenever I need something I know I can count on Granny," Magnuson would say in his first month directing the team. "He and Terry are always there to help."

Back in 1974, as a 17-year-old, Mulvey had been picked up at O'Hare Airport by Magnuson upon arriving in Chicago, and he could sense Maggie's enthusiasm for the Hawks from the moment he got into the car. Keith immediately took an interest in mentoring Mulvey, even asking about his plans for a post-hockey career. In the fall of 1980, newly acquired forward Peter Marsh was the latest arrival to be greeted near O'Hare by Magnuson—with Keith's toddlers Kevin and Molly in tow in the backseat.

The impressions that Magnuson as a coach—and earlier as a veteran teammate—made upon Mulvey made a lasting impact. Mulvey recalled a game in Montreal in which Magnuson got hit from the side, flew into the boards awkwardly, and actually broke his back. Magnuson returned to the lineup much quicker than anyone would ever have expected—wearing a back brace as he labored his way around the ice at practice, while suiting up for games when he could do so. At that point, Mulvey had yet to experience a significant injury during his time in hockey, but would ultimately deal with many later in his career. Magnuson's example had shown Mulvey the courage that was needed to keep playing in the NHL. "I saw that and I told myself, 'I have to give more,'" Mulvey said.

But as cerebral and prepared as Magnuson was in his approach to the game as a player, he found the new learning curve as a head coach even steeper. "There's so much to learn back there," Magnuson said of being behind the bench. "The most important thing is to be aware of the situation and be under control. If you're not under control, the players will sense it and they'll go out of control."

His openness with Cindy permitted him to accept her advice regularly, even on hockey matters—which included the idea of offering the players an occasional Monday off from practice if they worked hard in a Sunday night game—and which usually turned out to be the right move.

The hard work through which Maggie put the team in training camp paid off. The Hawks lost only one of their first six games, capped by an 8–4 shellacking of the Washington Capitals at the Stadium on October 19, the night Stan Mikita's jersey No. 21 was retired. Mikita, unable to return from the back surgery he had endured in November 1979, had retired after playing in only 17 games during the previous season. He left hockey owning essentially every scoring record in Black Hawks team history except goals, though his 541 in that category is still second only to Bobby Hull's 604.

Like the Hawks teams of the past years, however, the team would fall into a dreadful slump after their quick start, dropping to a 12–21–6 record by January 1.

"He began questioning himself and his own abilities," wrote *Tribune* columnist Skip Myslenski about Magnuson's first stiff test at the controls. "Frequently he spent full nights in his office watching endless reels of film and searching for a formula that would right the situation."

Often Koroll joined him for the marathon film sessions, and they watched tapes of the Canadiens, Islanders, Bruins, and even successful international teams, such as the Soviet and Czechoslovakian national teams, looking for patterns in their play. Once, while the coach of the Czechoslovakian team was in Chicago, Magnuson took him out to breakfast five straight mornings in an effort to get him to talk hockey strategy. At other times, players would knock on Magnuson's office door in looking to have a word with him—only to find the coach asleep on the sofa in front of a television, worn out from his work. "You kind of felt sorry for him," Ruskowski said. "You could see the red eyes from sleepless nights."

A spark was found, however, in the play of 19-year-old rookie center Denis Savard and the budding defenseman Doug Wilson, and a new winning streak soon began. By January 21, the Hawks had won seven in a row when the Montreal Canadiens came to town. Even though it was a Wednesday night in the dead of the Chicago winter, one of the few sold-out crowds of the year filled the Stadium. Maggie's boys beat the Habs 4–2 for their eighth straight victory. In Magnuson's tenure as a head coach, he would never be prouder of his young team.

"From the first shifts I could see that our players were up," Keith said that evening, "that they were confident, that they were in control, all the things I had been hoping for. And the crowd was solidly behind them. A lot of people may not realize how much that helps."

"They are growing into wanting to win and hating to lose," he would add later, "and that's something you can't teach them as a coach. They've got to experience it for themselves."

The team battled to reach the .500 mark by season's end in April 1981 but fell just short, finishing at 31–33–16. In spite of the impressive sprint at the end, the Hawks reverted to their old ways, again suffering yet another first-round sweep in the playoffs. This time it was the Calgary Flames eliminating them in three straight, despite taking the Flames to a knockdown, drag-out, Maggie-style game in the last contest in the Stadium, claimed by Calgary in two overtime periods by a 5–4 final score.

His first season as the head coach concluded, Magnuson immediately began his work again, insisting on building a long-lasting program—and staying positive for his charges. "As a player, I got down on myself after a loss," he admitted. "That's the way I prepared myself for the next game. But here, I have to pick everyone up and say, 'Hey, let's forget it.'"

In overseeing the Hawks draft a few weeks after the end of the playoffs, he approved the choice of Tony Tanti, a high-scoring forward who had posted 81 goals in his first season with the Oshawa Generals in the Juniors system, as a 17-year-old. As time went along, Magnuson was learning further about the proper balance that a head coach needed to find between admonishment and encouragement.

"The thing about coaching," he said, "your own character has to come out, but it can't come out so strong that you're forcing it on other people. They're all individuals, and to get the best out of everybody, you have to approach them on their own level."

A frustrating aspect of coaching for Magnuson was some players' lack of self-motivation necessary for success. "As a performer, he eternally played and practiced with fire in his soul," Myslenski had written in the midst of a troubling period for the team. "As a coach, he must accept that the fire doesn't burn so brightly in the souls of all his players." It was an element ever-present in his own play whenever he stepped onto the ice. "He's in a very tough situation," added Bob Murray early in the 1981–82 season. "He's used to experienced teams, which he played on, and this is an inexperienced team."

Every loss gnawed at him, as he was no longer able to jump on the ice a provide a hip check, a poke check, or a punch to jump-start his team. "Everybody feels the pressure," he said in an exasperated tone to Neil Milbert. "If anybody doesn't feel the pressure in this situation, he's not worth his salt. If you like your job and want to do well at it, you have to feel the pressure."

Cindy was starting to notice the difference in him as well. "She came to recognize and accept the moods that infected her husband after any defeat," Myslenski continued. "But even this didn't prepare her for the extremes he experienced as coach."

By the end of January 1982, the Hawks were mired in a devastating 10-game winless streak—their longest since December 1976, the point at which Reay was dismissed. Things came to a head after a 5–2 loss to Toronto at the Stadium on January 31, and Pulford was directed by Bill Wirtz to once again take the position behind the bench for a temporary six-game stint as the interim head coach (recently Pulford, from the press box, had been relaying strategic recommendations during games down to Magnuson and Koroll via walkie-talkie radio).

Three nights later, Mulvey set a Hawks record with five goals in one game against St. Louis. Magnuson returned to the head coaching spot for a 4–1 loss to Vancouver at the Stadium on February 15, after which he resigned from the job for good—a move which was called a "firing" in the press, but which was refuted by Pulford.

"Pully," Keith once told Pulford, "if you want to get rid of me, you're going to have to fire me. I'm not going to quit. I'm *never* going to quit."

Pulford held no hard feelings, and thought no less of the man. "I'll tell you one thing," Pulford asserted after the Vancouver game. "I am extremely proud of this man. He's not quitting; he's doing what he thinks he has to do for the good of the team. I hope he will always consider me his friend."

Magnuson truly was at peace with the decision; he had done all he could do. "It was killing me," Magnuson would admit years later about that time of his life. "My family was too young. Hockey is worth a lot to me, but it's not worth my family."

"Keith always said he loved his wife, Cindy, more than hockey," Koroll once said, "but knowing how much he loved hockey, he must have really loved Cindy a great deal."

Indeed, family was the only thing more important to Keith Magnuson than hockey.

Koroll, meanwhile, lasted several more years as an assistant, and then was assigned to coach the Hawks' minor league team in Milwaukee for part of a season until Orval Tessier (who succeeded Pulford) was fired in 1985. (Tessier, like Johnston, was promoted to the job from New Brunswick.) Early on as head coach, Koroll discovered that coaching was more difficult than playing—the same revelation that Magnuson had encountered.

"The player worries about himself," Cliff explained. "The coach has 22 headaches [players on the roster]. The player makes sure he gets himself to the airport. The coach has to worry about 22 people getting to the airport. The player has to make sure he's ready to play. The coach has to make sure 22 players are ready to play. Believe me, I see less of my family now than I did as a player."

Magnuson was not alone in his departure from the job in 1982; nearly half of the teams in the league during the 1981–82 NHL season (10 out of 21) lost their head coach due to resignation, dismissal, or retirement.

• • •

With hockey now behind him, Magnuson could now focus on his family, his business plans, and his philanthropic pursuits. "Maggie was someone you would trust with anything," said Paul Schrage, a senior executive vice-president with McDonald's whom Magnuson helped to get 7-Up served in the restaurant's chain.

As Keith made a name for himself in the business world, other opportunities came to the fore. In 1984, Magnuson left 7-Up and joined Bill O'Rourke at Coca-Cola's offices in the north Chicago suburb of Niles, Illinois. "O'Rourke sensed that changes were about to occur at 7-Up," Kevin Magnuson said. "Because my dad was loyal to a fault, he really struggled with making the move and leaving the company that gave him his start."

In the same year, Magnuson was elected to the Chicago Sports Hall of Fame, followed six years later by a spot in the City of Saskatoon Hall of Fame. And by 1998, Magnuson would rise to become vice-president of sales for Coca-Cola, looking every bit the part and taking great care in his appearance ("He owns just one pair of jeans," a Chicago writer was apparently told by Magnuson, "and will never wear them in public").

His success was little surprise to anyone; his total commitment to his new profession reminiscent of his circular skating sprints around the Chicago Stadium ice that set an example for everyone else. "I'm up by 5:30 every morning and put in an 8-to-10 hour workday," Maggie said of his job at Coca-Cola. "I believe the principles that apply to being successful in business are the same as they were in my hockey career." His son, Kevin, agreed with him. "My dad was so good at relating to every customer—from the stock boys in grocery stores to the CEOs. They all loved his down-to-earth mentality and passion for the business. His work ethic from the ice translated very well to the business world, and people really respected him for that."

As an example of Magnuson's combination of persistence and friendliness in the business world, Jim Wiste spoke of a time when they were on the golf course and a sales opportunity presented itself. When Maggie, Wiste, and the rest of the foursome had finished their 18 holes, they walked over to the beverage cart for a drink.

"I'll have a Coke," Magnuson told the server.

"We don't have Coke—we have other products," the server replied.

"Don't have Coke, eh? Well, here's my card. You have your boss call me."

Schrage was not surprised upon hearing this story. "He was always a gentleman," Schrage said, "but in business, he was also as aggressive and as forceful as he was on the ice. Keith was very persistent in getting a deal completed."

Schrage, who also participated in many charity golf outings with Magnuson, was always impressed with how Keith handled himself with control on the links. If someone in a foursome tried to shave a stroke off a hole or not permit Magnuson to take a "gimmee" putt when Keith had permitted the person to do the same on a previous hole, Keith would just shrug it off, as if it did not bother him.

In displaying success off the ice, it seemed that Magnuson's breadth as a person was finally being fully revealed to the public, and he demonstrated that breadth in many ways. "When I drive to practice in the morning," he had said back in 1977, while still playing, "if I can let somebody in ahead of me from another lane of traffic, that really makes me feel good. Maybe that person will feel better, and maybe he'll do it for somebody else up ahead."

To many who were previously unaware, his work with numerous charities around the Chicago area was coming to light for the first time. These pursuits did not slow down, despite his accelerated workload in the corporate world—pursuits which included visiting hospitals on a regular basis and helping to raise money for Mikita's hockey camp for deaf children. "People are sometimes surprised how even-tempered and relaxed I am off the ice," Magnuson revealed.

Those within the Hawks organization, however, had always known it. "I was a rookie broadcaster in 1980 [the same year as Magnuson's rookie year as a head coach]," Pat Foley said. "The timing of my arrival and Maggie's arrival to the Hawks was fortunate for me. He was someone I idolized as a kid [growing up in Glenview, Illinois]." Magnuson and Koroll, it turned out, would become personal guides for Foley around the league. "They helped me with travel issues," Foley continued. "Back in those days, we flew commercial flights. But Maggie and Cliff always made sure they saved a seat for me next to them. We would play gin, and they would win all of my meal money—'Circle around again,' they would tell the pilot, so they could take even more of it. But I gladly parted with it. They took care of me."

Magnuson also found time to spend with good friends. One day, Maggie appeared in the stands at a practice session with Koroll, Mikita, and Dale Tallon to watch a team that John Marks was coaching in Kalamazoo, Michigan. Waiting patiently for the workout to end and for Marks to emerge from his office, the trio then swept upon him and "abducted" their former Hawks teammate, pulling him into a car and driving him all the way to Canada to participate in yet another charity golf tournament. "He had no clothes, no golf clubs, or a chance to call home," Harvey Wittenberg recounted about Marks' dilemma. "He had fun and didn't file kidnapping charges." Added Marks about the story, "I came back home with three bucks in my pocket."

It was representative of Keith's inextinguishable sense of humor. On another such road trip a few years earlier, Magnuson had gone on a hunting expedition in Wisconsin with Tallon, Russell, Jim Harrison, and some others. The group's guide had a bird dog named Maggie, and when one of the men fired on some game, the guide yelled, "Maggie, go get it!"—at which point Magnuson darted off into the field ahead of the dog.

Most of all, Magnuson relished the time he could now spend with Cindy, Kevin, and Molly—time which had been limited in the midst of an NHL career. By 1993, Kevin was well on his way to crafting his own career in hockey, helping to lead Lake Forest High School in the Illinois state playoffs. "He's a better playmaker than I was at his age," Kevin's proud father said. "He has more offensive ability. He's also defensive-minded, blocks shots, and will stand up for himself and teammates. In high school and college you can only take that so far or you're out of the game [for fighting]. But defending the net you've got to take the body. I stress that with Kevin."

Kevin went on to become a defenseman for the University of Michigan where, in 1998, he played on a team that took home an NCAA title—just as his dad had done for Denver. "I had told him when he was a youngster that the greatest thing you can do is be on a hockey scholarship and win an NCAA championship," Keith had said. "As I was hugging him after the game, he said, 'Dad, we did it.'"

Molly took interest in another sport while in high school. "She can skate very well," Keith said, "but she's a good tennis player." Kevin went further in claiming that his sister was the best athlete in the family.

Tirelessly working on behalf of others, yet another of Magnuson's post-hockey passions would be to assist the ranks of the NHL's retired players, helping to secure more stable futures for those who played the game. It was a project that culminated in his founding and presidency of the Blackhawks' Alumni Association, with help from Koroll and Hawks front office man Jack Fitzsimmons. Tallon also assisted in organizing the luncheons for the Association. "When Maggie was at the microphone at the luncheon," Tallon said, "he wanted to thank everyone in the room personally. Everyone knew that the luncheon would then go from an hour to three and a half hours. But everyone loved Maggie, so nobody would mind."

Bill Wirtz was greatly in favor of the idea, and supported Magnuson as he got the association going. There was a closeness between Wirtz and Maggie that was unusual for an executive and a player during the era, a kinship that went beyond the business of hockey. While derisively nicknamed "Dollar Bill" for his alleged penny-pinching ways, there was a generous side to Wirtz that most people never saw.

"Everybody who has ever needed any help, he has always been there," said Tallon. "He has taken the criticism and passed on the praise." Denis Savard agreed, and cited a specific personal example. "When I was 19 years, old, I ran out of money," Savard reflected upon his first year with the Hawks. "I called Mr. Wirtz up and said, 'I need money. I gave money to my parents and I bought a house and I ran out of money.' I said, "I need $10,000,' and I said, 'You can take it off my check.' Guess what? He never took it off."

When the Ralston-Purina Company sold the St. Louis Blues (taking with it the city arena's name, the Checkerdome), Wirtz went door-to-door to the large businesses in downtown St. Louis, looking for a new benefactor for the club. In later years when Chicago Stadium was to be replaced, Wirtz wanted to make certain that the transition did not occur at taxpayer expense. "Bill Wirtz was much more than a man who paid men with sticks to shoot pucks," wrote Mike Downey of the *Tribune* upon Wirtz's death in 2007. "He was a humanitarian who gave away millions to charity without grabbing credit for it."

Magnuson lost his father in October 1996; Joe Magnuson passed away back in Saskatoon. With the memories and lessons of his mom and dad still firmly implanted in his mind, Keith returned to Chicago to dedicate himself to his family and work at an even higher level—which many thought for him was not possible, as he already set the standard.

"Winning isn't everything," Magnuson had reminded himself and others. "What's everything is whether or not you give 100 percent."

9

"I Probably Won More than I Lost"

"Maybe it's because hockey players were forced to become men quicker in Canada, but they are a breed apart from other professional athletes. They have none of the pretense of the American jock who gets pampered with a four-year scholarship to the University of Alabama. The hockey players talk better, tell a better story, are more fun than the other athletes. The hockey players don't have the formal education, maybe, but they are more street smart than the others. And, I suppose, more genuine."

—George Plimpton

On December 14, 2003, Keith Magnuson was preparing to head to the Toronto area for the funeral of former NHL player Keith McCreary—who, like Magnuson, had been a past president of the league's alumni association. During Magnuson's tenure in the position, he was instrumental in setting up a trust fund for disabled players, and saw to it that anyone needing assistance got the help he needed. Just before going to O'Hare Airport, Maggie had made a quick stop north of Chicago in Zion, Illinois, to help that community raise money for a new ice rink for its children—just as he had done for other towns during the past several years.

"He was just marvelous," organizer of the event and Magnuson's friend Bob Neal said in describing the scene in Zion that was awash in smiling faces, young and old. "He just loved those kids. I told him he missed his calling, [that] he should have been working with kids every day."

The next afternoon, Magnuson found himself in Bolton, Ontario, for McCreary's service. Afterward, a reception for the guests was held nearby at the Glen Eagle Golf Club. Driving Magnuson to the proceedings in a rented Chrysler Intrepid was 44-year-old Rob Ramage, 12 years younger than Magnuson and himself a retired NHL player. Ramage was also an officer with the alumni association, and had been working as a financial advisor in St. Louis, where he had spent six seasons in the mid-1980s with the Blues. Ramage's first season in the NHL had been Magnuson's last, the 1979–80 campaign, with the old Colorado Rockies, an organization that had made Ramage the first overall pick in the draft after he had played his rookie professional season in the final season of the WHA.

Like Magnuson, Ramage was a tough, hard-driving defenseman who captained his team, but Ramage also displayed a larger array of offensive skills than most defensemen who had entered the league for some time. After his successful start in the WHA, Ramage became a four-time All-Star in the NHL. In 1988, six weeks after his final All-Star Game, he was traded from the Blues to the Calgary Flames as part of the deal that brought Bobby Hull's son Brett to St. Louis. The following spring, Ramage would be part of a Stanley Cup winner in Calgary, and he hoisted another Cup, with the Canadiens in 1993, before retiring from the game.

Around 4:30 PM local time, Ramage and Magnuson left the reception in Bolton and headed back to the NHL Alumni Association headquarters near the Toronto airport. At approximately 5:00, Ramage approached a curve on Rutherford Road in the community of Woodbridge and lost control of the vehicle. Attempting to straighten the wheel, he clipped the bumper of a small car that was traveling ahead of them, causing Ramage to lose control once again. The Intrepid veered across the center line and struck an approaching sport-utility vehicle driven by a local woman named Michelle Pacheco.

Rushing to the scene to assist were Brian and Nancy McGran, who had been traveling behind Pacheco. They found Ramage unconscious, with his head at rest on the steering wheel. He would survive his injuries.

Hurrying over to the passenger side, they checked for Magnuson's pulse but found none. Paramedics soon arrived, and Magnuson was pronounced dead at the scene from head and chest injuries.

• • •

As night fell on the Chicago area on December 15, Bill Wirtz, Bob Pulford, and Dale Tallon made their way through the quiet north suburban towns to the Magnuson home in Lake Forest, arriving at the front step at 10:30 PM. With courage coming from their shared love of Maggie and support from the rest of the Hawks family, they informed Cindy and Molly of the horrible news. Other Magnuson family members, meanwhile, were gathering in Denver to inform Kevin, who was tracing his father's footsteps at DU in his first year of law school there. Tallon, sadly, had just missed seeing Keith the night before the crash; staying in the Toronto area to scout some games in the Juniors, Tallon had already gone to bed when Magnuson checked into the same hotel. Magnuson phoned Tallon and asked to meet him in the lobby for a chat. "I said I had to get up to catch a flight," Tallon recalled. "Regrettably, I never went down to see him."

Stan Mikita, several states away in Florida at the time, was awoken at 3:00 AM with a heart-wrenching ring of the telephone. "Peter Marsh phoned in the middle of the morning and told me Keith had been in a car accident in Canada," Mikita said. "Then Cliff [Koroll] called, bawling. It was terrible. Maggie was such a prince. I was crushed."

Koroll immediately went to the Magnusons' home to comfort the family, staying until 3:30 the next morning. He went back to his home at that point, slept for a couple of hours, and then returned with Tallon to help with the funeral arrangements—all of the costs of which would be covered by Bill Wirtz.

According to a *Chicago Sun-Times* report from December 17, the Hawks website had hundreds of e-mails submitted in just the first couple of hours, so many that a discussion board had been opened for fans' memories of Maggie. Several of the messages offered sympathy to Ramage as well.

"It's been a tremendous tragedy since the day of the accident," Ramage would say later. "Family and friends have been incredible throughout this. My heart and prayers and thoughts, as they have been since the day of the accident, is with Cindy and Kevin and Molly Magnuson."

• • •

More than 2,500 people had withstood the cold for more than six hours, lining up around the block at the visitation in Lake Forest on December 19, and over 800 mourners packed the First Presbyterian Church in town the following afternoon for the funeral service. Of these, 200 had to be placed in a separate room to view the ceremonies on closed-circuit television.

Mike Spellman was there as a representative of a local suburban paper, the *Daily Herald*. "Walking by outside the church was Bill Hermann of Lake Bluff and his young son, Liam," Spellman noticed, "each sporting a Blackhawks jersey and holding a red candle, silently strolling the sidewalk. 'Magnuson was one of my favorite players; he really gave his heart and his soul on the ice every game,' Hermann said. 'You don't see much dedication like that anymore to the sport or to life.'"

Moments later, a man and woman approached Molly with a gold medal, won by their son at a Special Olympics event that Magnuson had helped organize. Keith had so much of an impact on their son's life, they told Molly, that they wondered if the medal could be placed in the casket for the burial. The Magnusons were happy to honor the request. "We didn't even know these people," Molly said. "We were blown away."

Arriving three hours early, Pat Foley noticed that the church had already begun filling up. The entire 2003–04 Blackhawks team was there, in addition to former players Mikita, Grant Mulvey, Darcy Rota, Chris Chelios, Al Secord, Steve Larmer, Doug Wilson, Dennis Hull, and many others. Also present were several of Magnuson's old teammates from the University of Denver.

"I'll never forget the line around the funeral home, thousands of people waiting in freezing weather to pay their respects," Mikita said. Chelios said later in reflection, "He was my favorite player growing up, and one of the first guys I wanted to meet when I was traded to Chicago…at the age of 50, he still had the heart of a kid, and his family is a reflection of the kind of man he was."

Despite never having played with Maggie, Chelios was well aware of the love and dedication that Keith had for the Hawks. At a 75th anniversary game for team alumni in 2001, Chelios came onto the ice and decided that he would not put on the Hawks jersey, since he was playing for Detroit at the time. Magnuson understood, but was nonetheless disappointed.

While waiting for the service to begin, Foley and others respectfully shared quiet stories about Maggie while sitting in the nave. "The greatest captain the Hawks have ever had, or will ever have," Foley said of Magnuson. "He was everything a Chicago Blackhawk should be, and everything your son should grow up to be." Local writer Barry Rozner agreed. "The ultimate team captain in the only sport where the *C* means something," Rozner reflected when learning of the accident.

Just a month earlier, Foley had joined Hawks followers in mourning the death of one of his mentors—Lloyd Pettit, who called so many of Magnuson's exciting plays over WMAQ, and who had passed away on November 11. When Foley had his first professional broadcasting job in Grand Rapids in the old International Hockey League, the team played against Pettit's Milwaukee Admirals. In doing so, Foley had the opportunity to interview Pettit several times; once, in advance of one of those interviews, Pettit was standing behind Foley for the final five minutes of a period, with Foley unaware that he was there. When the period ended and Foley began his interview, the first thing Pettit said was, "You're doing a great job; keep doing what you're doing, and one day you'll be in the NHL." Pettit's words meant so much to him that Foley has kept the tape from that interview, which he has to this day.

As the proceedings commenced, Kevin Magnuson was the first to speak. He read a poem written by a friend of the family entitled "My First Christmas in Heaven," since the family would be keeping Keith in their hearts through the holiday in the coming week, and forever after. "Kevin talked about how Christmas was always his dad's favorite time of the year," Mikita recalled. Then, in a spirit of great forgiveness in the midst of an unimaginable ordeal, Kevin added a final thought: "My mom, my sister, and I would like to ask you to keep my dad's good friend Rob Ramage in your prayers."

Keith's brother, Dale, then walked to the podium, and spoke of their time growing up in western Canada. "In the game of life, Keith was our MVP," he said. "Very early in life it became apparent that he had a heart that most of us only dream of. He would always come through."

Koroll, Magnuson's best friend and roommate for so many years, added simply and appropriately, "Keith was a guy who lived 100 years in 56 years…he was as compassionate a person as there was. He never said 'no' to anyone."

While there is never enough in such situations, there seemed to be no shortage of prayers, comfort, and support from the hockey community for the Magnusons. "People say hockey players are the nicest people, and they are," Kevin had said during high school in 1993 after having virtually grown up at the Stadium.

Even one of Keith's most formidable foes lent his support in later years. "I used to wait at Gate 3½ [at the Stadium] for Keith and watch Dave Schultz walk by, and I used to hate him," Cindy admitted. "And then he sends me this note [after Keith's death] about how much Keith meant to him and to hockey, and how much he loved him. I mean, where else do you find something like that except hockey?"

Messages of admiration of Magnuson's life kept pouring in from around North America, and would for years to come.

"He was a Hawk," former New York Rangers goalie John Davidson said simply. "It's interesting today when you think of certain people. Mike Ditka was a Chicago Bear. Keith Magnuson was a Hawk."

Bob Pulford: "His great leadership on the ice was the way he was in ordinary life… As you travel through life, you meet very few people who are a notch above the rest. Keith Magnuson was one of those people."

Former Hawks goalie Darren Pang: "He epitomized what heart and soul was all about. He gave everything he had to the good of the team."

Former Hawks center Denis Savard: "We lost our chief. With Maggie, it was always, 'What can I do for you? How can I help you?' He was always positive, always happy. There's not too many human beings made that way."

Keith Brown: "Reputation is what people perceive you to be, but character is what you truly are. Keith Magnuson was a man of great character."

Darcy Rota: "Maggie was the best 'team guy' I've ever played with."

Grant Mulvey: "Keith was passionate toward others, and toward the concerns of others. He had commitment to the game and to life. Maggie was one of a kind."

Dale Tallon: "He was the heart and soul of this organization. He loved every second of it. You loved being in his company. It was infectious. He gave everything he had, every minute of the day, to the [Hawks] logo, to the cause, to the players, to his friends, to his teammates. There was nothing he wouldn't do for them, nothing… I never heard him say 'no' to anybody. He was just so generous with his time, almost to a fault."

John Marks: "Keith was fearless, and showed his heart every night out there on the ice. The world was a better place with him in it."

Phil Russell: "He was good a man as I've ever been in the trenches with. He took on all comers. And with Keith, it was never about himself—it was about what he could do for the team. There's an old cowboy saying: 'Be loyal to the brand.' The Hawks were always my brand, and they were always Keith's brand."

Stan Mikita: "Everything that came out of Keith's mouth was positive. He brought so much extra enthusiasm to our team."

Jim Wiste: "He had a heart of gold. Everybody loved Maggie. He did more work for charities and for other guys who played the game than any man I've ever known. He was a warrior on the ice and a total gentleman off of it."

Bobby Hull: "Keith's parents can be proud of how they raised him; Keith can be proud of his time on the ice and the family man he was."

• • •

The Blackhawks quickly established the Keith Magnuson Blackhawk Alumni Scholarship for three Chicago-area high school students each year—the number was a tribute to Keith's jersey No. 3. That tradition continues to this day, as Magnuson's legacy lives on through the lives of the people he has touched.

"Maggie used to tie his ties in these unbelievable double Windsor knots," Peter Marsh said. "Once, while we were doing a charity event in Florida, I asked Keith to tie one of those knots for me. To keep Keith in my memory, I never undid the knot, and to this day, I often wear that tie with the same knot."

Two days after the funeral, on December 21, the Hawks fought to an inspired 2–2 tie against the defending Stanley Cup–champion New Jersey Devils at the United Center, their new home since the demolition of Chicago Stadium in 1994. "The passion of the fans in the Stadium was unlike any other place," Bobby Hull said. "That was one of the things I missed so much when I left Chicago." Now, new memories were being made at the new building.

Before the game, a three-minute video of Keith's highlights was shown on the scoreboard; a standing ovation was given to a grateful Magnuson family as the spotlight shone on them. And while Magnuson's jersey No. 3—shared by fellow former great Hawks defenseman Pierre Pilote—had not yet been retired by the team, current

Chicago player Bryan Berard surrendered it and took No. 4 instead. "Out of respect to Maggie, I thought that No. 3 should not be worn," Berard told the local papers.

Murray Armstrong was fast approaching his 88th birthday at the time of Magnuson's death, and on Armstrong's special day, there was one thing on which he could always count. "Keith called me every year on my birthday, and sometimes a few times in between," Armstrong said. "He cared about his friends, but also about everybody. He was a very generous man, and we'll miss him terribly."

Armstrong himself passed away on December 8, 2010, at the age of 94, survived by his wife of 68 years, Freda, and his son, Rob, who had become a prominent journalist for CBS News. The man who had helped craft Keith Magnuson into an outstanding hockey player and young man, in addition to so many others, would be missed as well. "Aside from being a great coach, he was a great human being," Koroll would say in 2012. "He made me believe that I could play in the NHL."

Armstrong's legacy, and that of Magnuson's, would live on in the Mile High City. On April 10, 2004—just four months after Magnuson's accident—the University of Denver claimed its first national championship in hockey since Magnuson captained its previous one 35 years earlier. (Additionally, in 1997, *The Hockey News* named Magnuson the Western Collegiate Hockey Association's all-time best defenseman.) After Magnuson's death, the DU players had placed a sticker on their helmets that read KM2—denoting Keith's initials and his jersey number during his college days. In order to get to the championship game, the Pioneers had to overcome being knocked out of their conference tournament; they responded by upsetting top-ranked North Dakota 1–0, then scored four goals in the third period against Minnesota-Duluth for a 5–3 victory in the semifinals before downing the new No. 1 team, Maine, by a 1–0 score for the title.

In addition to the tales of valor they had heard over the years, the DU players had grown personally attached to Magnuson, after Keith had joined Koroll in attending DU's homecoming that same autumn in October 2003. Watching a hockey alumni game, the two were unable to help themselves as they jumped into the fray—even while wearing dress shirts and slacks and utilizing only skates, gloves, and a stick for equipment. The scene was loved by all. "Magnuson cross-checked players from the crease, hardly scared of getting hit by a slap shot from the point," reported Mike Chambers for the *Denver Post.* "He smiled the entire time. He didn't just participate in the event. He *was* the event."

As the Pioneers' 2003–04 season progressed, the impact that Magnuson and Koroll had on the team with their visit was immeasurable. "We had a lot of luck this season, and I'm sure Maggie had something to do with that," stated defenseman Ryan Caldwell after securing the NCAA championship. Fellow defenseman Matt Laatsch also felt the powerful effect. "Having Keith and Cliff Koroll for the alumni weekend was huge to us," Laatsch said. Then, Laatsch revealed that he had gotten the same advice Keith had given his own son. "Maggie was the biggest [alumnus] we had. He came in and gave us what ended up being our mission statement for the whole year. He said, 'When you get to the event, you'll know it.' He had been to the Frozen Four and national championship game, and he felt like we had the team to get there.

"No disrespect to any alumni, but he was larger than life. He was the guy you always hoped would come into the locker room when he was in town. To lose him was a pretty big blow to that team. But we always thought about 'getting to the event.'"

Some of the DU players even claim that Magnuson himself was there for the championship, an angel on the Pioneers' shoulders.

For at one point in that championship game, with Denver straining to hold on to their 1–0 lead, one of Maine's top scorers broke free with the puck at center ice and seemed to be on his way to the tying goal. However—with no DU player near him—the Maine player suddenly fell to the ice, inexplicably, as if hip-checked by an invisible force.

"We were on a bad change and the guy goes in all alone, then trips at the blue line," Laatsch said. "Explain how that happens."

• • •

If selflessness is the true measure of a team player, as it should be, then Keith Magnuson was the ultimate one—there has never been anyone better in any sport. He did not score many goals, but that did not matter to him; he absorbed punches that others on his team would not, never minding making that sacrifice. Everything he did on the ice was for the betterment of the Chicago Black Hawks, and everything he did off the ice was for the betterment of his family. Yes, Magnuson was known as a fighter—but he fought with more than just his fists. He fought daily for all the things he loved and valued.

Bob Verdi, who has seen it all with the Hawks, encapsulated it best in a piece written the day Maggie retired as a player, on November 1, 1979.

"How Keith Magnuson wanted to lug that jug [the Stanley Cup] around the Stadium ice just once. He won't ever be able to now, but a guy doesn't need a trophy case to be a winner."

The decisions on who "wins" and "loses" a hockey fight are always subjective. There are no weigh-ins, no judges, no points, no standing eight counts, no official knockouts, and no title belts. Those NHL followers who ponder such decisions are often of the opinion that Keith Magnuson lost more hockey fights than he won.

Even if that is true, it is of no consequence; as Theodore Roosevelt said, "The credit belongs to the man who is actually in the arena, whose face is marred by dust and sweat and blood—not the critic."

Magnuson himself seemed to agree. "I've thought about it since I retired," he said in 1996. "And I think I probably won more than I lost."

Other Magnusons also know the importance of standing up for one's teammates. "When you fight in hockey, 90 percent of it psychological," says Mark Magnuson, in the same words one could picture his uncle Keith using. "I fought guys where I knew I was likely to lose. You show up, try not to get hurt, and try to give your team some courage and energy. Your guys know they don't have to fight the other team's tough guys, because *you* will."

Or, as Keith once said, "I can't play it any other way."

Keith Magnuson's most lasting legacy, however, went far beyond the ice of Chicago Stadium. His qualities will continue to echo in eternity through the lives of the family he left behind.

"He was such a great son to his mom and dad, a great brother, a great husband, a great father, and great friend," as Cindy put it. "That says it all."

Epilogue

Even though he did not score touchdowns like Walter Payton, points like Michael Jordan, or even goals like Bobby Hull, Keith Magnuson was as recognizable walking down Michigan Avenue as any athlete in Chicago. And while many great athletes are long-forgotten after their playing days, Magnuson is long-*remembered*—doubtlessly due, at least in part, to his tireless work for Chicago's charitable needs.

"The public hears about a few of the good things Keith does, like visiting a hospital to see a sick kid," Bill O'Rourke said back in 1977. "But that doesn't even scratch the surface. Keith can hear about some problem in some family of a friend of a friend, and before you know it, he's on the phone. He's too good to be true."

As one example, that year Magnuson initiated a Black Hawk Roast to benefit Mike Schwass, a Chicago-area boy who had been partially paralyzed in a hockey game. "I thought maybe two or three players would show up," Magnuson remembered, "but they were all there." When the Hawks finished making light of themselves at the microphone, Maggie handed the Schwass family a check for $15,000 to assist with their medical bills. "Mike, we are all your friends and we are behind you," Magnuson encouraged the youngster at the end of the night, as Mike's long rehabilitation lay ahead of him. "Now it is up to you to climb the mountain. We know you will."

This was only one of the many instances in which Magnuson shifted the center of attention from himself to someone else.

It is ironic that Pioneers was the college team nickname for Magnuson, Cliff Koroll, Jim Wiste, Craig Patrick, and the many others who played for Murray Armstrong at the University of Denver, for they indeed blazed a trail into battle in the National Hockey League for other college players to follow. But Magnuson was also a pioneer in the development of the contemporary idea of a "policeman" in the sport, a player willing to check the intimidation that opposing players attempted to lay on his teammates. In doing so for such a long time, Magnuson remained the Hawks' career leader in penalty minutes for decades until Chris Chelios passed him in 1999 by a mere 53 (1,495 to 1,442). Moreover, the league records for single-season penalty minutes which Magnuson and Dave Schultz set in the early 1970s have been rarely approached in subsequent years. Daniel Carcillo's 324 minutes in 2007–08, in fact, is the most in the past 10 years in the NHL, and only two other players—Zenon Konopka and Peter Worrell—have surpassed 265 in a season since 2000.

As of 2013, Magnuson still ranked highly on many other career statistical lists for the Hawks; he has the third-best total for plus-minus in team history (170, behind Steve Larmer's 192 and Bill White's 176). Furthermore, his Defensive Point Shares from 1971–72—a newer figure kept by hockey statisticians designed to measure the overall value of low-scoring defenseman to a team—is the best in club history at 7.7.

But while the role of the policeman lives on, the debate over the need for fighting in professional hockey continues as well. Long eradicated from amateur levels in the sport, fighting has traditionally been balanced at the pro level between celebrating its existence and punishing its occurrence. In 1992, the "instigator rule"—also known as Rule 56(a)—went into effect in the NHL. The rule gave an extra two-minute minor penalty to the player who incites a fight, in addition to the standard five-minute fighting major (and a second instigator penalty in the same game for the same player results in an automatic ejection).

The rule immediately met with opposition from many NHL players, especially fighters like Marty McSorley. "It doesn't allow the players to police themselves," McSorley said, "and that is wrong."

However, there have also been many prominent voices surfacing in opposition to fighting in hockey—regardless of the scope, cause, savagery, or perceived need of any given fight. "They don't need fighting today in the NHL. It serves no purpose," said Lou Nanne, a longtime defenseman with the Minnesota North Stars and later a team executive. "Look at the Olympics or the world championships, or even the playoffs. Look at the college game, too. Why couldn't the NHL get by without it? I mean, fighting doesn't exist in any other sport except hockey. Players just have to learn to be disciplined, like in anything else in life."

The case against fighting in hockey has even had its flag carried by the most unlikely of sources: Dave Schultz himself. "Fighting does not have to be part of big league hockey any more than fisticuffs have to be a part of baseball, tennis, or football," Schultz wrote shortly after his retirement in the early 1980s. "For too many years, hockey has accepted brawls without questioning their validity or the damage that they have done to its image. The time has come for such questioning."

As stated earlier in this book, Schultz saw a larger issue with violence in hockey because of the dangerous ways in which the stick was being used as a weapon—not the least of which by Schultz's noted teammate and captain of the Flyers, Bobby Clarke. Thus, it might be concluded that the vast majority of serious injuries in hockey are the results of cheap shots; in other words, if the Code was followed by all, injuries from fighting would be minimal, and serious injuries extremely rare.

It is apparent that even modern players see the strategic role that fighting can serve in professional hockey. In a poll of 202 NHL players published by *Sports Illustrated* in March 2012, 99.5 percent of them—or 201—were against the league putting a ban on fighting altogether. "Those who don't want fighting probably never played," Phil Russell concluded. "And they don't understand the game."

• • •

The late 1960s and early 1970s were a turbulent era in American society, and within the Chicago sports scene as well. An interesting comparison can be drawn between Leo Durocher's Cubs and Billy Reay's Black Hawks of the same period. Both teams were mostly stocked with likable, friendly personalities; both teams came up just short of league championships in their respective sports; both teams were filled with talent, including future Hall of Famers; and both teams possessed unsung heroes, a supporting cast of role players who held each team together in the tough times while toiling in the shadows of the superstars.

The Cubs enjoyed the steadying forces of Glenn Beckert, Don Kessinger, Randy Hundley, and Bill Hands among marquee players Ferguson Jenkins, Ron Santo, Billy Williams, and Ernie Banks. The Hawks largely relied upon Magnuson, Koroll, and others who deferred much of the glory to Bobby Hull, Stan Mikita, and Tony Esposito.

Of course, it is mere speculation to wonder if holding on to players such as Jerry Korab or Rick Foley would have lightened the fighting load for Magnuson in the 1970s. With few exceptions, he remained on an island as the lone slugger, while opponents often sent more than one fighter after him each night, a new, fresh puncher ready to go against Magnuson in the third period when Keith was already worn down. Maggie took them all on, however, one at a time, and as often as they chose to come at him. "If you can beat them in the alley," Magnuson liked to say in quoting Conn Smythe, "you can beat them on the ice."

Just like the schoolteacher who is there for his or her students every day, Magnuson was always there for his teammates, as reliable as the sun rising in the east. Even after injuries had perforated the later years of his career, Magnuson would hobble on crutches down to the locker room to urge on his teammates in between periods. As Magnuson was fond of saying, "Whether you win or lose, it's all about showing up." Or, as Barry Rozner put it, "He lost more fights than he won, but he always showed up for the dance. If they had a Hall of Fame for showing up, Maggie would have his own wing."

On November 12, 2008, Magnuson's No. 3 jersey was retired by the Hawks, an honor he would share Pierre Pilote, another Chicago defenseman who preceded him in wearing it. A banner in Maggie's honor was raised to the rafters of the United Center before a standing-room-only crowd of 21,000. With his mother and his sister by his side, Kevin Magnuson walked to the microphone to speak at center ice on behalf of his father, and even though it was a packed house, Kevin felt an unexpected comfort. "It was as if I was sitting in my living room, having an intimate conversation with a few friends," he would say.

Just two weeks after Keith was honored at this ceremony, tragedy befell the Hawks family yet again. On November 30, 2008, Pit Martin was snowmobiling in rural Quebec. Following behind a friend's snowmobile, Martin's craft plunged into the icy waters of Lake Kanasuta. He was pronounced dead in the early hours of the next morning.

• • •

When the Blackhawks finally won the Stanley Cup in 2010—their first championship since 1961—many felt that a posthumous weight had been lifted off the shoulders of Magnuson, perhaps the most popular player ever to score only 14 goals in an 11-year career. Rozner was one of them, as he posted a magnificent summary of the many near-misses of the past decades, and how justice had finally been done.

It's [the 2010 championship] for the great players of the late '60s and early '70s, who came along too late for 1961 and only remember the pain of 1971, like Pit Martin, Jim Pappin, and Dennis Hull, Whitey Stapleton and Bill White, Doug Jarrett and Doug Mohns, Cliff Koroll and Phil Russell.

It is for Tony Esposito, perhaps the most underrated Hall of Fame goaltender in history, a man who never got the credit he deserved for making the playoffs every one of his 15 seasons in Chicago, about half of those years in his prime with some horrible teams when he did it entirely on his own.

But more than anyone, this is for Keith Magnuson, who wore his heart on his sleeve and the crest on his chest until the day he died, and no one would have taken greater pleasure in seeing his sweater stand last.

Maggie was the one who never left, not for any reason or anyone. No matter how much he may have hated what was done to his beloved team, and the men who did it, he never walked away.

He never wavered.

The man who bled for his team more than any player in Hawks history would have given anything to see this day, to see his boys dancing with Lord Stanley's sacred bowl.

He would have felt like he was part of it, because, well, he would have been.

Maggie wasn't just a legend of the fall and winter, and he didn't show up when paid to wave to the cameras.

He was always around the team, even in the worst of times, and he came to symbolize what love for the uniform meant.

Lord, how he would have loved this moment.

It is not the same without him, but of this we are certain:

You can rest in peace now, Maggie, for the ghost of Henri Richard is never more.

Your Chicago Blackhawks are Stanley Cup champions.

APPENDIX:
KEITH MAGNUSON'S CAREER STATISTICS

COLLEGE RECORD

				REGULAR SEASON		
SEASON	**TEAM**	**GP**	**G**	**A**	**PTS**	**PIM**
1966–67	University of Denver	30	4	17	21	77
1967–68	University of Denver	34	5	15	20	56
1968–69	University of Denver	32	7	27	34	48
	Totals	**96**	**16**	**59**	**75**	**181**

NHL RECORD

		REGULAR SEASON					PLAYOFFS				
SEASON	**TEAM**	**GP**	**G**	**A**	**PTS**	**PIM**	**GP**	**G**	**A**	**PTS**	**PIM**
1969–70	Chicago	76	0	24	24	213	8	1	2	3	17
1970–71	Chicago	76	3	20	23	291	18	0	2	2	63
1971–72	Chicago	74	2	19	21	201	8	0	1	1	29
1972–73	Chicago	77	0	19	19	140	7	0	2	2	4
1973–74	Chicago	57	2	11	13	105	11	1	0	1	17
1974–75	Chicago	48	2	12	14	117	8	1	2	3	15
1975–76	Chicago	48	1	6	7	99	4	0	0	0	12
1976–77	Chicago	37	1	6	7	86	0	0	0	0	0
1977–78	Chicago	67	2	4	6	145	4	0	0	0	7
1978–79	Chicago	26	1	4	5	41	0	0	0	0	0
1979–80	Chicago	3	0	0	0	4	0	0	0	0	0
	Totals	**589**	**14**	**125**	**139**	**1442**	**68**	**3**	**9**	**12**	**164**

Legend: GP: games played, G: goals, A: assists, PTS: points, PIM: penalties in minutes

COACHING RECORD

SEASON	TEAM	WINS	LOSSES	TIES
1980–81	Chicago	31	33	16
1981–82	Chicago	18	24	10
	Totals	**49**	**57**	**26**

Acknowledgments

THE GRACIOUSNESS OF THE MAGNUSON family in embracing this project has been overwhelming to me. Cindy, Molly, Kevin, Mark, David, Trystan, and the many more of you whom I have not met—I am honored that you opened your hearts and homes to me, and I will never forget it.

My attempt to capture the full spirit of Keith's life could not have been possible without the perspective of Cliff Koroll, his best friend from their grade-school days through their time with the Hawks and beyond.

It was also a great pleasure to speak with the many other interviewees for this book, who shared their admiration of Keith as a teammate and friend. They include former players and personalities such as Keith Brown, Chris Chelios, Pat Foley, Bobby Hull, John Marks, Peter Marsh, Stan Mikita, Grant Mulvey, Darcy Rota, Phil Russell, Paul Schrage, Dale Tallon, Doug Wilson, and Jim Wiste.

Adam Motin and Mitch Rogatz at Triumph Books have also been incredibly helpful; additionally, Adam Rogowin in the Blackhawks public relations department assisted tremendously in providing resources as well.

Finally, a word of thanks to the writers at the *Chicago Tribune* who covered the Hawks in the 1970s and early 1980s—including Ted Damata, Neil Milbert, and particularly Bob Verdi, who captured the magic of the old Stadium and all of its sights, smells, and sounds.

Sources

CHAPTER 1

"Fists that resembled a bunch of bananas"—Robert Bradford, *Signature* magazine, March 1973.

"On Saturday nights there, I remember"—Bob Verdi, *Chicago Tribune Magazine*, 11-20-77.

"I loved morning Sunday school"—Paul King, *Canadian* magazine (*Toronto Star* insert), 12-11-71.

"Where the rats hung out"—Magnuson and Bradford, pp. 63–64.

"A person's toughness must come from somewhere"—ibid., p. 47.

"There was a potbellied stove in the middle"—Dave Feschuk, *Toronto Star*, 12-21-03.

"Keith always had a checklist"—Dan Ralph, *Toronto Star*, 12-17-03.

"To my little friend, Keith—Magnuson and Bradford, p. 43.

"Because I was big when I was little"—ibid., p. 72.

"We don't want any farm boys"—ibid., p. 73.

"His ears stuck way out from his helmet"—ibid., p. 75.

"I remember this little redhead"—Dave Feschuk, *Toronto Star*, 12-21-03.

"He would always try to hit me in the corners"—Cliff Koroll, interview with author, 9-2-12.

"We played on different teams"—*Chicago Blackhawks Magazine*, 11-12-08.

"He was a small kid"—Neil Milbert, *Chicago Tribune*, 12-17-03.
"I was Blades property"—Magnuson and Bradford, p. 77.
"I'd cut two-by-fours"—ibid., p. 76.
"Juniors taught me the hard facts"—Schultz and Fischler, p. 30.
"There was no letter of intent"—Jim Wiste, interview with author, 9-5-12.

CHAPTER 2

"I wanted to become a hockey player"—Dan Moulton, *The Sporting News*, 12-19-70.
"Armstrong ran practices under NHL rules"—Norman MacLean, *The Sporting News*, 2-7-70.
"We often practiced from 1:00-4:30 PM for several days at a time"—Jim Wiste, interview with author, 9-5-12.
"I remember our freshman games"—Magnuson and Bradford, p. 91.
"By the way, Joe, the car's almost fixed"—ibid., p. 96.
"You know, if you play it right"—Magnuson and Bradford, p. 106–107.
"Maggie was very gullible at times"—Cliff Koroll, interview with author, 9-2-12.
"He would always screw up the punchline of jokes"—Dan Ralph, *Toronto Star*, 12-17-03.
"Jimmy, I've just hit six races in a row"—Jim Wiste, interview with author, 9-5-12.
"Maggie, can you eat 25 hard-boiled eggs?"—ibid.
"In a game against Air Force Academy"—Cliff Koroll, interview with author, 9-2-12.
"You never, ever worried about Keith being ready to play"—Adrian Dater, *Denver Post*, 12-17-03.
"It appears, Magnuson"—Magnuson and Bradford, p. 125.
"Sure it got monotonous"—ibid., p. 127.
"That really bugged me"—*Canadian* magazine (*Toronto Star* insert), Paul King, 12-11-71.
"A lot of times I'd be down to my last quarter"—Bob Verdi, *Chicago Tribune Magazine*, 11-20-77.
"Harry still felt that one hole remained in my training"—Magnuson and Bradford, p. 129.
"Wait 'til you get to Chicago"—ibid., p. 130.
"We'd get a bucket of pucks"—*New York Times* wire services, 4-3-71.

"We walked in Gate 3½ and stood by the opening"—Mike Spellman, Arlington Heights (IL) *Daily Herald*, 12-21-03.
"Keith Magnuson is a defenseman from Denver University"—Ted Damata, *Chicago Tribune*, 9-15-69.
"Be the best of them all"—ibid.
"Though I was still a naïve, gullible, red-haired western Canadian kid"—Magnuson and Bradford, p. 2.
"Dad always said that if you work for something"—Magnuson and Bradford, p. 8.

CHAPTER 3

"Here Come the Hawks"—Barry Rozner, Arlington Heights (IL) *Daily Herald*, 12-17-03.
"Right from our first exhibition game"—Mikita and Verdi, p. 114.
"Most guys skate rather easily at the start of practice"—ibid.
"After watching him for two days"—Stan Mikita, interview with author, 1-5-13.
"Talk about spirit—have you watched that Magnuson"—Bob Strumm, Saskatoon *Star Phoenix*, 10-17-69.
"Some of our best friends"—Cliff Koroll, interview with author, 9-5-12.
"When we hung our elbow pads and shin pads up"—Peter Marsh, interview with author, 10-29-12.
"When I was a rookie with Vancouver, it was an intimidating place to play"—Dale Tallon, interview with author, 11-2-12.
"Adjacent to the dressing room was a lounge"—Cliff Koroll, interview with author, 9-5-12.
"As soon as we came up the stairs"—Peter Marsh, interview with author, 10-29-12.
"With his fire-engine red hair flapping in the breeze"—Chuck O'Donnell, *Hockey Digest*, December 1996.
"His weight is forward, stance wide for balance"—Robert Bradford, *Signature* magazine, March 1973.
"We all file up that long, dark basement stairwell"—Magnuson and Bradford, p. 149.
"That building was a small structure with brick walls"—Pat Foley, interview with author, 10-19-12.
"I have been all over North America and Europe"—Bobby Hull, interview with author, 12-17-12.

"You can never be sure about players"—Dan Moulton, *The Sporting News*, 12-19-70.

"All of a sudden the puck became invisible"—Schultz and Fischler, p. 204.

"One of the bitterest cases of player-management friction"—Gary Ronberg, *Sports Illustrated*, 11-3-69.

"He asked me if there was anything he could be doing better"—Stan Mikita, interview with author, 1-5-13.

"Magnuson, the young pugnacious Hawks defenseman"—Ted Damata, *Chicago Tribune*, 11-22-69.

"I must say it was the worst beating I ever saw a player get"—Cheevers and Frayne, p. 65.

"Fighters are there to keep the peace"—Bernstein, pp. 32–33.

"If a guy like Gordie Howe"—ibid., p. 35.

"I stopped mouthing off to referees"—Mikita and Verdi, p. 82.

"I guarantee you, if you had placed a wager"—ibid., p. 83.

"Howe cuffed Magnuson's ears and turned away"—Mark Mulvoy and Gary Ronberg, *Sports Illustrated*, 4-6-70.

"Right in my face"—Bob Verdi, Blackhawks.NHL.com, "The Verdict: Brown Feels Truly Blessed," 3-10-10.

"I just can't hit a guy if he's turned sideways"—Magnuson and Bradford, p. 26.

"If a man goes down"—ibid., p. 32.

"Keith was not a bully"—Bobby Hull, interview with author, 12-17-12.

"To me, blood doesn't mean anything"—Magnuson and Bradford, p. 26.

"There's nobody who can quite hit like him"—ibid., p. 13.

"He could skate backward like the wind"—D. Hull, p. 70.

"Practice was at 10:00 A.M."—ibid., p. 67.

"Whitey always steps on the ice with just a few seconds left"—Magnuson and Bradford, p. 161.

"Without out a doubt he was the No. 1 practical joker"—D. Hull, p. 83.

"At least Bill got his skates back just before the game"—Bob Verdi, Chicago Blackhawks.NHL.com, "The Verdict: Bill White Was a Defensive Stalwart, Prankster," 12-22-10.

"You should know. You got your typewriter back"—ibid.

"I can't count the number of times Stapleton convinced Maggie"—Mikita and Verdi, p. 115.

"Once a week [Stapleton] would tell Magnuson he was traded"—Bob Verdi, *Chicago Tribune*, 11-1-79.

"Pat and I just seemed to click right away"—Bob Verdi, Chicago Blackhawks website, "The Verdict: Bill White Was a Defensive Stalwart, Prankster," 12-22-10.
"He was tall and he had long arms"—Chuck O'Donnell, *Hockey Digest*, December 1996, p. 78.
"You could feel it starting to build"—Magnuson and Bradford, p. 11.
"Usually I'm one of the first to congratulate Tony"—Mark Mulvoy and Gary Ronberg, *Sports Illustrated*, 4-6-70.
"Really, all that hurts is my lips"—ibid.
"The battle for the Cup returns to Chicago"—Ted Damata, *Chicago Tribune*, 3-30-70.
"The perfect cerebral and grounded half"—Bob Verdi, *Chicago Tribune*, 12-18-03.
"Not that we never had differences"—Magnuson and Bradford, p. 175.
"Until I finally kicked him out"—Neil Milbert, *Chicago Tribune*, 12-17-03.
"If you looked around, you'd see those lists"—Dan Ralph, *Toronto Star*, 12-17-03.
"It was if we had to win every night just to keep pace"—Verdi, p. 84.
"Fans, starved for hockey as they used to know it"—Mark Mulvoy and Gary Ronberg, *Sports Illustrated*, 4-6-70.
"Magnuson was playing spirited, flawless hockey"—ibid.
"It is interesting that in a hockey town like Boston"—Phil Elderkin, *The Sporting News*, 4-25-70.
"'I had a date with Jackie tonight,'"—Mark Mulvoy and Gary Ronberg, *Sports Illustrated*, 4-6-70.
"Sanderson was a classic example"—Schultz and Fischler, p. 62.
"You have to know Derek"—Cheevers and Frayne, p. 8.
"Every day the Bruins are Page One stuff"—Leo Monahan, *The Sporting News*, 5-9-70.
"The Golden Jet has seemed to have lost his zip"—Stan Fischler, *The Sporting News*, 5-9-70.
"If you were lucky enough"—Bob Verdi, *Chicago Tribune*, 12-18-03.

CHAPTER 4

"Pat Stapleton came up to me"—Luis Fernando Llosa, *Sports Illustrated*, 3-1-99.
"Our best game of the season"—Ted Damata, *Chicago Tribune*, 11-12-70.
"The hero of the masses was Keith Magnuson"—ibid.

"No one could believe it when my first punch landed"—Magnuson and Bradford, p. 175.

"A dynamite six-inch jab"—Stan Fischler, *The Sporting News*, 12-5-70.

"You don't see many like it"—ibid.

"Never before or since have a really injured a player"—Magnuson and Bradford, p. 31.

"Maggie's goal brought out a volume of cheers"—Ted Damata, *Chicago Tribune*, 11-12-70.

"Heiskala's career as an enforcer"—Schultz and Fischler, p. 71.

"Off the ice, Magnuson's bridgework gleams"—*Time* magazine, 1-11-71.

"Magnuson [has] set about establishing himself"—Dan Moulton, *The Sporting News*, 12-19-70.

"For the first time in memory"—John Ahern, *Boston Globe*, 12-2-70.

"Many of the fights he had"—Pat Foley, interview with author, 10-19-12.

"Last week the Bruins won 3–2"—John Ahern, *Boston Globe*, 12-2-70.

"He [Magnuson] does a lot."—ibid.

"He likes to play it rough and he provides a spark"—ibid.

"With 10 seconds left, no matter who's ahead"—Cheevers and Frayne, p. 65.

"If you're going to play in this league"—Magnuson and Bradford, p. 13.

"We insisted that our players get World Series tickets"—Dan Stoneking, *The Sporting News*, 11-4-72.

"Keith Magnuson, the robust Chicago defenseman"—Stan Fischler, *The Sporting News*, 2-6-71.

"Magnuson, who was greeted by a loud round of boos"—Kevin Walsh, *Boston Globe*, 1-20-71.

"There wasn't much hitting out there"—ibid.

"It is important to remember about Keith"—Jim Wiste, interview with author, 9-5-12.

"I sure can't complain about most of the fights"—Dan Moulton, *The Sporting News*, 12-19-70.

"I know I haven't played well this season"—Leo Monahan, *The Sporting News*, 5-15-71.

"We had let them win one"—Hull, p. 92.

"Chicago isn't an easy rink for a visiting goaltender"—Ken Dryden, *Canadiens Magazine*, vol. 22 (1), p. 31—as quoted in Denault, p. 62.

"For 20 minutes this afternoon"—Ted Damata, *Chicago Tribune*, 5-10-71.

"Destroyed the rhythm"—ibid.

"If Magnuson had retaliated"—Ted Damata, *Chicago Tribune*, 5-11-71.

"Spent most of the game anchored to the bench"—Denault, p. 67.
"The worst he ever had"—Bill Brennan, *The Sporting News*, 6-5-71.
"With the French-speaking Henri"—Denault, p. 68.
"The temperature outside the Stadium"—Ted Damata, *Chicago Tribune*, 5-19-71.
"Was on the ice for seven of the first 10 minutes"—Joyce, p. 22.
"Mr. Hull, one day I'll play against you"—ibid., pp. 24–25.
"I remember looking over to the Canadiens' bench"—ibid., p. 34.
"Uncorked a booming slapshot"—Denault, p. 68.
"Through a humid haze which hung over the ice"—Bob Verdi, *Chicago Tribune*, 5-19-71.
"Carried high into the net"—Ted Damata, *Chicago Tribune*, 5-19-71.
"It was the strangest goal I have ever scored"—Joyce, p. 39.
"I spent both intermissions praying"—Paul King, *Canadian* magazine (*Toronto Star* insert), 12-11-71.
"When Rejean got the puck to me"—Tom Fitzgerald, *Boston Globe*, 5-19-71.
"I didn't see Richard"—Bob Verdi, *Chicago Tribune*, 5-19-71.
"I made a move toward Esposito with the stick"—Tom Fitzgerald, *Boston Globe*, 5-19-71.
"Stan was as good as Wayne Gretzky with the puck"—Hull, p. 92.
"The Canadiens clung to their slender lead"—Bill Brennan, *The Sporting News*, 6-5-71.
"The best of the 10 Stanley Cups I've won"—Dan Proudfoot, Toronto Globe and Mail, 5-19-71.
"We played with confidence because he had confidence in us"—Joyce, p. 26.
"I never saw a goaltender"—Denault, p. 69.
"They gave everything they had"—Ted Damata, *Chicago Tribune*, 5-19-71.
"I'm mighty proud of this team"—Bob Verdi, *Chicago Tribune*, 5-19-71.
"The Hawks lost this game and the Cup by inches"—Ted Damata, *Chicago Tribune*, 5-19-71.
"I still wake up at night, wishing it was a nightmare"—Verdi, p. 98.
"You come across something like that seventh game"—Joe Falls, *The Sporting News*, 6-5-71.
"A play which brought from Keith Magnuson"—Bob Verdi, *Chicago Tribune*, 5-19-71.
"You get to know all its moods, its lights and shadows"—Magnuson and Bradford, p. 170.
"I suddenly realized that part of being a true professional"—ibid., p. 43.

CHAPTER 5

"Milk, a bowl of clam chowder"—Paul King, *Canadian* magazine (*Toronto Star* insert), 12-11-71.

"If you leave your label on a guy convincingly enough"—Robert Bradford, *Signature* magazine, March 1973.

"Slumped leeward and was saved from complete collapse"—Ted Damata, *Chicago Tribune*, 11-25-71.

"With cuts over both eyes that bridged the nose"—ibid.

"Keith even won the debate in the penalty box"—ibid.

"The greatest corner-man in the league"—Cheevers and Frayne, p. 65.

"The Bruins are gangfighters, or at least they used to be"—Stan Fischler, *The Sporting News*, 1-1-72.

"At least with this rule, we know who the fighters are"—Stan Fischler, *The Sporting News*, 3-25-72.

"It's a term we use to describe those"—Magnuson and Bradford, p. 25.

"As a fighter it was way better fighting at home"—Bernstein, p. 39.

"Let me tell you about Chicago"—Cheevers and Frayne, pp. 33-34.

"Back then, we never socialized off the ice"—Chuck O'Donnell, *Hockey Digest*, December 1996.

"In 1974, after the season, I had to fly to Detroit"—Rick Morrissey, *Chicago Tribune*, 12-17-03.

"I was shocked by the whole thing"—Bob Verdi, *Chicago Tribune*, 1-26-72.

"The [local newspapers] treat hockey"—Stan Fischler, *The Sporting News*, 2-5-72.

"A sophisticated team"—Magnuson and Bradford, p. 165

"Did Chicago's management at least buy a beer for Bobby?"—Dan Stoneking, *The Sporting News*, 4-8-72.

"If Winnipeg makes a sensational offer"—Stan Fischler, *The Sporting News*, 4-22-72.

"To be sure, Chicago owner Wirtz won't let Robert slip"—Dan Stoneking, *The Sporting News*, 4-8-72.

"Gives every decent player in the NHL"—Magnuson and Bradford, p. 168.

"When Hull was setting scoring records"—Joyce, p. 59.

"Ten or 15 years ago"—Joyce, p. 63.

"He has been the most glamorous shiny ambassador"—Stan Fischler, *The Sporting News*, 4-22-72.

"The players even said they'd give up a little bit of their salary"—Hull, p. 103.

"[Cliff] Koroll thinks that if we had won the cup in 1971"—Mikita and Verdi, p. 119.
"For a true professional"—Magnuson and Bradford, pp. 165–166.
"That irresistible wink and magnetic grin"—ibid., pp. 166–167.
"Bobby is like that wherever we play"—Stan Fischler, *The Sporting News*, 4-22-72.
"I've never seen him turn his back on a kid"—ibid.
"A year ago, Sanderson held out for $40,000"—Ted Damata, *Chicago Tribune*, 10-23-72.
"The World Hockey Association is banking on the premise"—ibid.
"Billy made sure that nobody thought"—Hull, p. 91.
"In the NHL, they treat you like cattle"—(Bob Verdi, special to *The Sporting News*, 8-11-73.
"I don't care if he signed with a team in China"—Joyce, p. 101.
"His objections to [Clarence] Campbell's"—ibid.
"Sinden, who had privately wished to have Hull"—ibid., p. 102.
"One of those rare shared moments in the history of a country"—Denault, p. 115.
"After the excitement of the just-concluded Summit Series"—ibid., p. 116.
"Pat and I were on the ice when Henderson scored"—Bob Verdi, Chicago Blackhawks.NHL.com, "The Verdict: Bill White Was a Defensive Stalwart, Prankster," 12-22-10.
"Magnuson flexed his muscles early"—*Chicago Tribune* (no author), 9-24-72.
"My first meeting with Magnuson was typical"—Schultz and Fischler, p. 71.
"I drove him in the mouth with my right"—ibid.
"I felt I had to prove myself"—ibid.
"Magnuson is just so busy all the time"—Stan Fischler, *The Sporting News*, 4-11-70.
"I have no doubt that Bobby Hull took more physical punishment"—Joyce, p. 28.
"Hull threw Fleming around like a bale of hay"—Joyce, p. 236.
"Hull and Fleming reprised the roles"—ibid.
"A few times I've had to slow down"—Magnuson and Bradford, pp. 147–148.
"We'd be creeping along, trying to hit it"—Podnieks, pp. 120–121.
"I hit another car on a freeway"—Paul King, *Canadian* magazine (*Toronto Star* insert), 12-11-71.
"One day, he walked into the apartment"—Bob Verdi, *Chicago Tribune Magazine*, 11-20-77.

"When they moved in last year"—Paul King, *Canadian* magazine (*Toronto Star* insert), 12-11-71.
"A minute later, in the center of a stadium"—Bob Verdi, *Chicago Tribune*, 3-15-73.
"I haven't won that many, have I?"—ibid.
"The Rangers, Bruins and Black Hawks had better win"—Stan Fischler, *The Sporting News*, 5-26-73.
"The rivalry ensured the series would be hotly contested"—Mark Magnuson, interview with author, 5-20-12.
"Keith left hours early for the Stadium that day"—ibid.
"You could hear it reverberate throughout the old stadium"—Chuck O'Donnell, *Hockey Digest*, December 1996.
"You couldn't hurt that kid's head with an axe"—Magnuson and Bradford, p. 43
"It was a five-on-three and it saved a goal"—Barry Rozner, Arlington Heights (IL) *Daily Herald*, 12-17-03.
"I thought I could be playing a week and a half ago"—Nolan Zavoral, *Milwaukee Journal*, 5-4-73.
"He reminded me a lot of Glenn Hall"—Mikita and Verdi, p. 112.

CHAPTER 6

"There's no excuse for one of the sport's richest franchises"—Stan Fischler, *The Sporting News*, 8-18-73.
"He was a gentleman"—Bob Verdi, special to *The Sporting News*, 8-11-73.
"The No. 1 order of business is getting Stan Mikita"—ibid.
"Able bodies who like Chicago"—ibid.
"Howatt is small"—Schultz and Fischler, p. 83.
"Magnuson said afterward that the brawl"—Bob Verdi, *Chicago Tribune*, 12-16-73.
"I grew up on the thin edge of poverty"—Schultz and Fischler, p. 23.
"I wanted no part of that rough stuff"—ibid., pp. 30-31.
"I used to hear stories from opposing players"—Bernstein, p. 44.
"Intimidation went both ways, though"—ibid.
"So many clubs are tough only in their own rinks"—Jack Chevalier, *The Sporting News*, 3-16-74.
"I believe referees get up for certain games"—ibid.
"So, if you were a goal scorer"—Bernstein, p. 46.
"It wasn't just two or three guys"—ibid., p. 45.

"If it's pretty skating the people want"—Schultz and Fischler, p. 74.
"We lose as many fights as we win"—Jack Chevalier, *The Sporting News*, 3-16-74.
"If I hadn't learned to lay on a two-hander once in a while"—Bernstein, p. 9.
"If ever a player led by inspiration"—Schultz and Fischler, p. 116.
"The unwritten rule was that he could dish out"—ibid.
"At times employing it in a manner of an infantryman"—ibid., p. 118.
"Any penalty involving the illegal use of the stick"—ibid., p. 196.
"It is an indisputable fact that Clarke"—ibid., p. 118.
"Bobby Clarke is a very dirty hockey player"—ibid., 119.
"My double triumph over so significant a foe"—ibid., p. 72.
"He showed me something by going down and helping out"—Dan Stoneking, *The Sporting News*, 1-19-74.
"How in hell do you sons of bitches ever win a hockey game?"—Schultz and Fischler, p. 127.
"I didn't do that to get things going necessarily"—Bob Verdi, *Chicago Tribune*, 4-24-74.
"A lot of people ask me if I'm bothered"—Gary Mueller, *The Sporting News*, 11-9-74.
"The fight and the goal not only gave us a win"—Schultz and Fischler, p. 78.
"You just can't get behind that team"—Gary Mueller, *The Sporting News*, 11-9-74.
"Overall, this is the most solid team we've had"—ibid.
"Long ago I gave up counting the stitches"—Magnuson and Bradford, p. 1.
"Almost all hockey players have missing teeth"—Magnuson and Bradford, p. 140.
"Tangled with a lot of noted pugilists"—ibid.
"Don't worry—you'll find her"—ibid., p. 158.
"If you're a pro athlete"—Paul King, *Canadian* magazine (*Toronto Star* insert), 12-11-71.
"I remember Maggie phoned me"—Dave Feschuk, *Toronto Star*, 12-21-03.
"That shows you the character and perseverance"—ibid.
"I've been lucky"—Bob Verdi, *Chicago Tribune Magazine*, 11-20-77.
"By far the best start of Magnuson's six-year fistic career"—Bob Verdi, *Chicago Tribune*, 9-30-74.
"I was still talking when they started punching"—*Toronto Star* (no author), 9-30-74.

"It's a long season, and we'll get Magnuson"—Bob Verdi, *Chicago Tribune*, 12-16-74.
"In the NHL jungle, an enforcer learns"—Schultz and Fischler, p. 78.
"Magnuson scored early"—Bob Verdi, *Chicago Tribune*, 12-29-74.
"There were no takers"—Bob Verdi, *Chicago Tribune*, 12-29-74.
"The players don't back each other up"—Gary Mueller, *The Sporting News*, 2-15-75.
"That might not be a very good thing to tell your own fans"—ibid.
"On the ice in the National Hockey League"—John Clayton, Beaver County (PA) *Times*, 2-18-75.
"You can't score if you don't get the puck"—ibid.
"I don't care how much the league tries to suspend the players for fighting"—ibid.
"This league isn't like it used to be in pre-expansion days"—Gary Mueller, *The Sporting News*, 4-5-75.
"There's no way a wing can keep from scoring"—Dan Moulton, *The Sporting News*, 11-4-72.
"Billy Reay would instruct me and Maggie"—Phil Russell, interview with author, 10-29-12.
"I remember Stan Mikita asking Ted Lindsay"—ibid.
"The NHL will continue to be plagued by a split personality"—Ray Kennedy, *Sports Illustrated*, 11-17-75.
"I don't think we need any of his legislation"—*Toronto Star*, 10-30-75.

CHAPTER 7

"Come contract time and all they talk about is the goals"—Gary Mueller, *The Sporting News*, 11-22-75.
"It just proves that against supposedly easier teams"—ibid.
"He was my first partner when I came to Chicago"—Tim Sassone, Arlington Heights (IL) *Daily Herald*, 11-12-08.
"Though the old guys were all Billy's players"—Hull, p. 137.
"Fitness was all the rage"—ibid., p. 140.
"Had the Black Hawks somehow persuaded Hull"—Stan Fischler, *The Sporting News*, 2-28-76.
"Were deluded into thinking they really were stars"—ibid.
"Stapleton not only didn't save the Cougars"—ibid.
"I believe it is the only way to develop the game"—*Toronto Globe and Mail* (no author), 6-10-75.

"In approximately seven weeks"—Al Strachan, *Montreal Gazette*, 11-11-75.
"If I were to rate the best hockey teams in the world today"—Magnuson and Bradford, p. 111.
"Watch Phil Russell"—*Chicago Tribune* (no author), 1-8-76.
"They gave him two minutes when they could easily have given him five"—ibid.
"The Black Hawks sometimes play as if they covet the Nobel Peace Prize"—Bob Verdi, *Chicago Tribune*, 1-8-76.
"What are we, last in the league in penalty minutes?"—ibid.
"A good and experienced one"—*Chicago Tribune* (no author), 1-8-76.
"When you get the kind of refereeing we saw tonight"—Bob Verdi, *Chicago Tribune*, 1-8-76.
"They just kept touching everything that was his"—Christie Blatchford, *Toronto Globe and Mail*, 1-9-76.
"For Fred Shero and his Flyers"—Denault, p. 270.
"No Red Army player wanted to play"—Tretiak, p. 98.
"The Black Hawks not only took the usual punishment"—Bob Verdi, *Chicago Tribune*, 1-19-76.
"He could have bumped Dick Daley in a mayoral election"—ibid.
"One thing you've got to have to be a success in this league can't be taught"—Magnuson and Bradford, p. 13.
"But Magnuson, Chicago's spiritual leader"—Bob Verdi, *Chicago Tribune*, 1-19-76.
"If I was a tough guy on another team"—Jim Wiste, interview with author, 9-5-12.
"He once said to me that I was nuts to keep coming back"—Chuck O'Donnell, *Hockey Digest*, December 1996.
"He wasn't dirty"—Rick Morrissey, *Chicago Tribune*, 12-17-03.
"We'll never forget what a good guy"—Michael Sneed, *Chicago Sun-Times*, 12-17-03.
"Going a hundred miles an hour"—Tim Sassone, Arlington Heights (IL) *Daily Herald*, 11-12-08.
"Bobby Orr was better on one leg than anyone else was on two"—McKenzie, p. 10.
"The record for pro hockey in Denver is not good"—Gary Mueller, *The Sporting News*, 10-30-75.
"It's the worst thing I've ever seen in hockey"—Bob Verdi, *The Hockey News*, 11-19-76.

"There's no place for what Watson did"—ibid.
"If I'd been going around the league doing things like that myself"—ibid.
"Bryan Watson isn't the most reliable guy I know"—ibid.
"Will be back with us in less than two weeks"—John Ahern, *Boston Globe*, 11-5-76.
"I looked at Bobby and asked him, in pantomime, what was going on"—Mikita, p. 124.
"In a 10-paragraph press release which not once mentioned Reay's name"—Bob Verdi, *Chicago Tribune*, 12-23-76.
"The best coach in the business"—ibid.
"It's against everything we stand for"—ibid.
"That's a rotten way to treat a guy"—ibid.
"Three years ago, almost no Hawk players would have dared"—ibid.
"Deep down, I really believed that if this group of players"—Mikita, p. 125.
"I called him [Magnuson] and asked to have dinner"—Bob Verdi, Chicago Blackhawks.NHL.com, "The Verdict: Bill White Was a Defensive Stalwart, Prankster," 12-22-10.
"I sort of had a feeling that, the way things were, there might be a change"—Bob Verdi, *Chicago Tribune*, 12-23-76.
"This year they gambled heavily on Bobby Orr's knees"—Robert Markus, *Chicago Tribune*, 12-23-76.
"Yeah, but like Tony Esposito says"—ibid.
"Teeth clenched and wired shut"—Grant Mulvey, interview with author, 10-26-12.
"The biggest hug and welcomed me into his inner circle"—ibid.
"Naw, I don't think that"—Neil Milbert, *Chicago Tribune*, 2-10-77.
"It's almost as though the people upstairs decided to write us off completely"—Neil Milbert, *Chicago Tribune*, 4-5-77.
"One afternoon, following a typically dull"—Bob Verdi, *Chicago Tribune Magazine*, 11-20-77.
"Pulford's defensive style should be"—Stan Fischler, *The Sporting News*, 10-15-77.
"I'm really excited about our new coach"—Bob Verdi, *Chicago Tribune Magazine*, 11-20-77.
"One night in the Forum"—Mikita, p. 109.
"I learned of that through my agent"—ibid., p. 130.
"I was never worried"—Bob Verdi, special to the *The Sporting News*, 2-18-78.

"You'd never get me to wear one of them"—Gary Mueller, *The Sporting News*, 12-3-77.
"He would still take a puck to the face"—Bob Verdi, *Chicago Tribune Magazine*, 11-20-77.
"Lewis told me later"—Bob Verdi, *Chicago Tribune*, 12-24-78.
"I was just sitting on the bench"—ibid.
"It bothered me this season"—Bob Verdi, *The Hockey News*, January 1979.
"There isn't a player on this team who doesn't completely respect him"—ibid.
"Was just starting to play as well as he ever had"—ibid.

CHAPTER 8

"There have been many finer athletes in Chicago, but not one finer person"—Bob Verdi, *Chicago Tribune*, 11-1-79.
"At first, it was just making appearances at food stores"—Neil Milbert, *The Hockey News*, June 1980.
"When a company such as ours takes on an athlete"—Bob Verdi, *Chicago Tribune Magazine*, 11-20-77.
"Maggie has been challenged"—ibid.
"It bothers me that I seem to be getting brittle"—ibid.
"He's one of those rare individuals"—Hollander, "The Great Gretzky's WHA-NHL Saga" (from *The Complete Handbook of Pro Hockey 1980* (Reyn Davis)).
"One of the biggest things about him is his intense desire"—ibid.
"Each year I've had to prove myself"—ibid.
"I was mentored by him as a roommate, teammate, and a coach"—Keith Brown, interview with author, 10-30-12.
"This is no good"—Bob Verdi, special to *The Sporting News*, 3-29-80.
"I felt my work with Joyce Beverages"—Neil Milbert, *The Hockey News*, June 1980.
"My family life was another consideration"—ibid.
"He's incompetent, has no business being a general manager"—*The Sporting News*, 8-16-80.
"I have no respect for that man"—Neil Milbert, *Chicago Tribune*, 6-14-80a.
"When it happened to Billy Reay"—Neil Milbert, *Chicago Tribune*, 6-14-80b.
"The Black Hawks have all the class"—Bob Verdi, *Chicago Tribune*, 6-15-80.
"That's not true"—Neil Milbert, *Chicago Tribune*, 6-14-80.
"The Black Hawks came to me."—ibid.

"I never thought I'd be a coach in the NHL"—ibid.

"You won't believe this"—Skip Myslenski, *Chicago Tribune Magazine*, 11-29-81.

"The changing of the guard behind the Hawks' bench"—Neil Milbert, *Chicago Tribune*, 6-15-80.

"Magnuson, whose 10-year career as a Chicago player"—*The Hockey News* (no author), 10-24-80.

"Keith is going to be successful"—ibid.

"It was a tough transition for both Maggie and me"—Cliff Koroll, interview with author, 9-2-12.

"Magnuson had said he would break his neck for the Wirtzes"—Bob Verdi, *Chicago Tribune*, 11-1-79.

"I think we're going into this season well prepared"—*The Hockey News*, 10-24-80.

"Whenever I need something I know I can count on Granny"—ibid.

"I saw that, and I told myself, 'I have to give more.'"—Grant Mulvey, interview with author, 10-26-12.

"There's so much to learn back there"—*The Hockey News*, 10-24-80.

"He began questioning himself"—Skip Myslenski, *Chicago Tribune Magazine*, 11-29-81.

"You kind of felt sorry for him"—ibid.

"From the first shifts I could see that our players were up"—George Vass, *Hockey Digest*, May 1981.

"They are growing into wanting to win and hating to lose"—ibid.

"As a player, I got down on myself after a loss"—Skip Myslenski, *Chicago Tribune Magazine*, 11-29-81.

"The thing about coaching"—ibid.

"As a performer, he eternally played and practiced with fire"—ibid.

"He's in a very tough situation"—ibid.

"Everybody feels the pressure"—Neil Milbert, *Chicago Tribune*, 2-1-82.

"She came to recognize and accept the moods"—Skip Myslenski, *Chicago Tribune Magazine*, 11-29-81.

"Pully, if you want to get rid of me"—ibid.

"I'll tell you one thing"—Neil Milbert, *Chicago Tribune*, 2-16-82.

"It [hockey] was killing me"—Luis Fernando Llosa, *Sports Illustrated*, 3-1-99.

"Keith always said he loved his wife, Cindy, more than hockey"—*Chicago Blackhawks* magazine, 11-12-08.

"The player worries about himself"—Skip Myslenski, *Chicago Tribune Magazine*, 11-29-81.
"Maggie was someone you would trust with anything"—Paul Schrage, interview with author, 10-15-2012.
"O'Rourke sensed that changes were about to occur at 7-Up"—Kevin Magnuson, interview with author, 5-15-12.
"He owns just one pair of jeans"—Skip Myslenski, *Chicago Tribune Magazine*, 11-29-81.
"I'm up by 5:30 every morning and put in an 8-to-10 hour workday"—Luis Fernando Llosa, *Sports Illustrated*, 3-1-99.
"My dad was so good at relating to every customer"—Kevin Magnuson, interview with author, 5-15-12.
"I'll have a Coke"—Jim Wiste, interview with author, 9-7-12.
"He was always a gentleman"—Paul Schrage, interview with author, 10-15-12.
"When I drive to practice in the morning"—Bob Verdi, *Chicago Tribune Magazine*, 11-20-77.
"People are sometimes surprised how even-tempered and relaxed I am off the ice"—Magnuson and Bradford, p. 150.
"I was a rookie broadcaster"—Pat Foley, interview with author, 10-19-12.
"He had no clothes, no golf clubs, or a chance to call home"—Wittenberg, p. 137.
"I came back home with three bucks in my pocket"—John Marks, interview with author, 11-2-12.
"He's a better playmaker than I was at his age"—David Southwell, *Chicago Sun-Times*, 3-9-93.
"She can skate very well"—ibid.
"I had told him when he was a youngster"—Luis Fernando Llosa, *Sports Illustrated*, 3-1-99.
"When Maggie was at the microphone at the luncheon"—Dale Tallon, interview with author, 11-2-12.
"Everybody who has ever needed any help"—Chris Kuc, *Chicago Tribune*, 9-27-07.
"When I was 19 years, old, I ran out of money"—ibid.
"Bill Wirtz was much more than a man who paid men with sticks to shoot pucks"—Mike Downey, *Chicago Tribune*, 9-27-07.
"Winning isn't everything"—Neil Milbert, *The Hockey News*, June 1980.

CHAPTER 9

"Maybe it's because hockey players are more fun"—Bob Verdi, *Chicago Tribune*, 11-1-79.

"He was just marvelous"—Associated Press (no author), 12-17-03.

"I said I had to get up to catch a flight"—Tim Sassone, Arlington Heights (IL) *Daily Herald*, 11-12-08.

"Peter Marsh phoned in the middle of the morning"—Mikita, p. 176.

"It's been a tremendous tragedy since the day of the accident"—Bob Mitchell, *Toronto Star*, 10-10-07.

"Walking by outside the church"—Mike Spellman, Arlington Heights (IL) *Daily Herald*, 12-21-03.

"We didn't even know these people"—Carol Slezak, *Chicago Sun-Times*, 11-10-08.

"We came back from Florida to attend the funeral"—Mikita, p. 176.

"He was my favorite player growing up"—Chris Chelios, interview with author, 9-20-12.

"The greatest captain the Hawks have ever had"—Len Ziehm, *Chicago Sun-Times*, 12-22-03.

"The ultimate team captain in the only sport where the *C* means something"—Barry Rozner, Arlington Heights (IL) *Daily Herald*, 12-17-03.

"Kevin talked about how Christmas was always his dad's favorite time"—Mikita, p. 177.

"My mom, my sister and I would like to ask you"—Dave Feschuk, *Toronto Star*, 12-21-03.

"In the game of life, Keith was our MVP"—Neil Milbert, *Chicago Tribune*, 12-21-03.

"Keith was a guy who lived 100 years in 56 years"—Mike Spellman, Arlington Heights (IL) *Daily Herald*, 12-21-03.

"He was as compassionate"—Jennifer Jones, *Chicago Sun-Times*, 12-17-03.

"People say hockey players are the nicest people, and they are"—David Southwell, *Chicago Sun-Times*, 3-9-93.

"I used to wait at Gate 3½ for Keith"—Barry Rozner, Arlington Heights *Daily Herald*, 2-4-04.

"He was a Hawk"—Bob Foltman, *Chicago Tribune*, 12-17-03.

"His great leadership on the ice was the way he was in ordinary life"—Jennifer Jones, *Chicago Sun-Times*, 12-17-03.

"As you travel through life"—*Chicago Tribune*, 12-17-03.

"He epitomized what heart and soul was all about"—Associated Press, 12-17-03.
"We lost our chief"—ibid.
"Reputation is what people perceive you to be"—Keith Brown, interview with author, 10-30-12.
"Maggie was the best 'team-guy' I've ever played with"—Darcy Rota, interview with author, 10-29-12.
"He was passionate toward others"—Grant Mulvey, interview with author, 10-26-12.
"He was the heart and soul of this organization"—Tim Sassone, Arlington Heights (IL) *Daily Herald*, 11-12-08.
"Keith was fearless"—John Marks, interview with author, 11-2-12.
"He was good a man as I've ever been in the trenches with"—Phil Russell, interview with author, 10-29-12.
"I never heard him say 'no' to anybody"—Bob Foltman, *Chicago Tribune*, 12-17-03.
"There's an old cowboy saying"—Phil Russell, interview with author, 10-29-12.
"Everything that came out of Keith's mouth was positive"—Stan Mikita, interview with author, 1-5-13.
"He had a heart of gold. Everybody loved Maggie"—Adrian Dater, *Denver Post*, 12-17-03.
"Keith's parents can be proud of how they raised him"—Bobby Hull, interview with author, 12-17-12.
"Maggie used to tie his ties in these unbelievable double-Windsor knots"—Peter Marsh, interview with author, 10-29-12.
"That was one of the things I missed so much when I left Chicago"—Bobby Hull, interview with author, 12-17-12.
"Out of respect to Maggie I thought that No. 3 should not be worn"—Tim Sassone, Arlington Heights (IL) *Daily Herald*, 12-22-03.
"Keith called me every year on my birthday"—Adrian Dater, *Denver Post*, 12-17-03.
"He made me believe that I could play in the NHL"—Cliff Koroll, interview with author, 9-5-12.
"Magnuson cross-checked players from the crease"—Mike Chambers, *Denver Post*, 10-11-09.
"We had a lot of luck this season"—Associated Press (no author), 4-12-04.

"Maggie was the biggest [alumnus] we had"—Mike Chambers, *Denver Post*, 10-11-09.
"No disrespect to any alumni, but he [Magnuson] was larger than life"—ibid.
"How Keith Magnuson wanted to lug that jug"—Bob Verdi, *Chicago Tribune*, 11-1-79.
"I've thought about it since I retired"—Chuck O'Donnell, *Hockey Digest*, December 1996.
"When you fight in hockey, 90 percent of it psychological"—Mark Magnuson, interview with author, 4-11-12.
"I can't play it any other way"—Magnuson and Bradford, p. 1.
"He was such a great son"—Carol Slezak, *Chicago Sun-Times*, 11-10-08.

EPILOGUE

"The public hears about a few of the good things Keith does"—Bob Verdi, *Chicago Tribune Magazine*, 11-20-77.
"I thought maybe two or three players would show up"—ibid.
"It doesn't allow the players to police themselves"—Bernstein, p. 149.
"They don't need fighting today in the NHL"—ibid., p. 203.
"Fighting does not have to be part of big league hockey"—Schultz and Fischler, p. 195.
"Those who don't want fighting probably never played"—Phil Russell, interview with author, 10-29-12.
"If you can beat them in the alley"—Magnuson and Bradford, p. 7.
"He lost more fights than he won"—Barry Rozner, Arlington Heights (IL) *Daily Herald*, 6-9-10.
"It was as if I was sitting in my living room"—Kevin Magnuson, interview with author, 10-13-12.
"It's for the great players of the late '60s and early '70s"—ibid.

References

Bernstein, R. (2006). The Code: The Unwritten Rules of Fighting and Retaliation in the NHL. Chicago: Triumph Books.

Cheevers, G., & Frayne, T. (1971). Goaltender. New York: Dodd, Mead, and Company.

Denault, T. (2010). The Greatest Game: The Montreal Canadiens, The Red Army, and the Night That Saved Hockey. Toronto: McClelland and Stewart.

Hollander, Z. (1980). The Complete Handbook of Pro Hockey. New York: Signet.

Hull, D. (1998). The Third Best Hull. Toronto: ECW Press.

Jackson, J. (2004). Walking Together Forever: The Broad Street Bullies, Then and Now. Champaign, IL: Sports Publishing.

Joyce, G. (2011). The Devil and Bobby Hull: How Hockey's Original Million-Dollar Man Became the Game's Lost Legend. Mississauga, Ontario: Wiley.

Magnuson, K., & Bradford, R. (1973). None Against! New York: Dodd, Mead, and Company.

McKenzie, B. (2000). "Full Speed Ahead" (in Dryden, Century of Hockey). Toronto: McClelland and Stewart.

Mikita, S., & Verdi, B. (2011). Forever a Blackhawk. Chicago: Triumph Books.

Podnieks, A. (2010). Hockey Superstitions: From Playoff Beards to Crossed Sticks and Lucky Socks. Toronto: McClelland and Stewart.
Schultz, D., and Fischler, S. (1981). The Hammer: Confessions of a Hockey Enforcer. New York: Summit Books.
Tretiak, V. (1987). Tretiak: The Legend. New York: Penguin Books.
Verdi, B. (2000). Chicago Blackhawks: Seventy-five Years. San Diego, CA: Tehabi Books.
Wittenberg, H. (2003). Tales from the Chicago Blackhawks. Champaign, IL: Sports Publishing.

WEBSITES

DropYourGloves.com
HockeyDB.com
Hockey-Reference.com
LegendsofHockey.com
NHL.com

NEWSPAPERS

Arlington Heights (IL) *Daily Herald*
Boston Globe
Chicago Daily News
Chicago Tribune
Chicago Sun-Times
Denver Post
Milwaukee Journal
Montreal Gazette
Philadelphia Inquirer
Toronto Globe and Mail
Toronto Star